Doing
Visual
Ethnography

Second edition

Doing
Visual
Ethnography

SECOND EDITION

Images, Media and
Representation in Research

Sarah Pink

Los Angeles | London | New Delhi
Singapore | Washington DC

First published 2001, reprinted 2002, 2003, 2004, 2005
This edition first published 2007
Reprinted 2010, 2011

SAGE Publications Ltd
1 Oliver's Yard
55 City Road
London EC1Y 1SP

SAGE Publications Inc.
2455 Teller Road
Thousand Oaks, California 91320

SAGE Publications India Pvt Ltd
B 1/I 1, Mohan Cooperative Industrial Area
Mathura Road
New Delhi 110 044

SAGE Publications Asia-Pacific Pte Ltd
33 Pekin Street #02-01
Far East Square
Singapore 048763

British Library Cataloguing in Publication data

A catalogue record for this book is available
from the British Library

ISBN13 978 1 4129 2347 7
ISBN13 978 1 4129 2348 4 (pbk)

Library of Congress Control Number 2006923195

Typeset by C&M Digitals (P) Ltd., Chennai, India
Printed in Great Britain by the MPG Books Group
Printed on paper from sustainable resources

Contents

Acknowledgements

When I wrote the first edition of this book in the late 1990s I did so with the conviction that a visual approach to ethnographic research was emerging as a key methodological strand. Through writing this book I drew together my own and other researchers' experiences along with theoretical and substantive interests in visual cultures and visual representations to propose a visual ethnographic methodology. The book's title, *Doing Visual Ethnography*, was proposed by Sage, and I think the idea of a Visual Ethnography sums up very well my intentions. In its original form this book was inspired greatly by my readings and viewings of and conversations about the work of other visual anthropologists, sociologists and visual artists. Since then, and often in relation to *Doing Visual Ethnography*, I have corresponded with and met many more ethnographers who share an enthusiasm for the visual. Some of the work incorporated in this new edition is of visual ethnographers who developed their own project-specific visual methods in dialogue with *Doing Visual Ethnography*. I am greatly indebted to them for both appreciating my initial text and for providing, through their own practice, a new body of work that this new edition is in turn created to dialogue with. I am especially grateful to those researchers and artists who have given me permission to reproduce their visual work in this book. Rather than listing their names here, each is mentioned in the text where their work is discussed. Being able to include their images and visual insights in this edition of the book has, I feel, greatly enhanced it. The book also draws extensively from my own experiences and would of course have been impossible without the support of the many people who have collaborated in my research, allowing me to photograph or video them. For the combination of visual and ethnographic training that has informed this work, and technical support in producing images for this book, I am indebted to the staff of the Granada Centre for Visual Anthropology at the University of Manchester, the Centre for Anthropology and Computing at the University of Kent, the Department of Social Sciences at Loughborough University and multimedia developers at the University of Derby.

Introduction

Photography, video and hypermedia are becoming increasingly incorporated into the work of ethnographers – as cultural texts, as representations of ethnographic knowledge and as sites of cultural production, social interaction and individual experience that themselves constitute ethnographic fieldwork locales. Visual images and technologies now form the areas, methods and media of ethnographic research and representations as well as the topics of university courses in visual anthropology, visual sociology or visual cultures. Simultaneously, the benefits of an ethnographic approach are being realized in visual arts and media studies. This includes developments such as 'media ethnography' (e.g. Crawford and Hafsteinnson 1996), using visual anthropology methods in media studies (e.g. Murdock and Pink 2005a, 2005b) and the use of ethnographic research methods and anthropological theory to inform photographic (e.g. da Silva and Pink 2004) and hypermedia (e.g. Coover 2004a, 2004b) practice and representation. In this contemporary context, ethnography and visual studies have much to contribute to one another. While photographic, film and digital hypermedia theory can inform our understanding of the potential of visual media in ethnographic research and representation, an ethnographic approach can also support the production and interpretation of visual images. This book is primarily for ethnographers who wish to incorporate the visual into their ethnographic work, but it is also for photographers, video makers and hypermedia artists who wish to gain a deeper understanding of how ethnographic research may inform their artistic practice.

For the past fifteen or so years I have worked with rapidly changing technologies and theoretical paradigms to use photography, video and hypermedia in my own ethnographic work. My involvement began in the late 1980s when proponents of the 'new ethnography' introduced ideas of ethnography as fiction and emphasized the centrality of subjectivity to the production of knowledge. Anthropology experienced a 'crisis' through which positivist arguments and realist approaches to knowledge, truth and objectivity were challenged. These ideas paved the way for the visual to be increasingly acceptable in ethnography as it was recognized that ethnographic film or photography were essentially no more subjective or objective than written texts and thus gradually became acceptable to (if not actively engaged with by) most mainstream researchers. During the 1990s, new innovations in visual technology, critical 'postmodern' theoretical approaches to subjectivity, experience,

Master Caravela. © Olivia da Silva 2000

Figure 1

Master Caravela is a member of the fishing community in Matosinhos (Portugal) represented in Olivia da Silva's photographic project, *In the Net* (2000). Da Silva uses anthropological methods to inform her photographic practice, writing how 'As a participant observer I worked closely with the subjects of my portraits as they lived out their everyday lives to access the personal and domestic arenas of fishing communities and to record individual histories and narratives' (see da Silva and Pink 2004). The relationship between arts practice and visual ethnography is a two-way process, while visual ethnographic practices can inform photographic representations, the visual practices of documentary artists also provide new and inspiring examples for visual ethnographers.

knowledge and representation, a reflexive approach to ethnographic fieldwork methodology and an emphasis on interdisciplinarity invited exciting new possibilities for the use of photographic technologies and images in ethnography. Emerging from that context, since the beginning of the twentieth century, there has been a flurry of new literature about and practical work involving visual methodologies. Traversing the social sciences and humanities these developments include work

Figure 2

Contemporary cultural events can be sites of visual production, representation and remembering. Since 2005 I have been doing research in Aylsham, Norfolk (UK), a Cittàslow town. Aylsham's carnival involved a series of sensory embodied performances and experiences that were represented visually in posters and displays before, during and after the event. It also hosted a photographic exhibition drawn from its local community archive that was evocative of 'the past'. The event was photographed and videoed by local people (including a professional photographer), by myself the researcher, and by the local community reporter. Afterwards images were used to represent it in various forms, including the local newspaper, and a digital slide show presentation in an international awards event, at which the town won a prize, in Spain.

© Sarah Pink 2005

In this still image from my own video recording of the carnival, Sue, who is involved extensively in the management of slow living in a professional and voluntary capacity, photographs the procession.

© Sarah Pink 2005

This still image from my video recording shows the exhibition of historical photographs of carnival displayed in the Town Hall. By viewing these images local people were able to remember past events, people and feelings. (See also Chapter 3.)

in social anthropology (Ruby 2000; Banks 2001; Grimshaw 2001; El Guindi 2004; Grimshaw and Ravetz 2004; Pink et al. 2004; MacDougall 2005; Pink 2005), sociology (Emmison and Smith 2000; O'Neill 2002; Knowles and Sweetman 2004; Pole 2004; Halford and Knowles 2005), and geography (Rose 2001) (see Pink 2005: ch. 2). Collectively these texts set a new scene for visual methods in an intellectual climate where the impact of the 'postmodern turn' has been assessed and put to rest leaving as its legacy, amongst other things, the reflexive approach to ethnographic and visual research that these works insist on. As will show through from the examples I discuss in this new edition of *Doing Visual Ethnography*, the current context is one that is influenced by three key factors. First, an enthusiasm for exploring new interdisciplinary themes, leading in particular to exciting connections between ethnography and arts practice, and as such for working at interdisciplinary boundaries (e.g. Grimshaw and Ravetz 2004; da Silva and Pink 2004; Schneider and Wright 2005; Bowman et al. forthcoming). Part of this interlinking is the increasing recognition that visual research must also accommodate embodiment and the senses (e.g. O'Neill 2002; Grimshaw and Ravetz 2004; Pink 2005). Secondly, in Britain at least, a new emphasis on research about and training in methodology and ethical scrutiny emanates from the institutional requirements now made by funding bodies and universities. This context on the one hand encourages innovative methodologies. On the other it emphasizes the importance of ensuring ethical practice through external scrutiny, and as such in ways often seemingly quite different from those suggested by the self-scrutiny of the reflexive ethnographer. In this environment visual ethnographers need to be not just self-reflexive about their methods, but also conversant about them in institutional languages. Finally, as the visual projects that have emerged since the publication of the first edition of this book demonstrate, visual ethnography is as much an applied as an academic practice (Pink 2004a, 2005, forthcoming).

An approach to theory, method and the visual in ethnography

The relationship between theory and method is important for understanding any research project. Similarly, an awareness of the theoretical underpinnings of visual research methods is crucial for understanding how those images and the processes through which they are created are used to produce ethnographic knowledge. The early literature on visual research methods has rightly been criticized for being 'centred on how-to manuals of method and analysis working within a largely unmediated realist frame (e.g. Collier and Collier 1986)' (Edwards 1997a: 33). Such manuals, like Prosser's notions of an 'image-based research' methodology (1996, 1998), propose problematically prescriptive frameworks that aim to distance, objectify and generalize, and therefore detract from the very qualities and potentials that the ambiguity and expressivity (see Edwards 1997a) of visual images offers ethnography. *Doing Visual Ethnography*, along with other new volumes published at the beginning of the twenty-first century (e.g. Banks 2001; Pink et al. 2004), signified a departure from this scientific and realist paradigm towards a new approach to making and understanding ethnographic images.

However, *Doing Visual Ethnography* is not intended as a recipe book for successful visual research, rather it suggests an approach. It is frequently emphasized that methodologies are developed for/with particular projects, they are interwoven with theory and 'as most good researchers know, it is not unusual to make up the methods as you go along'. Indeed, '[t]he methods should serve the aims of the research, not the research serve the aims of the method' (McGuigan 1997: 2). Moreover, as Lizette Josephides has stressed 'our ethnographic strategies are also shaped by the subjects' situations, their global as well as local perceptions, and their demands and expectations of us'. Therefore, 'There can be no blueprint for how to do fieldwork. It really depends on the local people, and for this reason we have to construct our theories of how to do fieldwork *in the field*' (1997: 32; original italics). The same applies to using visual images and technologies in fieldwork; specific uses should be creatively developed within individual projects. Therefore, rather than prescribing *how to do* visual research I draw from my own and other ethnographers' experiences of using images in research and representation to present a range of examples and possibilities. These are intended as a basis, or even point of contrast, from which new practices may be developed.

Different and competing methodologies, linked to specific theoretical approaches, co-exist in academic discourse. This forms a theme of this book as I consider the relationship between scientific-realist and what I call 'reflexive' approaches to the visual in ethnography. Although much recent work evidences a new openness to the visual, scientific approaches to social research still exist and students who wish to use visual methods should be familiar with the debates that surround the visual in social research. The theoretical agendas to which particular methods and practices are attached should be made explicit and questioned, and it is for this reason that scientific-realist and reflexive approaches are frequently contrasted in this book. The approach of those visual sociologists who have aimed to incorporate a visual dimension into an already established methodology based on a 'scientific' approach to sociology (e.g. Grady 1996; Prosser 1996; Prosser and Schwartz 1998), does not allow the potential of the visual in ethnography to be realized. Their proposal that visual images should support the project of a scientific sociology suffers from the problems of perspectives like equality feminism: it must subscribe to the dominant discourse in order to be incorporated. The advocates of this conservative strategy are thus obliged to prove the value of the visual to a scientific sociology that is dominated by the written word, thus effectively evaluating the worth of images to research on the terms of a sociological agenda that has rejected the significance of visual meanings and the potential of images to represent and generate new types of ethnographic knowledge.

In this book I take the contrasting view, that to incorporate the visual appropriately, social science should, as MacDougall has suggested, 'develop alternative objectives and methodologies' (1997: 293). This means abandoning the possibility of a purely objective social science and rejecting the idea that the written word is essentially a superior medium of ethnographic representation. While images should not necessarily replace words as the dominant mode of research or representation, they should be regarded as an equally meaningful element of ethnographic work. Thus visual images, objects, descriptions should be incorporated when it is appropriate, opportune or enlightening to do so. Images may not necessarily be *the* main research method or topic, but through their relation to other sensory, material and discursive elements of the research images and visual knowledge, will *become* of interest. As Stoller reminds us, 'it is representationally as well as analytically important to consider how perception in non-western societies devolves not simply from vision ... but also from smell, touch, taste and hearing' (1997: xv–xvi). This is in fact also the case for modern western cultures (Pink 2004b). Indeed, a multisensory approach to ethnography provides a useful context through which to reflect on the place of the visual in research and representation (Pink 2005). In some projects the visual may become more important than the spoken or written word, in others it will not. In this book I argue that there is no essential hierarchy of knowledge or media for ethnographic representation. Academic epistemologies and conventional academic modes of representation should not be used to obscure and abstract the epistemologies and experienced realities of local people. Rather, these may complement one another as different types of ethnographic knowledge that may be experienced and represented in a range of different textual, visual and other sensory ways. This, however, is not to say that images and words can play the same role in academic work. As I insist in Part 3 of this book, visual representations bear an important relationship to, but cannot replace, words in theoretical discussion.

Disciplinary concerns and ethnographic research

Anthropology, sociology, cultural studies, photographic studies and media studies are the key disciplines I shall refer to. With their shared interests in material culture, practices of representation, the interpretation of cultural texts and comprehending social relations and individual experience, each area of study has its particular theoretical and methodological heritage and offers its own understanding of the visual in culture and society. While different disciplines use visual images and technologies in ethnography to serve their own epistemological and empirical agendas, recently a number of significant interdisciplinary links have been implied.

In the 1990s the sometimes uncomfortable relationship between anthropology and cultural studies was a focus. For example, Penny Harvey suggested that although those anthropologists who were hostile to cultural studies approaches focused 'on the differences between studying texts and studying people, between representation and situated practice', in fact an 'awareness of a tension between text and everyday life is not exclusively anthropological' (1996: 14) and 'the discipline of anthropology cannot ignore the contributions from cultural studies' (1996: 15). An interlinking of cultural studies and anthropological approaches seems particularly pertinent to an ethnography that incorporates visual images and technologies. This approach recognizes the interwovenness of objects, texts, images and technologies in people's everyday lives and identities. It aims not simply to study people's social practices or to read cultural objects or performances as if they were texts, but to explore how all types of material, intangible, spoken, performed narratives and discourses are interwoven with and made meaningful in relation to social relationships, practices and individual experiences.

The idea of crossing disciplinary boundaries was also proposed by Elizabeth Edwards (1997a), who demonstrated how anthropological and photographic theories of representation may be combined to produce a deeper understanding of the expressive possibilities of photography for anthropological representation (see Chapter 6). Meanwhile, some photographers have developed an ethnographic approach to their photographic practice (see Chapter 3). More generally, anthropologists and artists have begun to explore what each might learn from the others' research and representational practices (see da Silva and Pink 2004; Grimshaw and Ravetz 2004; Schneider and Wright 2005). In contrast, sociological approaches to ethnographic uses of photography and video have been slower to incorporate ideas from outside, tending to looking inwards to their own discipline for approval. Concepts of 'validity', sampling and triangulation abound in sociological methods texts on ethnography (see, for example, Hammersely and Atkinson 1995: 227–32; Walsh 1998: 231). Correspondingly, many visual sociologists attempted to incorporate these conditions into their use of visual images, making their visual ethnographic 'data' succumb to the agenda of a scientific and experimental sociology (e.g. Grady 1996; Prosser 1996; Prosser and Schwartz 1998). This 'traditional' sociological approach failed to develop the full potential of the visual in ethnography. However, other visual sociologists, such as Elizabeth Chaplin (1994) and Maggie O'Neill (2002), have developed more interdisciplinary approaches that incorporate feminist, anthropological, cultural studies and other critical approaches. Two recent examinations of the work of documentary photographers also suggest both parallels between their interests and those of visual sociologists and anthropologists and lessons that academic researchers might learn from arts practice. First, in his analysis of the work of the

Japanese social documentary photographer Hashiguchi George, Richard Chalfen suggests that, although the photographer himself rejects the methodologies of the two subdisciplines, his work 'raises important questions that are relevant and even central to visual sociology' (2005: 155). Secondly, Katherine Hyde discusses the work of Wendy Ewald, a photographer, teacher and storyteller, who takes a collaborative approach to photographing children by 'sharing control over the process of visually representing children's lives, their stories and their faces'. Hyde suggests that Ewald's work is relevant to social scientists in two ways: both as a source of material that might be analysed as visual culture, and as a methodology of research and representation (Hyde 2005: 172).

The current interdisciplinary focus in visual methods is also represented in recent edited volumes that combine case studies in visual research from different disciplines, including social and cultural anthropology, sociology, cultural studies, social psychology and more. Good examples of these are Theo van Leeuwen and Carey Jewitt's *Handbook of Visual Analysis* (2001) and Chris Pole's *Seeing is Believing* (2004). The publication of work on visual methodologies is also growing in journal articles. Of particular interest is the interdisciplinary journal *Visual Studies* (formerly *Visual Sociology*) and guest edited issues such as Gerry Bloustein's (2003) special issue of *Social Analysis*.

A further motive for taking an interdisciplinary approach to the visual in ethnography is the idea that ethnography is an *aspect* of research and representation. Ethnography is rarely the sole means or end of a research project; different disciplinary uses of it are likely to situate ethnography differently within their processes of research and representation. Indeed projects are rarely purely ethnographic, but usually draw from ethnographic and other approaches to varying extents. Ethnography may be combined with textual, historical, narrative, statistical or a whole range of other research practices that intertwine and overlap or link conceptually as the research proceeds. Some of these connections are indicated in this book. For example, in Chapters 3 and 4 I discuss how studying local photographic and media cultures and histories can inform our understanding of contemporary ethnographic photography and video. Statistical sources or analysis of existing visual texts can inform the design and interpretation of visual research. In Chapters 6, 7 and 8, I emphasize the importance of understanding the media used for ethnographic representation by considering how photographic, video and hypermedia texts communicate and are interpreted.

Vision and images in social science: methodologies and theories

Ethnographers have long since used photography, film and more recently video in research and representation. However, historically and in different disciplines they have done so with varying degrees of acceptance and continuity. Moreover, both between and within disciplines the development of visual research methods has been informed by different theoretical approaches. A review of some of these developments traces both the distinctiveness of anthropological, sociological and cultural studies approaches to photography and video and their mutual complementarity.

Developments in visual anthropology

Historically, ethnographic uses of the visual were shrouded in controversy (see Pink 2005: ch. 1). From the 1960s to the early 1980s, debates focused on whether visual images and recordings could usefully support the observational project of social science (see, for example, Collier and Collier 1986; Hockings 1975, 1995; Rollwagen 1988). During this period many social scientists resisted the use of the visual in ethnography, claiming that as a data collection method it was too subjective, unrepresentative and unsystematic. Ethnographers like Margaret Mead, John Collier Jnr and Howard Becker set out to prove otherwise, in both their theoretical arguments and practical applications of photography and film. Visual ethnographers were forced to confront the accusation that their visual images lacked objectivity and scientific rigour. Mead's response was that cameras left to film continuously without human intervention produced 'objective materials' (Mead 1995 [1975]: 9–10). Others, suggesting that the specificity of the photographed moment rendered it scientifically invalid (see, for example, Collier 1995 [1975]: 247), endeavoured to compensate for this. For instance, Becker (following Jay Ruby) proposed that the photographs anthropologists and sociologists might take during fieldwork 'are really only vacation pictures' (Becker 1986: 244), indistinguishable from those of the anthropologist's – or anyone else's – vacation. He advocated a systematic approach to photography as the social scientists' key to success (Becker 1986: 245–50) in an echo of Collier, who warns that '[t]he photographic record can remain wholly impressionistic UNLESS it undergoes disciplined computing' (1995 [1975]: 248; original emphasis). Thus some disputed the validity of the visual on the grounds of its subjectivity, bias and specificity. Others responded that, under the right controls, the visual could contribute to a positivist social science as an objective recording method.

One of the most influential publications of this era is Collier's (1967) *Visual Anthropology: Photography as Research Method* (revised with Malcolm Collier and reprinted in 1986), a comprehensive textbook on the use of photography and video in ethnographic research and representation, with a lasting influence (e.g. on Prosser 1996; Prosser and Schwartz 1998). Collier and Collier advocated a systematic method of observation whereby the researcher is supported by visual technology. They asserted that 'good video and film records for research are ultimately the product of observation that is organized and consistent. The equipment, except in specialized circumstances, cannot replace the observer' (1986: 149). This approach depended on a realist interpretation of still and moving images and was criticized on this basis (for example, by Edwards 1997a). For Collier and Collier, the research plan was key to the ethnographer's project of recording an appropriate version of the reality he or she could observe. Therefore they distinguished between the fiction of the '"shooting scripts" often used in the photographic and film world' and research plans that purport to record reality. On their terms ethnography was an observation of reality, as opposed to the constructedness of the narrative-based communication 'stories' of scripted films (Collier and Collier 1986: 162). Also in 1986, in the now landmark collection *Writing Culture*, James Clifford suggested that, to the contrary, ethnographies themselves are constructed narratives: in a word, 'fictions'. He used the term 'fiction' not to claim that ethnographies are 'opposed to the truth' or are 'false', but to emphasize how ethnographies cannot reveal or report on complete or whole accounts of reality; that they only ever tell part of the story (1986: 6). For Clifford, not only was ethnography a constructed version of truth, but 'Ethnographic truths are ... inherently *partial* – committed and incomplete' (1986: 7; original italics). This can be applied to both research and representation. Clifford's ideas questioned Collier and Collier's claim that research shooting guides differ from 'fictional' shooting scripts because the 'systematic selectivity' of 'field shooting or observation guides' is concerned 'with defining procedure, structure, and categories for recording that produce data on which later research analysis and summations are built' (1986: 162). Clifford's very point was that 'cultural fictions are built on systematic, and contestable, exclusions' (1986: 6). The selectivity, predetermined categories and precautions that Collier and Collier assumed would prevent ethnography from being a 'fiction' rather than a realist observation were in fact the very cornerstones upon which Clifford's ethnographic 'fictions' were constructed. Collier and Collier recognized that the 'whole' view of a situation cannot be recorded on video, they urged the research photographer to confront 'the challenge of gathering a semblance of the whole circumstance in a compressed sample of items and events observed in time and space' (1986: 163). However, their work was inconsistent with the 'postmodern turn' in ethnography since they did not account for the possibility that any attempt to represent a 'whole view' itself constitutes a 'partial truth' or, in Clifford's terms, a 'fiction' based on 'systematic exclusions'. In this context, although Collier and Collier's (1986) work remains an important guide to visual ethnographic methods, it was a response to the demands of a scientific-realist twentieth-century anthropology.

In the 1980s Clifford's ideas helped to create a favourable environment for the visual representation of ethnography. The emphasis on specificity and experience, and a recognition of the similarities between the constructedness and 'fiction' (in Clifford's sense of the term) of film and written text, created a context where ethnographic film became a more acceptable form of ethnographic representation (Henley 1998: 51; Ruby 1982: 130). However, initially, little attention was paid to re-thinking the theoretical implications of photography and video as research methods. There were, of course, some exceptions. For example, Heidi Larson (1988) used photography and images reflexively to learn about her informant's views of reality through collaborative photography. But the greater focus on the mediation of meaning between anthropologists and informants was developed in the reflexive ethnographic film style of David and Judith MacDougall and their contemporaries (Loizos 1993).

In the 1990s a new literature approximated the historical debates and developments of the relationship between photography, film and the observational approaches of both anthropology and sociology (e.g. Chaplin 1994; Edwards 1992; Harper 1998a, 1998b; Henley 1998; Loizos 1993; Banks and Morphy 1997; Pink 1996, 1998b: CD). Edwards's (1992) and Marcus Banks' and Howard Morphy's (1997) volumes signified an intentional departure from the scientific-realist paradigm but recognized that the contemporary context was one in which '[m]any anthropologists still feel caught between the possibility of conceptual advances from visual anthropology and the more conservative paradigms of a positivist scientific tradition' (MacDougall 1997: 192). Rather than attempting to fit visual anthropology into a scientific paradigm, whereby visual research methods could support and enhance an objective anthropology, David MacDougall proposed a significantly different approach that would 'look at the principles that emerge when fieldworkers actually try to rethink anthropology through use of a visual medium' (1997: 192). This implied a radical transformation of anthropology itself that would 'involve putting in temporary suspension anthropology's dominant orientation as a discipline of words and rethinking certain categories of anthropological knowledge in the light of understandings that may be accessible only by non-verbal means' and 'a shift from word-and-sentence-based anthropological thought to image-and-sequence-based anthropological thought' (1997: 292). Therefore, rather than attempting to incorporate images into a word-based social science, MacDougall advocated that since '[v]isual anthropology can never be either a copy of written anthropology or a substitute for it ... [f]or that very reason it must develop alternative objectives and methodologies that will benefit anthropology as a whole' (1997: 292–3).

When I wrote the first edition of *Doing Visual Ethnography* in the late 1990s, MacDougall's analysis seemed an accurate characterization of the academic climate. There was increasing curiosity about visual methods as technology became more available and the visual more acceptable. Yet the question of how the visual might become part of ethnographic practice remained undetermined. Almost ten years later in 2006 a new context has emerged. Visual anthropologists have written reflexive books on visual ethnography (Banks 2001; Pink 2001 [1st edition of this book]; El Guindi 2004; Pink et al. 2004) and are exploring the relationship between visual anthropological and arts practice (da Silva and Pink 2004; Grimshaw and Ravetz 2004; Schneider and Wright 2005). The representational practices of visual anthropologists have taken new directions as further critiques of ethnographic documentary filmmaking (e.g. Ruby 2000; Chalfen and Rich 2004) have inspired both new forms of ethnographic documentary video (e.g. MacDougall 2005), the production of multimedia anthropological hypermedia representations (e.g. Ruby 2004: CD, 2005: CD; Kirkpatrick 2003: CD; and see Pink 2005), art and drawing (Ramos 2004), and applied visual anthropology practice (Pink 2004a, forthcoming). The challenge for visual anthropology as it re-establishes itself in the twenty first century is no longer the question of whether it will be accepted by the mainstream, but of how to connect with and contribute to mainstream anthropological debates. As I elaborate in *The Future of Visual Anthropology* (Pink 2005), the subdiscipline faces a number of opportunities and challenges that mean its practitioners need to engage a series of elements of the contemporary context, namely:

> the increasingly wide use of visual ethnographic methods of research and representation in 'visual' subdisciplines across the social sciences and humanities; the theoretical demands of, and shifts in, a mainstream anthropology in which the visual has now become acceptable and popular as a methodology and object of analysis; a reassessment of the aspects of human experience that images and writing best represent, and a related analysis of the relationship between the visual and other senses through an engagement with recent developments in the anthropology of the senses; the possibilities offered by digital video and hypermedia that invite visual anthropologists to develop new practices; and increasing use of visual methods of research and representation in applied anthropology. (Pink 2005: 3)

This second edition of *Doing Visual Ethnography* suggests a visual ethnographic process that is complementary to that wider project.

Developments in visual sociology

While from the late 1970s visual anthropologists, turning their attention to ethnographic film and video, began to question the notion of visual realism, visual sociologists (e.g. Wagner 1979) continued to develop their use of photography within the realist paradigm (Harper 1998a: 27; see also Pink 1999c). Some sociologists responded to feminist and postmodern critiques, in some cases developing interdisciplinary approaches to the sociology of visual culture (e.g. Crawshaw and Urry 1997) and the implications of photography for sociological understandings of the individual and self-identity (Lury 1998). However, some of those calling themselves visual sociologists engaged little with social theory or debates over reflexivity and subjectivity in research. Many sociologists continued to contest uses of visual images in research and representation (see Prosser 1996), arguing that their subjectivity and specificity rendered them invalid for a scientific sociology. The subdiscipline of visual sociology was, perhaps in response to this, correspondingly slow to engage with the visual beyond using it as a recording method and support for a word-based discipline. For instance, in the 1990s Jon Prosser and Donna Schwartz considered how photography could be incorporated into 'a traditional qualitative framework rather than adopt ideas emanating from postmodern critique' (1998: 115). Stephen Gold maintained a similarly close alliance with existing sociological methods. He saw visual sociology as divided into two camps that deal with either the interpretation or the creation of visual images. He defined this as a 'theory/method split' – and 'a major obstacle in the further development of visual sociology' – and proposed that theory and method may be brought together through the established 'grounded theory' approach (Gold 1997: 4).

Around the same time some visual sociologists began to account for the critique of ethnography. For example, Douglas Harper called for a redefinition of the relationship between researcher and informant in the form of a collaborative approach developed in the 'new ethnography' and the incorporation of the postmodern approach to documentary photography that 'begins with the idea that the meaning of the photograph is constructed by the maker and the viewer, both of whom carry their social positions and interests to the photographic act' (1998a: 34–5, 1998b: 140). Nevertheless, Harper did not propose a radical departure from existing sociological approaches to the visual. He recommended that visual sociology should 'begin with traditional assumptions and practices of sociological fieldwork and sociology analysis' that treat the photograph as 'data', and that it should open up to integrate the demands of the 'new ethnography' (1998a: 35). In fact, in the 1990s Elizabeth Chaplin was the main critic of traditional approaches to the visual in sociology. In her book *Sociology and Visual Representations* (Chaplin 1994) she engaged with post-feminist and post-positivist agendas to suggest a way forward for a 'visual sociology'. Chaplin advocated a collaborative approach that would reduce the distance between the discipline and its subject of study. Thus, unlike Harper, she argued that rather than the visual being 'data' that is subjected to a verbal 'analysis', the potential of the visual as sociological knowledge and critical text should be explored (1994: 16). Like those social anthropologists discussed above, Chaplin took a step further than most visual sociologists by engaging with the visual not simply as a mode of recording data or illustrating text, but as a medium through which new knowledge and critiques may be created. In the late 1990s some visual sociologists explored this potential in their practice (e.g. Barndt 1997; Barnes et al. 1997, whose work is discussed in Chapters 6 and 4, respectively). Nevertheless much visual sociology remained firmly rooted in existing sociological practice.

More recent sociological projects in visual methods have departed from the 1990s work in diverse ways. In 2000 Emmison and Smith, overlooking the extent of Chaplin's contribution, criticized visual sociology as 'an isolated self-sufficient and somewhat eccentric specialism' that was unable to connect with social scientific theory (2000: ix). They were to some extent correct that the connections between visual sociology practice and sociological theory had been limited, and their ambition to make visual research central to the sociological endeavour is laudable. However, for the reflexive vsisual ethnographer their own methodology is quite problematic (see Pink 2005). Emmison and Smith's approach is essentially an observational one. They treat observable human behaviour and material forms as 'visual data', finding interviewing often unnecessary. Moreover, their scathing critiques of visual anthropology are largely unjustified (see Pink: 2005: ch. 2). In contrast, participatory approaches recently developed by other sociologists place collaboration between researcher and informants at the centre of the ethnographic process. Of particular interest is the ethno-mimesis methodology developed by Maggie O'Neill (a sociologist developing work in cultural criminology). Linking sociological theory with performance art, O'Neill suggests that 'by representing ethnographic data ... in artistic form we can access a richer understanding of the complexities of lived experience which can throw light on broader social structures and processes' (2002: 70). The methodological implications of work like Chaplin's and O'Neill's are to stress collaboration, not solely between researcher and informants, but also between the visual, textual and performative and the producers of images and words. Their work, combined with two recent edited volumes by Caroline Knowles and Paul Sweetman (2004) and Susan Halford and Caroline Knowles (2005), signify new territory for visual sociology that makes fresh links between the subdiscipline of visual sociology and the concerns of mainstream sociologists (e.g. Knowles and Sweetman 2004: 5–11). These ideas form the basis of the discussions of the potentials of photography, video and hypermedia in research and representation in the following chapters.

The visual in cultural studies

Cultural studies approaches to photography and video have largely focused on the study of visual representation and visual cultures. For example, Stuart Hall's text *Representation* uses 'a wide range of examples from different cultural media and discourses, mainly concentrating on *visual* language' (1997: 9; original italics). It considered issues related to the negotiation of visual meanings, emphasizing the contested nature of meaning and 'the practices of representation' (1997: 9–10). However, the focus in cultural studies is on interpreting existing images and objects and the social and cultural conditions within which they are produced, rather than on how images and their production form part of ethnographic practices (see also, for example, Cooke and Wollen 1995; Jenks 1995; Evans and Hall 1999). Given the interest cultural studies has paid to visual cultures, representations and symbolism, and its increasing use of ethnography, it has incorporated the visual surprisingly little in its own research practices.

As an interdisciplinary subject, cultural studies does not identify with the development of a particular methodological tradition in the way that social anthropology, for example, is identified with participant observation: 'it still remains difficult to say quite what cultural studies amounts to methodologically'. Instead, 'cultural studies is eclectic in the methods it uses, drawing liberally from across the humanities and social sciences'; it thus deals with *methodologies* rather than a single methodology (McGuigan 1997: 1) and '[c]ultural studies methodology has often been described by the concept of *bricolage*: one is pragmatic and strategic in choosing and applying different methods and practices' (Alasuutari 1995: 2). This may explain why cultural studies guides to the use of visual images and technologies in ethnography are few and varied. Pertti Alasuutari suggested that 'to record nonverbal communication one needs a movie or video camera, and in a group discussion situation there should probably be several of them' (1995: 43), and recommends that video or tape recordings be made of interviews that may later be transcribed (1995: 179). Alasuutari's comments on the use of video in cultural studies research are not concerned with the development of the visual as a new form of knowledge, but are firmly embedded in a realist paradigm. In contrast though, Helen Thomas's discussion of her study of a youth and community dance group in south-east London (1997: 142) indicates the potential of video in cultural studies research. Asserting that ethnography is not about making truth claims, Thomas defined 'the construction of ethnographic descriptions' as 'an imaginative act which should bring us into touch with the lives of strangers' (Thomas 1997: 143). Her video work with dancers rehearsing, performing and in a group interview drew from feminist film theory to develop a participatory approach that sought to avert the oppressive 'masculine gaze' (see Chapter 4).

More recently, Martin Lister and Liz Wells formulated what they call a 'Visual Cultural Studies'. Mirroring the eclecticism of its parent discipline a *visual* cultural studies 'allows the analyst to attend to the many moments within the cycle of production, circulation and consumption of the image through which meanings accumulate, slip and shift' (2000: 90). As such, Lister and Wells would analyse photographs 'without separating them from social processes' (2000: 64). Rather than using images to produce knowledge (as in Thomas's work), they focus on the analysis of images and the contexts in which they become meaningful. Although this approach does not necessarily involve the researcher in collaborating with other social actors (as participant observation or participatory action research would), their methodology makes a welcome contribution to an ethnographic process that is attentive to visual aspects of culture and the embeddedness of images in society.

Common theoretical threads: the transformative potential of the visual

Across the ethnographic disciplines the use of visual images in research and representation is becoming more frequently written about and more rigorously theorized. Many researchers appear willing to scrutinize reflexively their own methods through explorations of how subjectivity, individual experience and negotiation with informants figure in the production of ethnographic knowledge. However, these developments are occurring at an uneven pace, both between and within the disciplines.

These changing disciplinary approaches to the visual can also be situated in relation to broader theoretical shifts. Publications of the 1990s situated the image and the camera as key elements in an intersection between modernity and a critique of modernity (McQuire 1998) and the relationship between photography and notions of the individual, memory and identity in Euro-American societies (e.g. Lury 1998). Both Scott McQuire and Celia Lury saw photography not only as a product of particular social and cultural environments, but also as a force that has itself encouraged shifts in ways of understanding and 'seeing'. McQuire argued that the ambiguity of the meaning of images not only questions the modern notion of truth, but destabilizes the basic premises of modernity. He proposed that the uncertainty of meaning implied by the camera questions the idea that there can be an 'ultimate goal' of a single, pure or 'untouched' meaning and this 'entrains a profound epistemological shift in which the meaning of meaning has itself been irreversibly transformed' (McQuire 1998: 47). McQuire emphasized the 'promiscuity' and ambiguity of the image: its simultaneous appearances of objectivity and subjectivity that became the basis upon which anthropologists rejected or accepted it and debated its usefulness to the social sciences in the 1970s. In McQuire's version of the history of the visual in modernity, he attributed power to the camera as an agent of change that overturns the realist paradigm. This implies that an appropriate application of visual images and technologies in ethnography may be developed as a force that will bring new meaning(s) to ethnographic work and social science. Suggesting, as MacDougall proposed for anthropology, a rethinking of social science 'through a visual medium' (1997: 293; and see also Grimshaw 2001; Grimshaw and Ravetz 2004). Moreover, as Lury's exploration of how 'the photographic image may have contributed to novel configurations of personhood, self-knowledge and truth' (1998: 2) suggests, the visual has implications not only for the discourses of modernity and ethnographic practice, but also for our understandings of the individuals who are the subjects of ethnography. Lury proposed that 'the photograph, more than merely representing, has taught us a way of seeing (Ihde, 1995), and that this way of seeing has transformed contemporary self-understandings' (1998: 3).

Approaches to the visual in anthropology, sociology and cultural studies have developed in rather different ways and have been informed by different understandings of the visual. However, reassessments of the relationship between vision, observation and truth influenced how the visual was approached across the disciplines, emphasizing the arbitrariness of visual meanings and the potential of the visual for the representation of ethnographic knowledge. The 1990s literature suggested that photographic and video images can act as a force that has a transformative potential for modern thought, culture and society, self-identity and memory and social science itself. This informs our understanding of a visual ethnography because it reminds us that by paying attention to images in ethnographic research and representation we are developing new ways of understanding individuals, social relationships, material cultures and ethnographic knowledge itself. The proliferation of publications in this area in the past ten years bears witness to the creativity and engagement that is developing in the use of visual ethnographic methods, itself an ongoing aspect of this transformation. When I wrote the first edition of *Doing Visual Ethnography* in the 1990s, a few studies stood out as obvious examples of the methods discussed. Reviewing the same field of literature in 2006, there is a wealth of work that could be cited. In the following chapters I point to those case studies that I consider are amongst the most valuable contributions to visual ethnographic practice.

The book

Chapter 1 outlines the theoretical approach of the volume, situating visual images and technologies in relation to a reflexive approach to ethnography that focuses on subjectivity, creativity and self-consciousness. It combines anthropological ideas about the individual in society with cultural theories of the visual and an exploration of consumption and material culture, to consider how visual images and technologies are interwoven with both the cultures ethnographers study and the academic cultures they work in. More practical uses of photography and video in ethnographic research and representation are the main foci of the following chapters, extending to a consideration of the potential of hypermedia representation in the final chapter.

In Chapter 2 the practical aspects of preparing for visual fieldwork are discussed, alongside project design, ethical considerations and gender issues. The following two chapters focus on different technologies and images in the research process. First, photography, which has been employed much more extensively by visual sociologists than in other ethnographic disciplines, is explored in Chapter 3. Ethnographic film, which has dominated the practice and literature of visual anthropology, is not my main concern here. Rather, I draw from this work to discuss video in Chapter 4. Chapter 5 focuses on the organization and interpretation of visual materials, while Chapters 6, 7 and 8 discuss the production of different types of text and how visual, written and other materials may be combined and interlinked in different representations. Digital media have opened up new and fascinating possibilities for the use of visual images in research and representation. However, these new potentials also raise a series of issues of representation, interpretation and the authoring of knowledge that need to be addressed at the outset of their use rather than retrospectively.

FURTHER READING

Banks, M. (2001) *Visual Methods in Social Research*, London: Sage. (An introduction to visual methods)

Chaplin, E. (1994) *Sociology and Visual Representations*, London: Routledge. (A critical and feminist approach to the visual in sociology)

Knowles, C. and Sweetman, P. (2004) (eds) *Picturing the Social Landscape: Visual Methods and the Sociological Imagination*, London: Routledge. (An edited volume of essays that demonstrate uses of visual methods in sociology)

Pink, S. (2005) *The Future of Visual Anthropology: Engaging the Senses*, London: Routledge. (An argument for a visual anthropology that engages anew with mainstream social anthropology and applied anthropology)

Van Leeuwen, T. and Jewitt, C. (2000) (eds) *Handbook of Visual Analysis*, London: Sage. (An edited volume that represents approaches to visual analysis across a range of disciplines)

Part 1
Thinking About Visual Research

Visual research and representation may sometimes unexpectedly become part of an ethnographic project that is already in progress. In other scenarios use of the visual will be part of a carefully prepared plan, although, as the examples in Chapters 3 and 4 indicate, new visual aspects of a project may develop. It is always important to be well prepared in the theoretical and practical possibilities raised by visual research methods. Part 1 offers a grounding in theoretical, practical and ethical issues that can inform a researcher whose uses of the visual in ethnography are either planned or (like many moments in ethnography) serendipitous.

1

The Visual in Ethnography:

Photography, Video, Cultures and Individuals

Images are 'everywhere'. They permeate our academic work, everyday lives, conversations (see Pink 1997a: 3), our imagination and our dreams (Edgar 2004). They are inextricably interwoven with our personal identities, narratives, lifestyles, cultures and societies, as well as with definitions of history, space and truth. Ethnographic research is likewise intertwined with visual images and metaphors. When ethnographers produce photographs or video, these visual texts, as well as the experience of producing and discussing them, become part of their ethnographic knowledge. Just as images inspire conversations, conversation may invoke images; conversation visualizes and draws absent printed or electronic images into its narratives through verbal descriptions and references to them. In ethnography images are as inevitable as sounds, smells, textures and tastes, words or any other aspect of culture and society. Although ethnographers should not be obliged to make the visual *central* to their work (see Morphy and Banks 1997: 14), they might explore its relation to other senses and discourses (see Pink 2005).

The visual has recently received much critical attention from scholars of the social sciences and humanities. It is now commonly recognized that, as Peter Crawford (1992: 66) recommended, notions of 'pure image' and 'pure word' are not viable. Instead we need to attend to the constructedness of this distinction. In this sense, even the term 'visual research methods' (see Banks n.d.) that refers to uses of visual technologies and images in research, places an undue stress on the visual. 'Visual research methods' are not purely visual. Rather, they pay particular attention to visual aspects of culture. Similarly, they cannot be used independently of other methods; neither a purely visual ethnography nor an exclusively visual approach to culture can exist. This chapter focuses on this interlinking of the visual with ethnography, culture and individuals.

Ethnography and ethnographic images

What is ethnography? How does one 'do' ethnography? What makes a text, photograph or video ethnographic? Handbooks of 'traditional' research methods tend to represent ethnography as a mixture of participant observation and interviewing. For example, Martin Hammersley and Paul Atkinson defined ethnography as 'a particular method or set of methods' that:

> involves the ethnographer participating, overtly or covertly, in people's daily lives for an extended period of time, watching what happens, listening to what is said, asking questions – in fact, collecting whatever data are available to throw light on the issues that are the focus of the research. (1995: 1)

Such descriptions are limited on two counts. First, they restrict the range of things ethnographers may actually do. Secondly, their representation of ethnography as just another method or set of methods of data collection wrongly assumes that ethnography entails a simple process of going to another place or culture, staying there for a period of time, collecting pieces of information and knowledge and then taking them home intact.

Instead, I shall define ethnography as a methodology (see Crotty 1998: 7); as an approach to experiencing, interpreting and representing culture and society that informs and is informed by sets of different disciplinary agendas and theoretical principles. Rather than a method for the collection of data, ethnography is a process of creating and representing knowledge (about society, culture and individuals) that is based on ethnographers' own experiences. It does not claim to produce an objective or truthful account of reality, but should aim to offer versions of ethnographers' experiences of reality that are as loyal as possible to the context, negotiations and intersubjectivities through which the knowledge was produced. This may entail reflexive, collaborative or participatory methods. It may involve informants in a variety of ways at different points of the research and representational stages of the project. It should account not only for the observable, recordable realities that may be translated into written notes and texts, but also for objects, visual images, the immaterial and the sensory nature of human experience and knowledge. Finally, it should engage with issues of representation that question the right of the researcher to represent other people, recognize the impossibility of 'knowing other minds' (Fernandez 1995: 25) and acknowledge that the sense we make of informants' words and actions is 'an expression of our own consciousness' (Cohen and Rapport 1995: 12).

There is, likewise, no simple answer or definition of what it is that makes an activity, image, text, idea, or piece of knowledge ethnographic. No single action, artifact or representation is essentially, in itself, ethnographic, but will be defined as such through interpretation and context. Anthropologists have noted the absence of concrete boundaries between ethnographic and fictional texts (see Clifford and Marcus 1986), and between ethnographic, documentary and fictional film (see Loizos 1993: 7–8). Similarly, there is no clear-cut way of defining an individual photograph as, for example, a tourist, documentary or journalistic photograph (see Chapter 3), or of deciding whether a piece of video footage is a home movie or ethnographic video (see Chapter 4). The same applies to the arbitrary nature of our distinctions between personal experience and ethnographic experience, autobiography and anthropology (see Okley and Callaway 1992; Okley 1996) and fieldwork and everyday life (Pink 1999a). Any experience, action, artifact, image or idea is never definitively *just one thing* but may be redefined differently in different situations, by different individuals and in terms of different discourses. It is impossible to measure the ethnographicness of an image in terms of its form, content or potential as an observational document, visual record or piece of data. Instead, the ethnographicness of any image or representation is contingent on how it is situated, interpreted and used to invoke meanings and knowledge that are of ethnographic interest.

Reflexivity and subjectivity

In their critique of natural science approaches, authors of traditional research methods texts emphasized the constructedness of ethnographic knowledge (e.g. Burgess 1984; Ellen 1984), usually coupled with a stress on the central importance of reflexivity (see also Fortier 1998; Walsh 1998). A reflexive approach recognizes the centrality of the subjectivity of the researcher to the production and representation of ethnographic knowledge. Reflexivity goes beyond the researcher's concern with questions of 'bias' or how ethnographers observe the 'reality' of a society they actually 'distort' through their participation in it. Moreover, reflexivity is not simply a mechanism that neutralizes ethnographers' subjectivity as collectors of data through an engagement with how their presence may have affected the reality observed and the data collected. Indeed, the assumption that a reflexive approach will aid ethnographers to produce objective data represents only a token and cosmetic engagement with reflexivity that wrongly supposes subjectivity could (or should) be avoided or eradicated. Instead, subjectivity should be engaged with as a central aspect of ethnographic knowledge, interpretation and representation.

At the end of the twentieth century postmodern thinkers argued that ethnographic knowledge and text can only ever be a subjective construction, a 'fiction' that represents only the ethnographer's version of a reality, rather than an empirical truth. Some proposed such approaches take reflexivity too far. For instance, David Walsh insisted the 'social and cultural world must be the ground and reference for ethnographic writing', that 'reflexive ethnography should involve a keen awareness of the interpenetration of reality and representation' and that researchers should not 'abandon all forms of realism as the basis for doing ethnography' (1998: 220). His argument presents a tempting and balanced way of thinking about the experienced reality people live in and the texts that ethnographers construct to represent this reality. Nevertheless, it is also important to keep in mind the centrality of the subjectivity of the researcher to the production of ethnographic knowledge. Anthony Cohen and Nigel Rapport's point that our understandings of what informants say or do is solely 'an expression of our own consciousness' (see above), problematizes Walsh's proposition. If the researcher is the channel through which all ethnographic knowledge is produced and represented, then the only way reality and representation can interpenetrate in ethnographic work is through the ethnographer's textual constructions of 'ethnographic fictions'. Rather than existing objectively and being accessible and recordable through scientific research methods, reality is subjective and is known only as it is experienced by individuals. By focusing on how ethnographic knowledge about how individuals experience reality is produced, through the intersubjectivity between researchers and their research contexts, we may arrive at a closer understanding of the worlds that other people live in. It is not solely the subjectivity of the researcher that may shade his or her understanding of reality, but the relationship between the subjectivities of researcher and informants that produces a negotiated version of reality (see, for example, Fortier 1998).

In relation to this, researchers should maintain an awareness of how different elements of their identities become significant during research. For example, gender, age, ethnicity, class and race are important to how researchers are situated and situate themselves in ethnographic contexts. Ethnographers ought to be self-conscious about how they represent themselves to informants and they ought to consider how their identities are constructed and understood by the people with whom they work. These subjective understandings will have implications for the knowledge that is produced from the ethnographic encounter between researcher and informants. In some fieldwork locations where photography and video are prohibitively costly for most local people, their use in research needs to be situated in terms of the wider economic context as well as questions of how the ethnographer's own identity as a researcher is constructed by her or his informants. Similarly, as I describe in Chapter 3, during my fieldwork in southern Spain, being 'a woman with a camera' was a significant aspect of my gendered identity as a researcher (see Pink 1999b). Gendered and economic power relations implied in and by images and image production have an inevitable influence on how visual images and technologies can be used in ethnographic research.

Reflexivity has been a key theme of the new visual methods literature that has emerged since the beginning of the twenty first century. It has been advocated strongly (although in slightly differing ways) in single author books (e.g. Ruby 2000a; Banks 2001; Rose 2001; and see Pink 2005: ch. 2 for a full review of this) and a number of good edited volumes containing case studies that demonstrate how contemporary researchers are reflecting on their visual methods in *practice* in visual anthropology (Edgar 2004; Grimshaw and Ravetz 2004; Pink et al. 2004; Schneider and Wright 2005) and visual sociology (Knowles and Sweetman 2004; Pole 2004). This period of methodological reflection, clearly informed by the postmodern turn of the 1980s and 1990s, has characterized not only the visual methods literature, but also qualitative research literature more generally.

Gendered identities, technologies and images

In the 1990s gender became a central theme in discussions of ethnographic research methodology. This included a focus on the gendered identity of the researcher, the intersubjectivity of the gendered negotiations that ethnographers have with their informants, the sensuous, sexualized and erotic aspects of fieldwork and the gendered nature of the ethnographic research process, or of the 'ethnographic narrative' (see especially Bell et al. 1993; Kulick and Willson 1995). A consideration of gender and other aspects of identity also has implications for ethnographic research with images.

Developments that took place in gender theory during the 1980s and 1990s have had an important impact on ethnographic methodology. A stress on the plural, rather than binary, nature of gendered identities and thus on *multiple* femininities and masculinities (see, for example, Connell 1987, 1995; Cornwall and Lindisfarne 1994; Moore 1994) has meant that differences *among* as well as *between* men and women are accounted for. Moreover, the fixity of both gender and identity have been questioned as researchers and theorists have begun to explore how the same individual may both experience and represent his or her masculinity or femininity differently in different contexts and in relation to different people (see Pink 1997a). It has been argued that the gendered self is never fully defined in any absolute way, but that it is only in specific social interactions that the gender identity of any individual comes into being *in relation to* the negotiations that it undertakes with other individuals. In this sense, as Kulick (1995: 29) has summarized, the gendered self is only ever completed in relation to other selves, subjectivities, discourses, representations or material objects. If we apply this to the fieldwork context, it implies that precisely how both researcher and informant experience themselves and one another as gendered individuals will depend on the specific negotiation into which they enter. If visual images and technologies are part of the research project, they will play a role in how both researcher and informant identities are constructed and interpreted. As part of most contemporary cultures, photography, video and other media also form part of the broader context in which researcher and informant identities are situated.

An understanding of gender relations as relations of power and a concurrent gendering of power relations has been developed in existing literatures on visual image production, representation and ethnographic research. In some instances gendered power relations become an explicit aspect of fieldwork experience. Deborah Barndt demonstrates this through a memorable example: 'Ever since that moment in 1969 when I took my first people picture and got threatened by my subject/victim (who in self-defense, wielded over me the butcher knife she had been using to carve her toe nails), I have understood that the act of photography is imbued with issues of power' (Barndt 1997: 9). In another project, photographing the staff of a sociology department, Barndt found also that the gendered and hierarchical power relations within the department corresponded with the access she had to different people:

> It seemed much harder to get into the space of the powerful than into the space of the less powerful: the (primarily female) secretaries in the departmental office were easier prey, for example, than the (usually male) full professors; you had to pass through two doors and get their permission before you could photograph them. (1997: 13)

An understanding of the intersection between image production, image-producing technologies and the ethnic, racial, gendered and other elements of the identities of those who use or own them is crucial for a reflexive approach. In more abstract discussions it has been argued that the modern or 'conventional' ethnographic research process itself constitutes a masculine pursuit that oppresses a feminine approach to knowledge. Don Kulick has likened the traditional narrative structure of ethnography to an exploitative and repressive act where the masculine ethnographer penetrates the feminized 'field' generalizing, abstracting and oppressing the 'feminine' objects of his study. He has argued for a different (and more feminine) approach to ethnography that focuses on negotiation and intersubjectivity (Kulick 1995). This perspective thus develops a model of masculinity as exploitative and repressive. This does not mean that all types of masculinity are always repressive or exploitative; in everyday life and experience many different types of masculinity exist (see Connell 1995). Rather, the abstracted models of feminine and masculine approaches to ethnography are important in that they stand as metaphors for particular approaches to ethics, epistemology and subjectivity.

These gendered models of ethnography as masculine, exploitative, observational and objectifying or feminine, subjective, sensuous, negotiating and reflexive have parallels in film studies and photography. In particular, notions of the gendered gaze, as developed by Laura Mulvey (1989) in film studies, and of the archive developed by Alan Sekula (1989) in photography, have suggested that women, or the less powerful, are oppressed by an objectifying masculine gaze that is implied by the way they are represented visually in both film and photography. Borrowed originally from Michel Foucault, these ideas have been re-appropriated to discuss visual representations in other cultures (e.g. Pinney 1992) and historically in western culture. For example, studies of colonial photography have characterized the 'colonial gaze' on other less powerful cultures as an exploitative and objectifying project to catalogue and classify the colonized (see Edwards 1992, 1997b). As a response to this, feminist approaches to the production of ethnographic knowledge and of ethnographic images and the uses of technology have been developed in Chaplin's work with photography (1994) and Thomas's research with video (1997). As well as video-recording dancers in rehearsals and performances which they too scrutinized, in a group interview Thomas moved to the other side of the camera so that 'the researcher would also be put into the "actual" research frame under the gaze of the camera' (Thomas 1997: 146). This informed how power relations were structured within the group and in particular between Thomas and the group members, with the camera as a democratizing technology, breaking down one dimension of the research/researched distinction by 'observing' the researcher along with her informants. Other research methods that have been used to 'reinscribe the power relations of fieldwork' include giving respondents video cameras with which to make their own video diaries (Holliday 2004).

Doing ethnography in contemporary contexts

The themes of reflexivity and subjectivity discussed above have certainly shaped contemporary ethnographic methodologies. However, today's research practices are also influenced by the specific political, technological and material contexts in which ethnographers work as well as new understandings of what might constitute an ethnographic 'field'. These situations mean that research now often becomes multisited, new relationships and ethical and personal responsibilities come to the fore and ethnographic narratives are contingent on these variables rather than following the conventional structure that, as I noted above, has been criticized from a feminist perspective. Ethical questions are covered in Chapter 3. Here I reflect on the nature of contemporary fieldwork contexts by way of examples that reveal how multisitedness, political contexts and technological and experiential factors also impinge on the

spaces of ethnography. The four areas singled out for discussion below
do not constitute an exhaustive list of contemporary fieldwork contexts –
that in itself would require a whole book. Rather, I have selected four
scenar   research. These contexts are followed up in
the ca   re I examine in more
detail

First   g carried out inside
the do   iplinary interest. In
these   dividuals or groups
living   , for example, social
anthr   ogy (Da Silva 2000)
and c   working for indus-
try a   doing ethnographic
resea   ise of visual media
and r   nmas as the camera
enter   e the object of public
scrut   nities to create data
archi   ce and practice, and
encou   and sensory prompt
throu   d experiences. Visual
meth   embodied experiences
and materiality of the home (Pink 2004b, 2005) and homelessness (Radley
et al. 2005). As the extract from Alan Radley et al.'s research in Figure 1.1
shows, photography can inspire people to represent and then articulate
embodied and material experiences that they do not usually recall in verbal interviewing. More generally, visual explorations produce useful data
for understanding how people experience their social and material environments, be this urban transport systems (e.g. Patton 2004) or a
children's playground (Loescher 2004), and for representing how 'social
processes are objectified in material objects' (MacDougall 2005: 240).

Secondly, contemporary ethnographers also need to account for the
mobility of their informants. As Vered Amit has pointed out, 'the people
whom they [ethnographers] are trying to study are increasingly likely
to be as mobile if not more so than the ethnographers trying to keep up
with them' (2000: 12). Research projects might cross short distances or
national boundaries as informants move according to their own circumstances. Our studies thus might include the new political and economic
contexts that economic migrants, refugees and asylum seekers find
themselves in and their strategies for coping with these.

Thirdly, Christine Hine's book *Virtual Ethnography* outlines an approach
to doing ethnographic research on-line: where the 'field' is located in electronic space, on the internet (2000). This has been followed by a number of
interesting ethnographic studies of, for instance, on-line social practices
and relationships. For example, Elisenda Ardevol's ethnographic study on
a dating website inevitably includes analysis of both written and photographic representations of self (see Ardevol 2005). In other cases fieldwork

© *Darrin Hodgetts, Andrea Cullen and Alan Radley 2003*

Figure 1.1

As part of a study of homelessness in Britain, Alan Radley, Darrin Hodgetts and Andrea Cullen asked research participants to photograph their everyday experiences of being a homeless person. Jean, who had been homeless for more than twenty years, took the photograph below and afterwards discussed it in interview with the researchers. Radley et al. write:

She described this photograph as follows:

> That's opposite the step where I used to sleep. These cardboard bits, I took a photograph of the cardboard bits because we use these cardboard bits and we flatten them out along the steps to sleep on so, soft you know it covers the concrete and the wet and the damp and everything so. You know we rely very much on the cardboard being left out for sleeping on, You know that it is important that we have cardboard. Other than that we have to go out and put big newspapers if there's no cardboard around.

Detailed descriptions of sleeping rough were relatively rare among the participants' responses. However, Jean felt it was important to communicate the sense of degradation that sleeping rough involves. Perhaps for that reason, many of her pictures centred upon litter and rubbish bins, as well as doorways and steps on which she had to sleep. About the last, she complained, was the annoying habit that people have of pissing on them, something that can be interpreted as a metaphor of displacement, of the abject situation in which rough sleepers find themselves ... She returned to the matter of cardboard later on in the interview when she spoke of homeless people building 'little cardboard houses around them at night' so that, as she said,

> You know, that cardboard is so close to you, it could almost be a person and there's lots of times that homeless people have been considered a piece of cardboard themselves. We've often been called 'cardboard people'.

(Radley et al. 2005: 289–90)

Moroccan Immigrant Praying, Barranquete, Almería, January 2004.
© *John Perivolaris 2004*

Figure 1.2
Migration and movement is part of the context in which contemporary
ethnographers work. John Perivolaris's photographic project *Migrados* focuses on
narratives of migration to Spain. The man photographed here collaborated with
Perivolaris as his guide and host, showing him what it was important for him to
photograph (Perivolaris 2005, personal communication). See an on-line exhibition
and discussion of this work at www.flickr.com/photos/dr_john2005/.

might be split between face-to-face social relationships in one locality and other contexts where the same people meet on-line in internet discussions, lists or forums. In many contemporary research projects ethnographers are finding that their informants' everyday relationships have an on-line component, this might mean not simply the exchange of e-mail but also of digital photography, the construction of websites or using on-line forums (e.g. Postill 2005). Such on-line contexts are likely to be composed of a combination of photographic and written elements, not to mention the iconography of on-line communication (see Ardevol 2003; Trias i Valls 2003).

Finally, researchers are increasingly attending to the idea of the human imagination and dreams as a site of ethnographic fieldwork. Visual methodologies have a key role to play in this research space. Of particular interest is Iain Edgar's approach to accessing and analysing the images that are produced through our imaginations and dreams. His imagework and dreamwork methods are similar since 'both refer to the mind's spontaneous production of imagery that people may consider "good to think with"' (2004: 10). However, as Edgar points out, although imagework is itself largely non-verbal, it tends to produce verbal narratives about intangible images (although in some scenarios informants produce visual representations of their dreams or imaginations – see for example Orobitg 2004), which form the materials that the researcher then analyses.

As these examples suggest, contemporary 'new' fieldwork domains are saturated with visual images. Indeed, as the ethnography shows, researchers working in these contexts are increasingly likely to be using visual images and media as part of their practices of research and representation.

Unobservable ethnography and visual culture

In the Introduction I described the realist view of visual technologies as tools for creating visual records. This view persists in some social science research methods textbooks. For example, Uwe Flick has referred to 'the use of visual media for research purposes' as 'second-hand observation' (1998: 151). While this may prove a useful means of undertaking some forms of social research, this 'observational' approach depends on the problematic assumption that reality is visible, observable and recordable in video or photography. However, as writers such as Johannes Fabian (1983) suggested, the epistemological and ethical principles of the observational approach should be rethought. In particular two issues need to be addressed. First, is it possible to observe and record 'reality'? For instance, just because something appears to be visible, this does not necessarily mean it is true. Secondly, the observational approach implies that we can observe and extract objective information (data) about our informants. This can be problematized as an 'objectifying' approach that does research *on* but not *with* people.

The relationship between the visual, the visible and reality has been explored in cultural studies as well as anthropology. As Chris Jenks argued, while material objects inevitably have a visual presence, the notion of 'visual culture' should not refer only to the material and observable, 'visible' aspects of culture (Jenks 1995: 16). Rather, the visual also forms part of human imaginations and conversations (Edgar 2004; Orobitg 2004). As Ivo Strecker has emphasized, images play a central role in the human mind and in human discourse which is 'metaphorically grounded' (Tyler 1987; Lakoff and Johnson 1980, quoted in Strecker 1997). The material and visual cultures that we encounter when we do ethnographic fieldwork may therefore be understood from this perspective: material objects are unavoidably visual, but visual images are not, by definition, material. Nevertheless, the intangibility of an image that exists as verbal description or is imagined makes it no less real. This approach to images presents a direct challenge to definitions of 'the real in terms of the material, which can be accessed through the visible' (Slater 1995: 221). This rupture between visibility and reality is significant for an ethnographic approach to the visual because it implies that reality cannot necessarily be observed visually. Therefore, rather than recording reality on video tape or camera film, the most one can expect is to represent those aspects of experience that are visible, or that the person being represented/representing themselves seeks to visualize or make visible. Moreover, these visible elements of experience will be given different meanings as different people use their own subjective knowledge to interpret them.

Strecker criticized existing treatments of images in ethnography by pointing out that ethnographers have tended to 'stand between' their informants and audiences/readers by translating images into words. In doing so ethnographers would impose one (their own) interpretation on the images, thus dismissing the possibility that the images may have more than one potential meaning. Instead, he proposed that since ethnography is 'largely to do with the interpretation of images' it should pay greater attention to 'the rhetorical contexts in which they are embedded' (Strecker 1997: 217). This theme is taken up again in the following chapters as I consider how visual images are given new meanings in a range of different contexts. Just as reality is not solely visible or observable, images have no fixed or single meanings and are not capable of capturing an objective reality. The most one can expect is that observation and images will allow one only to interpret that which is visible and the other elements of experience that are evoked through this.

Photography and video do nevertheless bear some relationship to 'reality'. The connection between visual images and experienced reality is constructed through individual subjectivity and interpretation of images. As Terence Wright pointed out, this may be because '[a]s products of a particular culture, they [in this case photographs] are only perceived as real by cultural convention: they only *appear* realistic because we have been taught to see them as such' (Wright 1999: 6; original italics). As ethnographers, we may suspend a belief in reality as an objective and observable experience, but we should also keep in mind that we too use images to refer to certain versions of reality and we treat images as referents of visible and observable phenomena: 'As Alan Sekula (1982: 86) has pointed out, it is the most natural thing in the world for someone to open their [*sic*] wallet and produce a photograph saying "this is my dog"' (Wright 1999: 2). Such realist approaches to photography and video are embedded in the experience and everyday practices of most ethnographers. Indeed, as I argue later in this book, in some cases realist uses of photographic and video images may be appropriate in ethnographic research and representation. However, realist uses of the visual in ethnography should be qualified by a reflexive awareness of the intentions behind such uses and their limits as regards the representation of tuth.

Images, technologies, individuals

Photography and video have been appropriated in varying forms and degrees by many individuals in almost all cultures and societies. However, visual images and technologies are not only elements of the cultures that academics study, they also pertain to the academic cultures and personal lifestyles and subject positions from which contemporary ethnographers approach their projects. As Chaplin has argued for sociology, ethnographic disciplines should not distance themselves from the topics they study (1994: 16). This means thinking not simply of 'the sociology *of* visual representation' but of sociology *and* visual representations as elements of the same cultural context. Thus ethnographers should treat visual representation as an aspect of the material culture and practice *of* social scientists as well as a practice and material culture that is researched *by* social scientists.

Most ethnographers, and an increasing number of informants (depending on the fieldwork context), own or have some access to still and video cameras. The inevitable interlinking between personal and professional understandings, agendas and intentions means that ethnographers' professional approaches to visual images and technologies cannot essentially be separated from their personal approaches and a reflexive approach to one's own visual practices is important for ethnographic and artistic work. Rather than there being a single corporate ethnographic approach that all ethnographers take on, the practices of individual ethnographers are attached to a combination of personal and professional elements. Anthropologists (e.g. Kulick and Willson 1995;

Okely 1996; Okely and Callaway 1992) have stressed the inseparability of personal from professional identities and the importance of autobiography and personal experience in the production of ethnographic knowledge. Some existing work develops this in practice, showing that there are inevitably continuities between the different personal and professional uses to which visual images and technologies may be put. For example, Okely has written anthropological text that uses autobiographical information as what she has called 'retrospective fieldwork'. This article, based on Okely's experiences of attending a boarding school, uses her memories and photographs from this period of her life (1996: 147–74). Likewise, Strecker and Jean Lydall's ethnographic film *Sweet Sorghum* (1995), about their daughter's childhood experiences of living with the Hamar people in Ethiopia while her parents were doing fieldwork, cut their own old 'home movie' footage with a more recently shot interview with their daughter. In such ways personal uses and experiences of visual technologies as well as actual images may later become part of a piece of professional work. Here a reflexive awareness of not only the visual dimensions of the culture being researched, but also of ethnographers' own cultural and individual understandings and uses of visual images and technologies, is important.

In my own fieldwork I have had to recognize that I have been just as much a consumer of photographic images and technologies as my informants (although maybe in different ways). Consumption and style have become the focus of multidisciplinary projects (e.g. Miller 1995; and preceding this Appadurai 1986), usually about the practices of 'other' people. Ethnographers' subjectivity and fieldwork styles may be theorized similarly: ethnographers are also consumers and apply certain practices of consumption to their visual technologies and images. Ethnographers' photography or video making may be related equally to their professional fieldwork narratives or personal biographies. Moreover, photography and photographs can represent an explicit meeting point (or continuity) between personal and professional identities; as material objects they pass through, and are invested with new meanings in, situations where individuals may wish to express different aspects of their identities. For example, when is a photograph of one's informants/friends kept in a 'research archive'? And when does it remain in one's personal collection? When I first returned from fieldwork in southern Spain in 1994 I had two sets of photographs: one of friends and one of 'research'. As time passed these photographs shifted between categories. They moved out of albums and eventually into a series of envelopes and folders. The personal/professional visual narratives into which I had initially divided them gradually became dissolved into other categories as I worked through the experience of fieldwork in an attempt to translate it into ethnographic knowledge. Thus my anthropological analysis began to appropriate my personal experience and possessions. Concurrently my informants and friends, both in 'the field' in Andalusia and 'at home' in the UK, appropriated my 'anthropological' and personal photographs, incorporating them into, and making them meaningful in terms of, their own material and visual cultures as they included them in their own photograph albums.

Consuming technology and practising photography

Photographers and video makers, whether or not they are ethnographers, are individuals with their own intentions working in specific social and cultural contexts. In order to understand the practices of both ethnographers and informants as image-makers it is important to consider how relationships develop between individuals, visual technologies, practices and images, society and culture. Pierre Bourdieu (1990 [1965]) made an early attempt to theorize photographic practices and meanings to explain why individuals tend to perpetuate existing visual forms and styles in their visual work. Bourdieu proposed that while everything is potentially photographable, the photographic practice of individuals is governed by objective limitations. He argued that 'photography cannot be delivered over to the randomness of the individual imagination' but instead 'via the mediation of the *ethos,* the internalization of objective and common regularities, the group places this practice under its collective rule' (Bourdieu 1990 [1965]: 6). According to this interpretation, images produced by individual photographers and video makers would inevitably express the shared norms of that individual's society. Thus, Bourdieu argued 'that the most trivial photograph expresses, apart from the explicit intentions of the photographer, the system of schemes of perception, thought and appreciation common to a whole group' (1990: 6).

Individuals undoubtedly produce images that respond and refer to established conventions that have developed in and between existing 'visual cultures'. However, the implication of this is not necessarily that individual visual practices are dictated by an unconsciously held common set of beliefs. Bourdieu's explanation represents a problematic reduction of agency, subjectivity and individual creativity to external objective factors. It is difficult to reconcile with more convincing theories of agency and self-hood, such as Cohen's proposition that individuals are 'self-driven' (1992: 226) 'thinking selves' and the creators of culture (1994: 167), thus viewing 'society as composed of and by self-conscious individuals' (1994: 192). This focus on individual creativity has been brought to the forefront in some anthropological work. In particular, Rapport has argued in favour of a recognition of the individual 'as a seat of consciousness, as well-spring of creativity, as guarantor of meaning' as opposed to 'the *dissolved, decentered, deconstructed* individual actor and author as he or she appears in Durkheimian, Structuralist and Post-Structuralist schools of social science' (Rapport 1997: 7; original italics). This suggests that while it is likely that individuals will reference known visual forms, styles, discourses and meanings through the content and form of their own visual images, this does not mean that they have simply internalized and are reproducing these formats. It is also probable that, as Evans and Hall have noted (1999: 3), their practices will intersect with camera and film manufacturing industries and developing and processing companies. Thus in creating images that reproduce or reference 'conventional' compositions and iconographies, individuals draw from personal and cultural resources of visual experience and knowledge. They thus creatively compose images that they intend to represent particular objects or meanings; moreover, they do so in particular social and material contexts. In the following chapters I emphasize the importance of attending to the intentionality of ethnographic photographers and video makers as creative individuals.

Images and image producers: breaking down the categories

Existing social scientific literature on photography tends to distinguish between family, snapshot, amateur and professional photographies. Similarly, distinctions are made between home movies and professional videos. For photographers themselves these categories and the distinctions between them can be important. To mistakenly put a photographer/amateur/snapshotter in the 'wrong' category can imply problematic assumptions about his or her knowledge of both photographic technique and his or her subject matter. For instance, in Spain bullfight *aficionados* associate different types of bullfight photography with particular gendered identities and corresponding understandings of the bullfight (see Pink 1997a). Work on photography in North American and European cultures implies that similar categories of image and image producers often appear to be assumed by both informants and researchers, and are not usually questioned (e.g. Bourdieu 1990; Chalfen 1987; Pink 1997a; Slater 1995). However these, like all categories, are in fact culturally constructed, and individually understood and experienced. Individual photographers, video makers or visual images may not fit neatly into just one of the identities that is implied by the distinction between categories such as domestic, amateur, professional (or ethnographic) images and producers. No photographic or video image need have one single identity and, as I have noted above, no images are, for example, essentially 'ethnographic' but are given ethnographic meanings in relation to the discourses that people use to define them.

The categorization of different types of photography and photographer also raises issues concerning professional identity for ethnographers who use still photography or video. For example, if categories of 'domestic', 'tourist', 'documentary' or 'ethnographic' are used to define a fieldwork photograph, each implies different types of knowledge and intentionality for the photographer. Some criticisms of the value of ethnographers'

John Postill (for right) doing fieldwork at the opening of a Chinese school in Malaysia.
© *John Postill 2003*

Figure 1.3
In 2003–4, when, with our son, I accompanied John Postill during his fieldwork in
Malaysia, my photographs of them taken at events that John was attending as part
of his fieldwork (recorded on my family photography CD) had personal meanings as
memories of our stay in Malaysia (where I was not doing research myself), and as
such of a similar status to vacation photography. For me the memories associated
with this photograph are to do with the taste of the meals in the containers in the
foreground and of exploring with our son. For John (filed in his digital research archive)
these same images were evocative of fieldwork experiences and knowledge.

photography have suggested that it is 'unlikely to be professional', 'mere
vacation photography', 'unsuitable for exhibition' or 'less relevant as representation' than images produced by professional, commissioned photographers (all comments social scientists have voiced). These opinions
assume there is an essential difference between professional ethnographic
and personal leisure photographs or video. However, during ethnographic
fieldwork the distinction between leisure and work is frequently ambiguous, for both ethnographers (especially anthropologists, for whom it
raises the question of whether one is ever 'off duty') and 'informants' who
may find it difficult to regard some 'research' activities as 'work'. Often
an ethnographer's research is structured by other people's leisure time
(among other things). Correspondingly, a proportion of 'ethnographic'

photography may be centred on leisure activities in which the ethnographer participates. I found that in Spain (in 1992–4), when photographing the professional and social life of bullfighting culture, many of my photographs and much of my photographic activity was structured simultaneously by my own work and leisure or my informants' leisure (see also Chapter 5). Thus the photographs I took at birthday parties, bullfights and official receptions were simultaneously ethnographic, anthropological, family and leisure photographs. While fixed categories imply that if an ethnographer's photography or video is classified as 'tourist' or 'leisure' images, then they are not 'ethnographic', my experiences indicate that a fieldwork photograph or video need never be fixed in any single category and that it would be mistaken to distinguish categorically between leisure and professional images and situate ethnographers' images accordingly. Ethnographers' own photographs are often worked into a range of different personal and professional narratives and subject positions (of ethnographers and their informants). They do not belong in any one fixed category and may be incorporated differently as the same individuals re-negotiate their gendered identities in different situations (see Chapter 2).

Fieldwork photographs often simultaneously belong to the different but connected material cultures of visual anthropology or sociology and of the culture being 'studied' (see Chapter 5). This may raise certain issues. For instance, what happens when ethnographers start to produce the very material culture they are studying; what impact do ethnographers have when they participate in and contribute to the visual discourses they are analysing; and what are the effects of informants' appropriations of ethnographers' images. I explore some of these scenarios in the following chapters.

A note on terminology

In the first edition of this book I referred to the people who take part in our research as 'informants'. This has been the standard term used by anthropologists for many years, but as Amit has pointed out it is nevertheless one that a good number of anthropologists do not feel comfortable with. She suggests that because of the intimacy and familiarity of the relationships that develop between anthropologists and the people whose lives their research becomes based on as the result of long-term fieldwork there exists 'the discomfiture that many anthropologists have with using terms such as informant, respondent or research subject as textual references for people they have known as friends, neighbours, advisers, etc' (2000: 3). The same can also apply to the collaborative work ethnographers develop in shorter-term projects. The relationships we develop with the people we work with to produce ethnographic knowledge do not involve our extraction of information from them, but the co-production of knowledge. This relationship is inevitably unequal, even if as in the examples I discuss in the following chapters the 'informants' also stand to gain something from it. In this sense changing the terminology does not necessarily represent any qualitative shift in the potentially exploitative nature of the relationship (cf. Amit 2000: 3). Nevertheless other terms have, across different disciplines, become popular recently. Two that seem particularly appropriate are those of 'research participant' and 'interlocutor'. The former is usefully open in that it can refer to any number of different forms of participating in ethnography. The latter, because it implies that the person is in dialogue or conversation with the ethnographer, stresses the intersubjectivity of the encounter. However the most likely scenario of any ethnographic research is that the ethnographer will interact with different 'informants' in ways that might represent any one of these potential relationships. For example, some people might behave as respondents, others will enter into extended dialogues with the ethnographer and others might participate by actively shaping the form the research takes. In this book I do not make a commitment to any one term, but use that which appears most appropriate for the situation discussed.

Summary

Ethnographers themselves are members of societies in which photography and video are already practised and understood in particular ways. The ways in which individual ethnographers approach the visual in their research and representation are inevitably influenced by a range of factors, including theoretical beliefs, disciplinary agendas, personal experience, gendered identities and different visual cultures. Fundamental to understanding the significance of the visual in ethnographic work is a reflexive appreciation of how such elements combine to produce visual meanings and ethnographic knowledge.

FURTHER READING

Amit, V. (2000) *Constructing the Field*, London: Routledge. (An edited volume of case studies that discuss the contemporary fieldwork context)

Bell, D., Caplan, P. and Jahan Karim, W. (1993) *Gendered Fields*, London: Routledge. (An edited volume that offers a very useful series of case studies of the gendered nature and relationships of fieldwork)

Edgar, I. (2004) *Guide to Imagework: Imagination-Based Research Methods*, London: Routledge. (An introduction to Edgar's imagework methodology, which could be used as a complementary method to the visual ethnographic methods described in this volume)

Howes, D. (2005) *Empire of the Senses: The Sensory Culture Reader*, Oxford: Berg. (A volume of key readings about sensory aspects of culture, which usefully contextualizes the place of vision)

2

Planning and Practising 'Visual Methods':

Appropriate Uses and Ethical Issues

Why use visual methods?

It is impossible to predict, and mistaken to prescribe, precise methods for ethnographic research. Similarly, it would be unreasonable to 'require that visual methods be used in all contexts'. Rather, as Morphy and Banks have suggested, 'they should be used where appropriate, with the rider that appropriateness will not always be obvious in advance' (1997: 14). In practice, decisions are best made once researchers are in a position to assess which specific visual methods will be appropriate or ethical in a particular research context, therefore allowing researchers to account for their relationships with informants and their experience and knowledge of local visual cultures. Nevertheless, certain decisions and indicators about the use of visual images and technologies in research usually need to be made before commencing fieldwork. Often research proposals, preparations and plans must be produced before fieldwork begins; the fieldwork may be in an area where technologies are difficult to purchase or hire; if the project is to be funded and equipment purchased from a research grant, technological needs must be anticipated and budgeted for. Most researchers work with or for or study in universities and other organizations. Usually such institutions also require that their committees should formally scrutinize and approve of research ethics that any project involves before fieldwork begins.

The appropriateness of visual methods

Banks has divided visual research methods into three broad activities: 'making visual representations (studying society by producing images)'; 'examining pre-existing visual representations' (studying images for information about society); 'collaborating with social actors in the production of visual representations' (Banks n.d.). These activities can, in a general way, be anticipated before one begins fieldwork. However, in reality our specific uses of visual images and technologies tend to develop as part of the social relationships and activities that ethnographers engage in during fieldwork. Some of these will be purposefully thought out and strategically applied. In Chapters 3 and 4 the specific applications of general models of visual research methods are discussed in detail. In other cases unanticipated uses of the visual may be discovered by accident and retrospectively defined as visual methods. Ethnographers might repeat such activities (sometimes in collaboration with informants), thus developing and refining the method throughout the research. However, methods developed within one research context may not be transferable to, or appropriate in, others. For example, when I started to research Spanish bullfighting culture I began photographing people at the many public receptions held to present trophies, exhibitions and book launches. After my first reception I showed my photographs to the organizers and participants and they asked me for copies of certain photos, some of which they gave to their colleagues. By keeping note of their requests and asking questions about the images I gained a sense of how individuals situated themselves in relation to other individuals in 'bullfighting culture'. As I attended more receptions I consciously repeated this method and developed my use of the camera and the photographs in response to the relationship that developed between my informants, the technology, the images and myself as photographer (see Chapter 3; Pink 1999b). This method of researching with images was appropriate in bullfighting culture partly because it imitated and was incorporated into my informants' existing cultural and individual uses of photography. Yet in other fieldwork contexts it will not work in the same way. The ethnographer needs to consider both local photographic conventions and the personal meanings and both economic and exchange values that photographs might have in any given research context. An increasing number of social scientists do research with people who are more technology literate and (especially for doctoral students) wealthier than them. For example, in John Postill's research about ICT uses in Malaysia he found that many of his informants, who were mainly middle class Chinese suburban residents, had more sophisticated photographic technology than he was using himself. At public events he was often surrounded by local people photographing the proceedings with their mobile phones and key local actors tended to use digital cameras to produce images for their own websites. One local politician had a portable printer that he used to print out a photograph of himself photographed with Postill at a community basketball match (an enviable technology to any visual researcher) (Postill, personal communication).

Here Postill was able to sometimes share his own digital images of events with his informants.

In other research contexts ethnographers' equipment might well exceed the economic possibilities of their informants. This might be the case both in developing countries or when researching less powerful groups of people in modern western countries. Radley, Hodgetts and Cullen's photographic study of how homeless people both survive and make their home in the city is another example of how in a context where photographic practice was not part of the everyday lives of their informants, photography was in fact an appropriate research method. In this study they asked twelve homeless people to take photographs, using disposable cameras, of 'key times in their day, of typical activities and spaces, or anything else that portrayed their situation' (Radley et al. 2005: 277). Their photographic production was both preceded and followed by an interview. The researchers argue that their emphasis on the visual 'as a way of engaging the participants' (2005: 292) meant that for this research that had a particular focus on appearance, materiality and the use of space (2005: 293) the data provided more information than simply interviewing would have. Importantly, they also report that 'the participants said that they enjoyed making the pictures, enjoyed having the opportunity to show as well as to tell about their lives, their constraints and their possibilities' (2005: 292).

Before attempting visual research it is useful to read up on visual methods used by other ethnographers. However, it is also crucial to evaluate their appropriateness for a new project. This includes considering how visual methods, images and technologies will be interpreted by individuals in the cultures where research will be done, in addition to assessing how well visual methods suit the aims of specific projects. In some situations visual methods appear inappropriate. Moreover researchers should not have fixed, preconceived expectations of what it will be possible to achieve by using visual research methods in a given situation. Sometimes visual methods will not support the researcher's aims. Hastrup's (1992) description of her attempt as a woman anthropologist to photograph an exclusively male Icelandic sheep market demonstrates this well. She described the difficulty and discomfort she experienced while photographing this event but notes that having accomplished the task she felt a sense of satisfaction 'to have been there and to have been able to document this remarkable event' (1992: 9). She had left with the sensation that she 'even had photos from the sacred grove of a male secret society' (1992: 9). However, her photographic method was not appropriate for recording the type of information she had anticipated and she wrote of the disappointment she experienced on later seeing the printed photographs: 'they were hopeless. Ill-focused, badly lit, lopsided and showing nothing but the completely uninteresting backs of men and rams' (1992: 9). She emphasized the difference between her experience of photographing and the end results: 'While I was taking them I had the impression that I was making an almost pornographic record of a secret ritual. They showed me nothing of the sort but bore the marks of my own inhibition, resulting from my transgression of the boundary between gender categories' (1992: 9). Hastrup's expectations of what she might obtain by using this visual research method were not met. She anticipated that her photographs would represent ethnographic evidence of her experience of the event: 'a record of a secret ritual'. To assess why this was not achieved she generalized that 'pictures have a limited value as ethnographic "evidence"', and the 'secret' of informants' experiences can only be told in words (1992: 9). While I would agree that as ethnographic 'evidence' photographs indeed have limited value (see Chapter 1), this does not necessarily indicate that one may only represent ethnographic knowledge with words (see Chapters 6–8). The potential of photography or video as a realist recording device or a way of exploring individual subjectivities and creative collaboration will be realized differently in every application.

Sometimes using cameras and making images of informants is inappropriate for ethical reasons (see below). In some situations photographs or videos of informants may put them in political danger, or subject them to moral criticism. The appropriateness of visual methods should not simply be judged on questions of whether the methods suit the objectives of the research question and if they fit well with the local culture in which one is working. Rather, such evaluations should be informed by an ethnographic appreciation of how visual knowledge is interpreted in a cross-cultural context. Therefore decisions about the particular methodologies and modes of representation to be used should pay attention to intersections between local visual cultures, the ways in which the visual is treated by wider users or audiences of the research and ethnographers' own knowledge, experience and sensitivity. By thinking through the implications of image production and visual representation in this way ethnographers should be able to evaluate how their ethnographic images would be invested with different meanings by different political, local and academic discourses.

Planning visual research

Without good knowledge of the context in which one is planning to do ethnographic research it is very difficult to predict how and to what extent visual images and technologies may be used. Similarly, the basis upon which one may judge if visual methods will be ethical, appropriate, or a useful way to participate or collaborate with the people with whom one is working, will be contingent on the particular

The women bullfighter Cristina Sanchez performing. © *Sarah Pink 1993*

Figure 2.1

When researching gender and bullfighting in Spain, one of the roles I played was as amateur bullfight photographer. My photographic prints, taken mainly in black and white, using a traditional stills camera, provided me with a way to fit in with and share one of the activities that local bullfight *aficionados* were involved in at that historical moment. Since doing that research both technologies and local practices have shifted. Were I to begin similar fieldwork now in 2006 I would not be able to take for granted that exactly the same method would be appropriate. I would need to review the extent to which amateur bullfight *aficionados* now use digital photography and the implications of this for their practice.

research context. Plans to use visual methods made before commencing the research may appear unnecessary or out of place once the research has begun. For example, my original proposal to do research about women and bullfighting in southern Spain anticipated the extensive use of video. However, once in the field I found my informants only occasionally used video cameras. I was working in a culture where photography was a dominant source of knowledge and representation about bullfighting. In this situation it was usually more appropriate to participate in local events as a photographer than as a video maker. Since some of my informants also participated in their 'bullfighting culture' as amateur photographers, I was able to share an activity with them as well as producing images that interested them. At the time photography fitted the demands of the project. However, retrospectively, I was able to identify ways in which video could have supported the research, fitted into the local bullfighting culture and also served my informants' interests. Such insights could be used as the basis of future research plans, but would need to be reviewed on the basis of any changes in contemporary local practices at the point that new research commenced.

Usually ethnographers with some experience of working in a particular culture and society already have a sense of the visual and technological cultures of the people with whom they plan to work. Ethnographers should have an idea of how their photographic/video research practices will develop in relation to local practices and a sense of how they may learn through the interface between their own and local visual practices. Such background knowledge makes it easier to present a research proposal that defines quite specifically how and to what ends visual technologies and images are to be employed. This may entail developing insights from prior research in the same culture, doing a short pilot study, or researching aspects of visual cultures from library and museum sources, ethnographic film and the internet. This need not be solely a traditional literature review about visual culture. The first stage of the research process may be an interactive exploration of websites and e-mail contacts where elements of the visual culture of a research area are represented. For instance, if I was to begin research into the visual representations of bullfighting culture now, in the first decade of the twenty-first century, rather than the early 1990s, the starting point from my base in England would be to examine the now numerous bullfighting websites and on-line magazines. E-mail communications and electronic exchanges of digital images are clear options for researchers working with informants who are technology users themselves. When starting research about the 'slow living' movement in Britain in 2005, all my initial contacts were made on-line. My web searches included reading on-line materials but also discovering the snail logo of the movement and the visual images that form part of its internet presence. In some cases, a desk-based analysis of web pages can form the first stage of ethnographic fieldwork (see Figure 2.2).

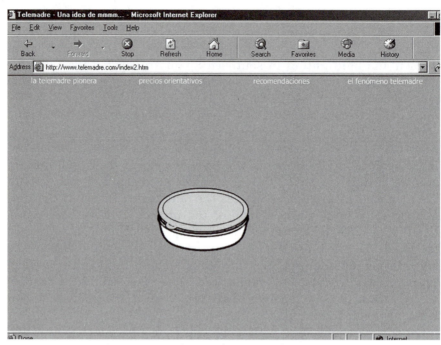

A page from the telemadre.com *Website. Reproduced with permission of mmmm...*

Figure 2.2

In collaborative research with Ana Martinez Pérez, I am analysing social and gendered relationships that are produced in relation to a Spanish website: www. telemadre.com. The web site represents what its producers call a 'social model', by which, for a fee, unemployed mothers (the *telemadres*) cook meals for young professionals (the *telehijos*) who do not have time to cook for themselves. Our wider research will include visual ethnographic fieldwork with the *telemadres* and *telehijos*. However, as a precursor to this we have developed an analysis of the visual and written texts of this website (Pink and Martinez Pérez 2006). The analysis both builds on existing theoretical and ethnographic research about Spanish gender and domestic life and will inform the research questions that guide our fieldwork.

For example, in our analysis of the web page above that represents a Tupperware® container as the preferred method of storage for the prepared food we note how we have learnt from our existing ethnographic experience that: 'When adult sons still living at home worked away from the parental home it was common on their weekend visits for them to leave with a set of Tupperware containers of prepared home-cooked meals to be reheated from Monday to Friday, to be returned and re-filled by their mother the following weekend. This occurred even in cases of sons who lived relatively independently in their own homes' (Pink and Martinez Pérez 2006). The Tupperware container thus becomes a culturally relevant image. The implication is that when we follow this study up with our fieldwork we will need to attend to this question of the meaning of Tupperware to our informants and the extent to which this helps to embed the economic exchanges between *telemadres* and *telehijos* with sentiments of kinship.

More generally, the internet is part of many contemporary ethnographic field sites.

Pre-fieldwork surveys of literature, electronic and other visual texts and examples of how other ethnographers have successfully worked with visual images and technologies in specific cultures can indicate the potential for using visual methods in particular fieldwork contexts. Combined with some considered guesswork about people's visual practices and discourses, this can form a basis from which to develop a research proposal. However, neither a researcher's own preparation, nor other ethnographers' accounts can predict how a visual method will develop in a new project. Just as ethnography can only really be learned in practice, ethnographic uses of visual images and technologies develop from practice-based knowledge. Moreover, as projects evolve novel uses of photography or video may develop to explore and represent unexpected issues. Indeed, some of the most thought provoking and exciting instances of visual research have emerged unexpectedly during fieldwork. A good example is Gemma Orobitg's research amongst the Pumé Indians of Venezuela. Orobitg, who notes that 'During the initial design of my fieldwork ... I did not consider using a camera. Rather it was a fortunate coincidence that led me to first experiment and then reflect methodologically on the value of visual technologies in anthropological research and for anthropological analysis' (2004: 31). Orobitg was asked to take photographs for some documentary filmmakers who wanted to develop a film project in the area and needed some images to support their application. However, from the moment she showed these photographs to the Pumé people she was working with, the images began to inform her research in some key ways: as a visual note book; as a way of communicating with the Pumé; and as a medium through which to reconstruct the imaginary sphere of Pumé life (Orobitg 2004: 32). In Chapters 3 and 4 I discuss a series of examples that are intended to offer ideas and inspirations through which ethnographers may develop their own styles.

Choosing the technology for the project

Like images, and any material object, technologies are also interpreted differently by individuals in different cultures. If possible, ethnographers should explore the meanings informants give to different visual technologies before purchasing equipment.

The selection of a digital or 'traditional' camera, a semi-professional video camera or the cheapest hand-held domestic model may be related to economic factors, but should also account for how the equipment one uses will become part of one's identity both during fieldwork and in academic circles. Individuals constantly re-situate themselves and construct their self-identities in relation to not only other individuals but also to material objects and cultural discourses. The visual technologies ethnographers use, like the images they produce and view, will be invested with meanings, inspire responses and are likely to become a topic of conversation. Some informants may have a shared interest in photography or video (in some cases they will have better cameras and skills than the researcher). For example, in Spain my amateur interest in bullfight photography was shared with several local people. This led us to discuss technical as well as aesthetic aspects of bullfighting photography. Then, in the early 1990s, this included themes such as the best film speeds, zoom lenses and seating in the arena. Later in 1999 and 2000, in video interviewing projects in the United Kingdom and Spain, interviewees appeared relaxed with my domestic digital video camera, simply seeing it as one of the latest pieces of new video technology. In comparison to solitary field diary writing, photography and video making can appear more visible, comprehensible activities to informants, and may link more closely with their own experience. Photographs and video tapes themselves become commodities for exchange and the sites of negotiation, for example, among informants, between researchers and informants, between researchers and their families and friends at home and among researchers. In short, the visual technologies and images associated with ethnographers will also be implicated in the way other people construct their identities and thus impact on their social relationships and experiences.

Therefore, when selecting and applying for funding for technology it is important to remember that a camera will be part of the research context and an element of the ethnographer's identity. It will impinge on the social relationships in which he or she becomes involved and on how informants represent themselves. Different technologies impact on these relationships and identities in different ways. In some cases image quality may have to be forsaken to produce images that represent the type of ethnographic knowledge sought. For example, the relationship between ethnographer and subjects that can develop in a photographic or filmic situation created by the use of professional lighting and sound equipment will differ from when the ethnographer is working alone with just a small hand-held camcorder or stills camera. The images may be darker and grainier, the sound less sharp, but the ethnographic knowledge they invoke may be more useful to the project.

In tandem with the social and cultural implications of the use of visual technologies, practical and technical issues also arise. How will a camera and other equipment be powered and transported? (Will there even be electricity?) What post-production resources will be available? Finally, what resources will be available for showing the images to informants? In some locations cameras can be connected to TV monitors and video recorders. In others, a solar-powered laptop computer might be used to screen digital still and video images. When purchasing equipment it is important to keep track of technological developments and also of post-fieldwork equipment requirements. How and where will editing be carried out? Will any extra computing hardware, software or expertise be needed? The precise technology available and skills needed can change within a year or so. For example, for my 1999 video ethnography research I needed to ask skilled computing staff to support me by digitalizing my video footage and saving it on CD. In contrast, in 2006 I am able to do this myself using the software that was supplied with my domestic digital video camera and laptop computer. However, both equipment and additional production facilities, if they are used, can be costly and it is important to budget realistically for the cost of tape transfer, use of editing facilities, printing and computing equipment.

Ethics and ethnographic research

A consideration of the ethical implications of ethnographic research and representation should underpin any research project. Most guides and courses on research methods dedicate a section to ethics. Such texts usually cover a standard set of issues such as informed consent, covert research, confidentiality, harm to informants, exploitation and 'giving something back', ownership of data, and protection of informants. These indisputably relevant issues are critically reviewed later in this chapter. However, the issue of ethics in ethnographic work refers to more than simply the ethical conduct of the researcher. Rather, it demands that ethnographers develop an understanding of the ethical context(s) in which they work, a reflexive approach to their own ethical beliefs, and a critical approach to the idea that *one* ethical code of conduct could be hierarchically superior to all others. Because ethics are so embedded in the specific research contexts in which ethnographers work, like decisions about which visual research methods to employ in a project, ethical decisions cannot be concluded until the researcher is actually in the field.

In practice, ethics are bound up with power relations between ethnographers, informants, professionals, sponsors, gatekeepers, governments, the media and other institutions (see Ellen 1984: 134). Ethical decisions are ultimately made by individual ethnographers, usually with reference to personal and professional codes of ethical conduct and the intentionalities of other parties. Researchers from different disciplines will need to refer to the ethical guidelines of the professional association that they feel most closely aligned with, and at times to those of other related disciplines when their work crosses disciplinary boundaries. Most professional associations now keep their ethical codes and other guidelines and discussions relating to this on-line. In Britain the Association of Social Anthropologists (ASA) and the British Sociological Association (BSA) provide important documents. The ethical practices of academic researchers are now often also scrutinized by both the research ethics committees that have been set up in the institutions in which they work and the research funding councils that support their work. The personal dimension of ethnographic research, the moral and philosophical beliefs of the researcher and his or her view of reality, also impinge greatly on the ethical practices that he or she applies in research and representation.

Ethics are also bound up with the epistemological concerns of academic disciplines – they both inform and are informed by theory and methodology. For instance, a research methodology that is informed by a relativist approach requires that ethics becomes not simply a matter of ensuring that research is done in an ethical way (that is, conforms to a fixed ethical code or set of rules), but that ethics becomes an area of philosophical debate in itself. If difference denotes plurality and equality rather than hierarchy, then it would seem unreasonable to argue that one ethical code would be superior to another. This problematizes the idea that there is one set of rules that defines *the* ethical way to undertake ethnographic research and challenges the assumption that ethnographic research may be guided by one code of ethical conduct rather than by another. However, such a relativist approach to ethics raises difficult questions. For instance, how relativist can ethnographic research and representation afford to be in relation to ethics while remaining an 'ethical' activity? Should ethnographers accept all ethical codes as being equally permissible? Clearly there are some activities that ethnographers would wish to render 'unethical'.

Rapport has suggested that the inadequacy of a relativist approach for dealing with ethics may be resolved by a focus on the individual. He argues that '[i]nstead of relativistic making of allowances for different cultures maintaining different traditions – whatever the consequences to their individual members – I want to outline a liberal basis for social science which recognises individuals as universal human agents above whom there is no greater good, without whom there is no cultural tradition' (Rapport 1997: 181). For Rapport, the ethical approach of social science should be one that responds against 'the violation of individual integrity, the threat to the individual's conscious potential, the ideological prioritising of community above and beyond the individuals who at any one moment constitute it' (1997: 181). Therefore he is able to argue that social scientists should be able to see a number of practices (such as 'Naziism, religious fundamentalism, female circumcision, infanticide and *suttee*') as unethical 'because of the hurt they cause to individuals, because of the harm which accrues in those social milieux where an ethic of interpersonal tolerance is not managed' (1997: 181).

Rapport's principle offers a basis upon which ethnographers may evaluate the ethical practices of themselves as researchers, their informants
and other individuals, agencies and institutions with whom they come
into contact during research. Ultimately, the decision will be a personal
one for each ethnographer has to decide whether his or her research
practices and representations are ethical before these are held up to the
scrutiny of others who will then interpret this question for themselves.
Similarly, the question of the ethics of those whom we study, and the
ethics of studying and/or making moral judgements about them, is one
that individual ethnographers must address for themselves at some
stage in their research. It will also be addressed by those who read or
view their representations at another stage. During my research about
bullfighting I was often confronted with the question 'was bullfighting
morally right or wrong?' While carrying out this research I felt morally
able to 'stand on the fence'. I did not commit myself to a moral judge-
ment either way, and still maintain that I don't. However, I was aware
that some of my Spanish informants and some acquaintances in the
United Kingdom felt that not only bullfighting, but also my research
and my participation in bullfighting culture by attending (and sometimes enjoying) bullfights was unethical. They felt that by researching
and writing on the subject I was effectively condoning what they
regarded as an unethical practice. On occasion I could empathize with
their subject position, but I felt I was doing nothing more than shifting
subject positions; I was never making a personal commitment to either
standpoint. Aware that some people, especially animal rights activists,
would judge my informants' practices as unethical, and having heard
their views that bullfighting fans were 'blood thirsty', 'violent' and 'bar-
baric', I felt obliged to 'protect' my informants by attempting to represent them as sensitive and moral human beings and to describe their
understanding of bullfighting in a way that indicated they did not fit
the unethical profile others had associated with them. The ethics that
guide ethnographers may be a critical discourse on the ethics of the
people they study, or of an individual or institution who has power over
them. Rapport admits that his perspective on ethics (see above) is personal. Similarly, my own approach to the ethics of bullfighting was
based on a personal conviction. Another ethnographer might argue that
any activity that causes harm or hurt to animals is unethical, thus
taking a different approach to the representation of ethnographic work
on bullfighting.

As Peter Pels has pointed out for anthropology, in the contemporary
world:

> Globalizing movements have resulted in a situation in which the ethics of
> anthropology can no longer be thought of simply in terms of the dyad between
> researcher and researched: anthropology is placed squarely within a more

complex field of governmentality, cross-cultural conflict and global mobility. Some of these developments seem threatening to anthropology, others seem to provide new opportunities, and all raise novel questions about the ethics of anthropological research. (Pels 1996: 8)

It is not solely ethnographers and informants who are implicated in the ethical issues researchers confront during fieldwork. Indeed, there may be a whole range of other interested parties and agendas that shape the ethical conduct of ethnographers and their informants either by enforcing their own guidelines, or by posing a threat to the safety of those represented in ethnographic work. Ethnographers therefore need to understand how plural moralities are at play in any ethnographic situation, and the extent to which these different ethical codes are constructed and interpreted in relation to one another. Ethnographers should seek to identify where the ethics of the research fit in with these other ethical codes with which it intersects. Ultimately, ethics in ethnography is concerned with making decisions based on interpretations of the moralities and intentionalities of other people and the institutions they may represent.

Visual research methods and ethical ethnography

The theoretical underpinning of my approach to ethics and visual research methods is based on the relationship between vision and reality discussed in Chapter 1. This emphasizes the specificity of the visual meanings that operate in the different cultures and societies in which ethnographers work and in the different ways ethnographers' images can be interpreted by other bodies such as academics, informants, professionals, sponsors, gatekeepers, governments, the media and other institutions. However conscious ethnographers are of the arbitrary nature of photographic meanings, ethnographic images are still likely to be treated as 'truthful recordings' or 'evidence' by non-academic viewers. Ethnographers should pay particular attention to how different approaches to the visual and different meanings given to the same images may coincide or collide in the domains in which we research and represent our work.

Below I critically review existing approaches to ethics in ethnographic research methodology, to consider their implications for the use of visual images.

Covert research and the question of informed consent

As a scientific-realist strategy, covert research was assumed to enable ethnographers to better observe an 'objective truth'. In the case of the covert use of video recording and photography the same principle was applied: the use of a hidden camera was thought to allow researchers to produce images of an objective reality, less 'distorted' by their own subjectivity and by the self-consciousness of their informants (see Chapter 1 and also Banks 2001: 120–1). Nevertheless, as I have noted in Chapter 1, such objectivity can never actually be achieved. Although some would argue that not all covert research is necessarily unethical (see, for example, Hammersley and Atkinson 1995: 263–8), any type of covert research requires a careful consideration of ethics and any decisions made should be contingent on the specific research context. In my view, however, it would be extremely difficult to justify undertaking covert research as part of a visual ethnographic project.

The approach to photography and video in ethnographic research I propose in Chapters 3 and 4 emphasizes the idea of collaboration between researcher and informant (which is also fundamental to Banks's approach to visual research [see Banks 2001]). Covert research implies the researcher videoing and photographing the behaviour of informants in a secretive rather than collaborative way, for example, using a hidden camera or using the camera under the guise of a role other than that of researcher. A collaborative method, in contrast, assumes that researcher and informant are consciously working together to produce visual images and specific types of knowledge through technological procedures and discussions. As such, in my view, a collaborative method provides a more appropriate ethical approach to visual ethnography.

The distinction between overt and covert research is, however, further complicated by challenging the notion of 'informed consent'. First, because cross-culturally consent may take different forms, involve different individuals and relationships and have different meanings. Secondly, informants may be keen to collaborate without actually engaging fully with *why* a researcher would want to video-record certain activities. Even if informants collaborate or participate in the production of ethnographic video and photography, it is unlikely that their understanding or intentions *vis-à-vis* the project will coincide exactly with the ethnographer's. In such cases it could be argued that even if consent is given, it is not *informed* consent, and the researcher is (even if unintentionally) keeping his or her real agenda hidden from the informants.

The ethical implications of covertly shot video or photography vary at different stages of the project at which the images may become accessible to different parties. If the ethnographer is to publish covertly produced images, this raises a range of new issues (see below).

Permission and the right to photograph/video at public events
It is good practice to ask permission to photograph in any public context or event, as well as seeking the consent of the individuals

photographed, and in some situations official permission is required. Permission to photograph and video at public events may be granted in a variety of ways. During my fieldwork in Spain, like many of my informants, I often photographed the bullfight. While it was not allowed to video-record a bullfight without formal permission, photography was usually freely permitted. Much of this involves photographing individual performers, however their permission is rarely asked and their fans tend to assume their right to photograph a public figure. Bullfighters are frequently photographed before and after as well as during their performances. Fans queue up at their hotels, hoping for a chance to pose with the performer, while the arena is packed with many aspiring bullfight photographers with a range of different types of camera and skills. In this research context public photography was freely permitted and acceptable. In other field contexts formal permission might be needed before photographing in any public place or event. It is best to seek guidance locally, both regarding the public rules and regulations *and* local cultural conventions. Both when formally permission is not required, or when it has been given formally, it is nevertheless polite to ask people if they would mind being photographed in public contexts.

The question of whether an ethnographer has permission to photograph or video differs from situation to situation and according to who we listen. Often it seems obligatory initially to negotiate official permission to video or photograph with institutional gatekeepers. However, permission to video or photograph individuals in their capacity as participants in events is usually best negotiated with each individual or group. The ethics of obtaining permissions vary in different research contexts, according to project aims and the agendas of researchers, informants and other interested parties. To clarify permissions to photograph or video and the possible future uses of any images produced, some researchers use consent forms that the subjects of their images are asked to sign. However, getting an informant's signature on a consent form should not be considered to give the researcher the moral right to then use the image in unrestricted ways; as I detail below, ethical questions will continue to be considered as the process of representation begins.

Harm to informants

While ethnographic research is unlikely to cause harm as, for example, drugs trials may, it can lead to emotional distress or anxiety (Hammersley and Atkinson 1995: 268). Sensitivity to how individuals in different cultures may experience anxiety or stress through their involvement in research is important in any ethnographic project. However, rather than prescribing actual methods of preventing harm to informants in visual research, my intention is to suggest a way of thinking about how research, anxiety and harm are understood and experienced in different ethnographic contexts. General methods of preventing harm to informants may not be locally applicable. First, there are culturally different ways of understanding harm and of causing it with images. Therefore, in order to prevent harm being caused, a researcher needs a good understanding of local notions of harm and anxiety, how these may be experienced and how they relate to images. Secondly, the idea that informants may find the research process distressing is usually based on the assumption that the informants are having the research *done to them*. In this scenario the researcher is supposed to be in control of the research situation and therefore also assumes responsibility for the potential harm that may be done to the informants. This approach requires that in taking responsibility to protect their informants, researchers should be sensitive to the visual culture and experience of the individuals with whom they are working. For instance, ethnographers need to judge, or ask (if appropriate), if there are personal or cultural reasons why some people may find particular photographs shown to them in interviews or discussions offensive, disturbing or distressing, or if being photographed or videoed themselves would be stressful.

Anxiety and harm to informants can often be avoided through a collaborative approach to visual research and joint ownership of visual materials. Here researchers and informants should maintain some degree of control over the content of the materials and their subsequent uses.

Harm, representation and permission to publish

Above I have discussed the issue of permission to video or photograph during ethnographic research. The publication of the research raises new issues. Sometimes this is already a concern when the images are shot, especially if the ethnographer's project is to produce a documentary or photographic exhibition. These intentions should be made clear to the subjects of the images. Some ethnographic filmmakers ask the subjects of their films to sign consent forms (see Barbash and Taylor 1997; Banks 2001: 131–2; Marvin 2005). However, if this is not done, moral and legal issues of ownership of the images and of consent may arise. If the images were produced covertly, without the permission of their subjects, the moral right of the video maker or photographer to publish them could be questioned. Moreover, it cannot be assumed that people have consented to being in a publicly screened video or to have large images of themselves exhibited in a gallery simply because they have allowed the images to be taken or have responded to the camera. This raises questions such as should the subjects of photographs and video be allowed to see printed or edited copies before they consent to their images entering a public domain?

Different filmmakers, photographers and ethnographers have their own opinions and practices regarding this. Much of ethnography is about making private aspects of people's lives public. Therefore, who should be responsible for deciding the content of the visual representation of other people's lives?

Questions of harm to individuals or institutions become pressing when it comes to publication. For photography and video this is particularly important since it is usually impossible to preserve anonymity of people and places. Ethnographers have to make choices regarding if and how video footage will be incorporated into the final publication of the research. This requires a serious consideration of ethical issues and possibly the participation of the informants or the subjects of the images. The publication of certain photographic and video images may damage individuals' reputations; they may not want certain aspects of their identities revealed or their personal opinions to be made public. People express some things in one context that they would not say in another, and in the apparent intimacy of a video interview an informant may make comments that he or she would not make elsewhere. Institutions may also be damaged by irresponsible publication of images. The public front of any institution is often a veneer that holds fast the conflicts and organizational problems that are part of its everyday order.

Finally, once visual and other representations of ethnographic work have been produced and disseminated publicly neither author nor subjects of the work can control the ways in which these representations are interpreted and given meanings by their readers, viewers or audiences. In Chapters 6, 7 and 8 these issues are raised in a discussion of the visual representation of ethnographic work.

Exploitation and 'giving something back'

Usually ethnographers stand to gain personally from their interactions with informants, through an undergraduate or masters' degree project, PhD thesis, consultancy project or other publication that will enhance their career. In contrast, informants may not accrue similar benefits from their participation in research projects. Conventional responses to this ethical problem focus on how ethnographers may 'give something back'; how the participants in the research may be empowered through their involvement in the project, or that research should be directed at the powerful rather than the weak (Hammersley and Atkinson 1995: 274–5). None of these responses, however, provide satisfactory solutions to the exploitative nature of research (see Hammersley and Atkinson 1995).

The idea of 'giving something back' implies that the ethnographer extracts something (usually the data) and then makes a gift of something else to the people from whom he or she has got the information.

Rather than making research any less exploitative, this approach merely tries to compensate for it by 'giving something back'. Ironically, this may benefit the ethnographer, who will feel ethically virtuous, while the informants may be left wondering why they have been given whatever it was they 'got back', and what precisely it was they got it in return for. Rather than try to redress the inequalities after the event, it would seem better advised to attempt to undertake ethnography that is less exploitative. If ethnography is seen as a process of negotiation and collaboration with informants, through which they too stand to achieve their own objectives, rather than as an act of taking information away from them, the ethical agenda also shifts. By focusing on collaboration and the idea of 'creating something together', agency becomes shared between the researcher and informant. Rather than the researcher being the active party who both extracts data and gives something else back, in this model both researcher and informant invest in, and are rewarded by, the project. Recent work with video and photography shows how these media can be used to develop very successful collaborative projects. In some cases this has empowered informants/subjects and can serve to challenge existing power structures that impinge on the lives of informants and ethnographers. In a project developed by Barnes, Taylor-Brown and Weiner (1997), a group of HIV-positive women collaborated with the researchers to produce a set of video tapes that contained messages for their children. This use of video allowed the women to represent themselves on video tapes to be screened in the future. Simultaneously, the agreement allowed the researchers to use the tapes as research materials (see Chapter 4).

As I have suggested above, the concept of 'giving something back' often depends on the idea of ethnography as a 'hit and run' act: the ethnographer spends a number of months in the field gathering data before leaving for home where this data will be written up. Very little remains once ethnographers leave their field sites, apart from (in the case of overseas fieldwork) those domestic and other things that did not fit into a suitcase. Field notes and papers are of little use or interest to most informants, and at any rate researchers may feel these are personal documents. However, video tapes and photographs are usually of interest to the people featured in them and the people who were involved in their production. If an ethnographer is working on the 'giving something back' principle, copies of video and photography of individuals and activities that informants value could be an appropriate return for the favours they have performed during fieldwork. However, a collaborative approach to ethnographic image production may do more to redress the inequalities that inevitably exist between informants and researchers. Beate Engelbrecht's collaborative work with ethnographic film shows how visual work can become a product in which both informants and ethnographer invest. Engelbrecht (1996) describes a number

© Sarah Pink 2005

Figure 2.3
As part of my research in Aylsham, Norfolk, I provide copies of my own photographs of the Slow Food and Cittàslow events to the people who are developing local projects. In 2005 the town was a finalist in the international LivCom Awards (see www.livcomawards.com/), where it won a silver award. As part of the preparation for the event, I sent a set of photographs and video clips of the town and from its carnival and regional agricultural show which, combined with images produced by other peoples, provided a range of materials used to develop the presentation given at the awards event in Spain.

of filmmaking projects that involved the collaboration of local people in both filmmaking and editing. In some cases people wanted their traditional festivities or rituals to be documented, and were pleased to work with the filmmakers to achieve these ends. Others realized the commercial potential of their participation in film projects. For example, Engelbrecht notes how the artisans who were represented in her film *Copper Working* (1993) participated actively in the film and 'were also thinking of the potential of film as a marketing instrument [for their copper artifacts]' (1996: 167). In this case, the subjects of the film had their own agenda and were able to exploit the project of the film makers for their own purposes: 'it was agreed upon that one copy of the film should be given to the local museum exhibiting the best of the recent copper work of the village so as to use it for tourist information' (1996: 167).

A further problem with the notion of 'giving something back' is that it neglects the interlinkages between the researcher's personal autobiographical narrative and the research narrative. Fieldwork, everyday life and writing-up may not necessarily be separated either spatially or temporally in the ethnographer's life and experience (see Chapter 1). Ethnographic research may not entail the researcher going somewhere, taking something away and being morally obliged to 'give something back'. Instead, the ethnography may be part of a researcher's everyday interactions. There may be a continuous flow of information and objects between the ethnographer and informants. This might include the exchange of images, of ideas, emotional and practical exchanges and support, each of which are valued in different ways.

Ownership of research materials

In some cases visual research materials are jointly owned by a set of different parties such as the researcher, informants/subjects, funding bodies, bodies involved in post-production and other institutions and universities or organizations. While researchers may consider their own practices to be ethical, this may be challenged by any joint owners of the photographs or tapes. Such problems may arise if a project is sponsored by an institution that claims ownership of the data, or the project has involved teamwork and photographs or video tapes are joint possessions of the members of the project team. Moreover, if video or photographic images have been produced in collaboration with informants, the collaborators may wish to use the images in ways that the researcher feels are unethical. To attempt to avoid such problems it is advisable to clarify rights of use and ownership of video and photographic images before their production. This will inevitably bear on the ethical decisions taken during the research and may influence the types of images that are produced. In some cases it is appropriate to use a written agreement that states who will use the video or photographic materials; the purposes for which it will be used; and whether the participants have consented to its use.

Visual research with children

In recent years the ethics of doing research with and about, and of producing visual images of, children have come under increasing scrutiny. This, of course, has important implications for visual ethnographic research. As I have noted above, much contemporary research is scrutinized by institutional ethical committees, and these will pay specific attention to research involving children. It is important to gain consent not only of the children themselves but also of their parents or guardians in order that they should participate in research. Phil Mizen provides a useful discussion of this in an article about research about children's labour in which children were asked to photograph the contexts in which they worked. Through this research, he notes that

> our approach had been to carry through the belief that children are rational agents actively engaged with the social world around them … , and thus capable of providing informed consent or, conversely, of withdrawing this at any time. Even so, we were equally mindful of their subordinate status; a fact reinforced from the outset by our need to obtain prior consent from parents and guardians before any of the fieldwork activities could begin. (2005: 126)

Questions surrounding photographing and video-recording children are important not only amongst researchers but also in wider society. This will vary in different cultural contexts but, for example, in Britain photographing children in schools and for press reports is becoming increasingly complex. As a modern Western parent myself, I feel the importance of this when I am asked for sign consent forms for my children to be photographed during activities organized by my childcare provider. Researchers create similar paper-trails of documentation of consent when they wish to photograph a young person who is someone else's son or daughter.

Here I discuss briefly some recent visual research projects involving children and young people as examples that will provide useful case studies in existing practice. In some research projects it is the children themselves who are depicted visually during the research process and in representations. For example: David MacDougall (2005) discusses both his own ethnographic documentary film work with children in his 'Doon School' projects in India, and examples of other documentary approaches to representing children; Rossella Ragazzi's (2006) video work on migrant children in Paris involved screening back 10-minute episodes of her footage at the school, generating comments and new understandings; in Chapter 1 I noted Hyde's (2005) discussion of Wendy Ewald's portraits of children as an interesting example that suggests how social researchers might also engage collaborative photographic practices to both understand and represent children's experiences; Andrea Raggl and Michael Schratz have used their own photographs of children, taken in school, to inform a rather different type of collaboration with children – as a way to ask pupils to 'recall learning situations' and to 'reflect *on* or *about* action' (2004: 151); other projects like Mizen's cited above ask the children themselves to photograph their own worlds. In the case of Mizen's research the children became 'researcher photographers' who were invited to make a 'photo-diary', 'in which they were encouraged to use photography to illustrate, document and reflect upon their work and employment' (2005: 126) (see also Chapter 3).

These projects cited above all take children and their experiences as the main focus of their research. However, it is worth noting that children will be implicated in many of the social and cultural contexts in which visual ethnographers work, even if it is the adults with whose lives theirs are interwoven who are the key individuals a researcher is collaborating with. Therefore it is advisable to gain an awareness of the methodological and ethical issues involved with working with children before embarking on any project.

Summary

Preparing for ethnographic research is a complex task. It is impossible to predict exactly how fieldwork will proceed and many decisions about using visual methods and the ethical questions they raise are taken during research. Often ethnographers cannot answer the questions that inform the use of photography and video in particular social and cultural contexts, until they have experience of the visual culture and social relationships with which they will be working.

FURTHER READING

Banks, M. (2001) *Visual Methods in Social Research*, London: Sage. (Provides a useful discussion of the ethics of visual research that could be used alongside that given in this text)

Pink, S., Kurti, L. and Afonso, A.I. (eds) *Working Images,* London: Routledge. (An edited volume of case studies about the use of visual research methods. The first set of chapters in particular tell the stories of how different types of visual research projects developed)

Ruby, J. (2000) *Picturing Culture,* Chicago: University of Chicago Press. (Offers an approach to visual anthropology that equates a reflexive with an ethical approach to research and representation)

Part 2
Producing Knowledge

Doing fieldwork is a unique and personal experience. While different ethnographers may purport to use the same methods, they will in fact do so in different ways. In Chapters 3 and 4 I draw from some of my own and other ethnographers' experiences of doing research with photography and video to offer some ideas and possibilities for a reflexive approach to visual methods. Analysis can take place at any point in the research process, and may be combined with some of the methods described in Chapters 3 and 4. In Chapter 5 I focus more specifically on the storage, analysis and interpretation of research materials.

3

Photography in Ethnographic Research

Photography has a long and varied history in ethnography. Supported by different methodological paradigms, a camera has been an almost mandatory element of the 'tool kit' for research for several generations of ethnographers. During the colonial period in the late nineteenth and early twentieth centuries, photography, seen as an objective recording device, flourished as a method for the 'scientific' documentation of cultural and physical difference (see Edwards 1992, 1997b). Around this time early anthropological uses of photography in research were also developed by Britain's Alfred Cort Haddon (Banks's on-line catalogue of this work is discussed in Chapter 8), Franz Boas in the United States and Baldwin Spencer and Frank Gillen in Australia (Jacknis 1984; Morphy 1996), and from 1915 to 1918, Bronislaw Malinowski used photography as part of his long-term fieldwork method (Young 1998). Later, in the mid-twentieth century, Bateson and Mead (1942) used photography to record and represent Balinese culture (see Chaplin 1994: 207ff; Banks 2001). Between the 1970s and the end of the twentieth century photography was initially employed to fit the needs of scientific-realist approaches to ethnography, which were then critiqued by the reflexive stance that has endured and now informs most visual research. Attempts to connect ethnographic and collaborative documentary photography practices signify recent innovations. It is not my intention here to analyse the historical context of these developments (see Pink 2005: ch. 1). Rather, in this chapter I draw from my own and other ethnographers' experiences to explore two inextricably interconnected themes in contemporary visual ethnography practice: the study of local photographic cultures and uses of photographic images and technologies in ethnographic research.

Photographic practices have formed the subject matter of academic work across the social sciences and humanities. In the 1990s anthropologists critically examined the history of their own discipline, highlighting the ethnocentric, oppressive agendas in which scientific anthropological uses of photography during the colonial period were implicated (see Edwards 1992, 1997b) and the primitivizing tendencies of 1970s and 1980s photographic representations of ethnographic realities (Brandes 1997). Other studies focused on photography in consumer culture (e.g. Bourdieu 1990 [1965]), family photography (e.g. Chalfen 1987), tourist photography (e.g. Chaney 1993; Crawshaw and Urry 1997; Edensor 1998; Hutnyk 1996; Urry 1990), the relationship between digital and 'traditional' photography (e.g. Lister 1995; T. Wright 1998) and ethnographic studies of local or ethnic photographic cultures (e.g. Pinney 1997; Pink 1997b, 1999b). Since 2000, new studies have focused on historical aspects of photographic practice and culture. For instance, Edwards (2001) interrogates the situated and historical meanings that can be produced through the analysis of historical and archival photographs; and Pinney and Peterson's edited volume (2003), *Photography's Other Histories*, demonstrates how photography has, historically and in the present, been appropriated in different cultural contexts. Other anthropological studies of photographic culture are represented in ethnographic films. For example, *Photo Wallahs* (MacDougall and MacDougall 1991) represents photography in an Indian hill town, while *Future Remembrance* (Wendl and Du Plessis 1998) is a study of studio photography in Ghana. These two films represent existing photographic practices in specific localities. *Future Remembrance* should be viewed alongside Tobias Wendl's (2001) writing about studio photography in Ghana, and *Photo Wallahs* with MacDougall's (2005) and Pinney's (1997) books.

In Chapter 2 I proposed that visual research methods should be informed by ethnographers' knowledge of the visual cultures they work in, including knowledge about local and academic uses of photographs. Using photography in ethnographic research is not simply a matter of studying visual culture on the one hand, and on the other adding to disciplinary and personal resources of visual materials by photographing exotic situations and persons. Rather, ethnographic photography can potentially construct continuities between the visual culture of an academic discipline and that of the subjects or collaborators in the research. Thus ethnographers can hope to create photographic representations that refer to local visual cultures and simultaneously respond to the interests of academic disciplines. To do so requires research into uses and understandings of photography in the culture and society of the fieldwork location. In some cases empirical and theoretical studies may be available, in others local photographic cultures may be virtually undocumented.

The ethnographicness of photography

As I pointed out in Chapter 1, no visual image or practice is essentially ethnographic by nature. Accordingly, the ethnographicness of photography is determined by discourse and content. For instance, Edwards rightly suggested that 'an anthropological photograph is any photograph from which an anthropologist could gain useful, meaningful visual information' (Edwards 1992: 13). She emphasized how viewers subjectively determine when or if a photograph is anthropological, pointing out that '[t]he defining essence of an anthropological photograph is not the subject-matter as such, but the consumer's classification of that knowledge or "reality" which the photograph appears to convey' (1992: 13). Similarly, using as his example the categories of visual sociology, documentary photography and photo-journalism, Becker noted that the definition of the genre of a photograph depends more on the context in which it is viewed than its pertaining to any one (socially constructed) category (Becker 1995: 5).

Therefore the same photograph may serve a range of different personal and ethnographic uses; it may even be invested with seemingly contradictory meanings. As Edwards noted, '[m]aterial can move in and out of the anthropological sphere and photographs that were not created with anthropological intent or specifically informed by ethnographic understanding may nevertheless be appropriated to anthropological ends' (1992: 13). Similarly, a photograph created by a researcher with a particular ethnographic agenda in mind may travel out of 'the research' and into the personal collections of informants or other individuals, therefore being appropriated for *their* own ends (see Pink 1996). For example, one photographic slide that I took of Encarni, a friend and informant during fieldwork, was duplicated as a print and used in a variety of ways: in her personal collection and family album, in my discussions with other informants, in my PhD thesis (Pink 1996), my book (Pink 1997a), in a conference paper (Pink 1996), as well as being part of my own personal collection of photographs of friends. Similarly, my photograph of the woman bullfighter Cristina Sanchez entitled 'The Bullfighter's Braid' was in one context an 'ethnographic photograph' that appeared on the front cover of my book *Women and Bullfighting* (1997a). This photograph also won a prize for artistic journalistic photography, was used to publicize the visit of a female bullfighter to Cordoba and became part of the personal collections and wall displays of my informants. Therefore, during the fieldwork this photograph had no single meaning, but it was re-appropriated and given new significance and uses in each context. In Chapter 5 I discuss how the diversity of meanings invested in these two images was fundamental to my subsequent analysis of them and informed the academic meanings I gave to them.

Thus there are no fixed criteria that determine which photographs are ethnographic. Any photograph may have ethnographic interest, significance or meanings at a particular time or for a specific reason. The meanings of photographs are arbitrary and subjective; they depend on who is looking. The same photographic image may have a variety of (perhaps conflicting) meanings invested in it at different stages of ethnographic research and representation, as it is viewed by different eyes and audiences in diverse temporal historical, spatial and cultural contexts. Therefore it seems important that ethnographers seek to understand the individual, local and broader cultural discourses in which photographs are made meaningful, in both fieldwork situations and academic discourses. Photographs produced as part of an ethnographic project will be given different meanings by the subjects of those images, local people in that context, the researcher, and other (sometimes critical) audiences. Edwards's work on historical photography (1992, 1997b) is a good example of this. The contributors to her edited collections discussed mainly colonial archival photography. They critically deconstructed the theories, philosophies and political agendas that informed the intentions of those who produced and used these images. By revealing the historical meanings that these photographs were given, the authors thus gave them new meanings by embedding them in new discourses. At the turn of the twentieth century such images were assumed to represent objectively collected scientific knowledge about 'inferior', dominated peoples. Almost 100 years later, the contributors to Edwards's collections largely viewed them as documents that represent the subjectivity of a particular theoretical scientific perspective on reality and the ethnocentric, racist and oppressive ramifications of this. Re-situated, the images were made to represent a critique of the intellectual and scientific environment and framework of beliefs in which they were produced (see also Chapter 5).

However, it is not only historically that the meanings given to photographs may be re-negotiated. When I showed a class of students a series of slides of a woman bullfighter's performance, some members of the group reacted by interpreting them in terms of an anti-bullfighting discourse. The meanings they invested in them were quite different from the ways in which they were interpreted by bullfight *aficionados,* who focused on the details of the bullfighter's technique and her female body. Other students in the group situated the images in another moral discourse. Taking a more relativist approach, they argued that we should try to understand what the photographs would mean in a Spanish cultural context. For me, however, the slides are also ethnographic photographs. They were shot as part of ethnographic fieldwork with dual intentions that related to my research; as an attempt to document the performance of a woman bullfighter and as part of my project to learn the art of bullfight photography (see Figure 3.1).

Ethnographer as photographer

When ethnographers take photographs, like any professional or lay photographer, they do so with reference to specific theories of photography and in the context of particular social relationships. As Terence Wright has pointed out, 'anyone who uses a camera or views a photograph, will most probably be subscribing, albeit unwittingly, to some or other theory of representation' (1999: 9). A reflexive approach to ethnographic photography means researchers being aware of the theories that inform their own photographic practice, of their relationships with their photographic subjects, and of the theories that inform their subjects' approaches to photography. This is an important issue for portrait photography, as Lury noted (citing Homberger 1992), 'at the heart of the photographic portrait is a contract between the subject and the photographer, a contract in which the former negotiates the term of the latter's appropriation of his or her property rights in the self' (Lury 1998: 45). Yet the nature of this contract varies. For example, on the one hand, the commercial contract whereby the photographer 'makes especially clear the rights of the individual to self-possession created in portraiture: so for example the individual has the right to accept or reject the portrait' (Lury 1998: 45). On the other hand, in different circumstances 'other epistemological and judicial principles ... provided the authority for the abandonment of the contract and undermined the function of the uniqueness of the self as a possession of the individual' (Lury 1998: 46). These principles were those that operated in the construction of the photographic archives of government bureaucracies and colonial systems.

Therefore, it is useful to pay attention to the subjectivities and intentionalities of individual photographers, coupled with the cultural discourses, social relationships and broader political, economic and historical contexts to which these refer and in which they are enmeshed. Edwards's (1992) volume contains historical examples of this (e.g. Hockings 1992; Tayler 1992). Macintyre and Mackenzie demonstrate how in Papua New Guinea the 'cultural distance' between different colonial photographers and their local subjects varied according to 'the range of photographic genres and the varying degrees of control exerted by those behind the lens' (Macintyre and Mackenzie 1992: 163). Their comments remind us that for both historical and contemporary photography, '[t]he experience, the motivations and the social positions of the photographers are intrinsic to the images' (1992: 163). Archival research about vintage photographs should therefore investigate not solely the content of the image, but also the personal and professional intentions of photographers and of other institutions and individuals with whom they negotiated. Ethnographic research into local contemporary photographic cultures should refer to the same principles. Therefore, when possible, analysis of the content or iconography of photographs should be informed by a consideration of the photographers' personal and professional intentions, the historical development of photographic practices in any particular cultural context, the institutional agendas to which they were obliged to respond, how they have used photography to refer to specific cultural discourses and construct

The woman bullfighter Cristina Sanchez waited at the ringside
for her turn to perform.

Once she had finished performing with the pink cape Cristina switched to the red
muleta and sword.

She tossed her hat over her head to signify that she was dedicating her
bull to the audience.

Then she performed with the red *muleta* ...

... using the same cape passes and poses that are practised by her
male colleagues ...

... and holding the audience's attention.

Just before the end of the performance Cristina's cape was caught by the bull's horns, she was tossed in the air, and fell to the ground ...

... but got up, kicked off her shoes and went on successfully to kill the bull.

In recognition of her success she was awarded one of the bull's ears as a trophy ... and was thrown flowers from the audience.

© Sarah Pink 1993

Figure 3.1

These slides were taken at Cristina Sanchez's performance in Valdemorillo in 1993. They are usually projected in sequence. Bullfight *aficionados'* interpretations of them would focus on the women bullfighter as performer – her poses, her performance skills and achievements – thus understanding them in terms of specific gendered narratives on bullfighting. Some UK viewers invested quite different meanings in the images, understanding them in relation to a narrative on animal rights and cruelty. One viewer situated this further in terms of her personal narrative as a vegetarian. Each viewer used his or her own cultural and experienced-based knowledge and moral values to give meanings to the images. For bullfight *aficionados* this was often concerned with the question of whether or not women should be bullfighters; for others it referred to whether bullfighting should be allowed at all.

particular aspects of self-identity, and the theories of representation that informed their practice. Ethnographic photographers may create their own photographs as a critical response or vindication of the power relations represented in such existing bodies of photographic work.

In Chapter 1 I discussed the difficulty of distinguishing between ethnographers' personal and professional lives, relationships and activities. When it is difficult to distinguish between parts of one's life that are strictly research, leisure or social life, it is similarly hard to classify photographs as belonging to just one of these categories. Much of my fieldwork in southern Spain and in Aylsham in England has been at social events, festivities and celebrations, where it can be difficult for informants to comprehend what I was doing as 'work'. In Spain I frequently took 'ethnographic' photographs while socializing. For me these photographs are ethnographic because I was interested in people's visual self-representation, and I usually photographed informants on their request. These photographs were simultaneously visual representations of my own social experience and personal documents that belong to both my own collection and those of friends for whom I copied them. Ethnographers can have dual (or multiple) intentions when photographing during fieldwork. For example, these intentions could be personal, artistic or ethnographic, and could combine to determine the content of the image, possibly in collaboration with the subjects of the photograph. To understand how these personal and professional intentions intersect, inform each other and combine to produce and represent ethnographic knowledge visually, a reflexive approach is necessary. This involves: first, developing a consciousness of how ethnographers play their roles as photographers in particular cultural settings, how they frame particular images and why they choose particular subjects; secondly, a consideration of how these choices are related to the expectations of both academic disciplines and local visual cultures; and thirdly, an awareness of the theories of representation that inform their photography. Sometimes it is useful to keep a reflexive diary about the development of one's photographic practice and the intentions and ideas that informed taking each image.

Below I discuss existing uses of photography as a research method. These can be broadly divided into three themes: photography as a visual recording method; collaborative photography; and interviewing with photographs. Each method covered is not usually used in isolation but often interlinks and overlaps with other visual and non-visual methods.

Getting started: taking the first picture

The question of when to take the first photograph varies from project to project. Sometimes photographing can form a way of getting the research off the ground and establishing relationships with informants. In other situations researchers may have to wait several months before beginning to photograph, or may decide not to use the camera themselves at all, but to hand it over to their informants. Above I have stressed the importance of developing knowledge about the visual culture in which one works. This knowledge should inform such decisions. For ethical reasons ethnographers should consider not only where their photography fits into local visual cultures, but also how their photographic practices may affect local economies and other individuals (see Chapter 2).

Several examples demonstrate how photography may initiate and support research. Collier and Collier (1986) describe the idea of the camera as a 'can-opener' in two ways that can help establish rapport with one's informants. First, they note how playing a photographer role can put researchers in an ideal position to observe the culture or groups they are researching. Secondly, showing photographs to their subjects can provide both feedback on the images and their content while also forging connections with members of the 'community'. This can provide excuses for further meetings and photography and may be a reason to visit informants in their homes. While it will not always be appropriate to use photography in this way, ethnographers often find that photographing and photographs provide a useful method of representing their own identities and communicating with informants at the early stages of fieldwork. Taking the first images with a Polaroid® or a digital camera may speed up the process, allowing informants to gain an idea of what the ethnographer is doing almost instantly, and (hopefully) to engender their trust and interest.

Sometimes, to be able to photograph the activities they are interested in, ethnographers first have to establish themselves locally as someone who is trusted to take photographs. Shanklin (1979) has described her role as ethnographer/photographer during research in rural Ireland. She had intended to take photographs of people working, that she could subsequently discuss with her informants, but initially she found this was inappropriate. However, she learnt, by observing her informants' domestic displays of family photography, that photographing children was an appropriate activity and would provide parents with valued images: 'Just as I had to learn something about patterns of social interaction in order to become more a member of the culture I studied, so too I had to learn something about their use of photographs in order to integrate my own picture taking into the roles to which I had been assigned' (Shanklin 1979: 143). Once she had established herself as someone who took photographs within the local community, she found she could proceed by photographing agricultural workers at work and interviewing as she had originally intended.

In some projects photographing may come first and can be a means of making contact with local people. For example, Schwartz (1992) began her research by photographing the physical environment of Waucoma, the town she was studying. On arrival, she began photographing buildings to both inform the residents of her presence and to observe the goings on of everyday life. This provided her with an entry point into local interaction – seeing a stranger photographing the town made many people curious enough to approach her and ask what she was doing. The local people became interested in and supportive of Schwartz's work and the photographic aspect of the project became a key point of communication between her and her informants.

In my own research in Spain I began to photograph as soon as I made contact with the groups I was interested in working with. Photography provided me with an appropriate activity to engage in at the beginning of my research into bullfighting culture. As an unaccompanied woman at bullfighting receptions and public occasions and, at the time, still learning the language and unable to engage in any detailed conversation, I was grateful to have a role as 'photographer'. My photography was endorsed by the organizers and was not problematic for participants since at any such public event a number of press photographers were expected to be present. Once my photographs of the receptions were printed, I showed them to the organizers and other participants with whom I was in contact. We discussed the event and the people who were present, and my informants often asked for copies of particular images, usually of themselves with particular people, so that they could pass them on to their friends, colleagues or contacts within the bullfighting world. In this way I could not only gain feedback about the events I participated in as a photographer, but also a sense of how social relationships and alliances were mapped out and constructed within the bullfighting world. I did this by studying who wanted to be photographed with whom during the events, and by tracking the collection and distribution of the copies of the images that people asked for.

As these examples show, the camera can lead us into fieldwork situations as our photographic practices themselves are interwoven with the whole sets of relationships we build during research.

Photography as a recording device: the potential of the photographic survey

The photographic survey has a long history in social science, from the colonial archive and the archives of photographs of criminals produced in the early twentieth century, to more recent studies where ethnographers have collaborated with informants photographically to document aspects of their culture. The creation of photographic records has often been based on the assumption that the artefacts photographed have finite, fixed symbolic meanings. For example, Collier and Collier proposed a 'cultural inventory', where, for example, by producing a systematic photographic survey of visual aspects of the material content and organization of a home, one may answer questions relating to the economic level of the household, its style, decor, activities, the character of its order and its signs of hospitality and relaxation (Collier and Collier 1986: 47–50). Collier and Collier's approach provides a way of visually comparing specific material aspects of different households or even cultures. However, such photographic records are limited because they do not indicate how these objects are experienced or made meaningful by those individuals in whose lives they figure. Since then, this photographic survey approach has been employed mainly by visual sociologists. For example, Secondulfo's (1997) study of the symbolism of material items within the home and Pauwels's (1996) study of the material environment of the Brussels office of a Norwegian chemical multinational. Pauwels has sought to contexualize his visual survey through interviews and an analysis of other aspects of office life. These types of realist survey provide useful materials that can be used to provide statistical data and background knowledge, and in some cases this will be sufficient, when related to other data to justify their use. However, combining photographic surveys with a subjective collaborative approach can bring further benefits. Schwartz's (1992) collaborative approach to photographic survey work in the North American Waucoma farming community led her to define her survey photographs as neither 'objective visual documents' nor 'photographic truth'. Rather, they 'represent a point of view' – in this case her 'initial inferences about life in Waucoma' (1992: 14). She used her survey images of the Waucoma physical environment, together with old photographs of the same places, in interviews with local people. Rather than basing her analysis of the images on their content, her interpretation 'is informed by insights gained through ethnographic fieldwork and informants' responses to them'. Schwartz assumed that her photographs 'would prompt multiple responses'. She 'sought to study the range of meaning they held for different members of the community' (1992: 14). Therefore, she made the idea that visual meanings are arbitrary a key element of her research method.

Photographic surveys or attempts to represent physical environments, objects, events or performances can form part of a reflexive ethnography. However, such photographs are most usefully treated as representations of *aspects* of culture; not recordings of whole cultures or of symbols that will have complete or fixed meanings. This also has implications for the way ethnographers store, categorize and analyse photographs (see Chapter 5).

Participatory and collaborative photography

Ethnographers collaborate with informants to produce photographs in a variety of ways. Existing examples involve working alone with a single informant (e.g. Collier and Collier 1986), with groups engaged in creative (e.g. Chaplin 1994) or ceremonial (e.g. Larson 1988) activities, in eclectic ways within wider ethnographic projects (e.g. Banks n.d.; Pink 1999b), and in ways more systematically built into a research design (e.g. Radley et al. 2005). When photographs are produced collaboratively, they combine the intentions of both ethnographer/photographer and informant and represent the outcome of their negotiations.

Collaborative photography usually involves ethnographers engaging in some way with the photographic culture of their informants. For instance, an ethnographer might try to produce the kinds of images that are popular in informants' photographic cultures, or that refer to local photographic conventions but simultaneously conform to the demands of an academic discipline. The intentions and objectives of researchers and informants combine in their negotiations to determine the content of the photographs in ways that vary in different projects. For instance, informants may seek family photographs, images that will provide legal evidence, documentation of local traditions or of work processes, artistic exhibits, souvenirs or photographs that may be used for publicity. Ethnographers may wish to produce images that they can publish with academic text or exhibit. They may wish to learn local photographic styles, conform to the conventions of their academic discipline, or produce images that follow a particular photographic tradition, such as realist documentary, expressive or art photography.

Existing ethnographic examples indicate that people are usually quick to teach a potential photographer what kinds of images they would like to have taken. Sometimes the photographs informants request challenge the assumptions behind the ethnographer's original intentions and initiate a shift in the anticipated use of photography as a research method. For example, Pinney described how, during fieldwork in India in 1982, he learnt how local people wanted to be represented through his attempts to photograph his informants in terms of his own aesthetic designs. He took a photograph of his neighbour that fitted the type of image he wanted to produce: 'candid, revealing, expressive of the people I was living among' (Pinney 1997: 8). This photograph was a half-length image taken around 5pm in the fields: 'a good time to catch the mellowing sun' (1997: 8). But his informant was not satisfied with the image. He 'complained about the shadow and darkness it cast over his face and the absence of the lower half of his body. The image was of no use to him' (1997: 9). Pinney's informants wanted a different type of photograph, one that was taken according to another procedure. These photographs 'could not be taken quickly since there were more lengthy preparations to be made: clothes to be changed, hair to be brushed and oiled (and, in the case of upper-caste women, the application of talcum powder to lighten the skin)' (1997: 9). Moreover, their content and symbolism conformed to different expectations: 'These photos had to be full-length and symmetrical, and the passive, expressionless faces and body poses symbolised for me, at that time, the extinguishing of precisely that quality I wished to capture on film' (1997: 9). Here the portraits indicated informants' existing expectations of photography and their personal and cultural uses of images. One way to learn about these is to pay attention to the personal photograph collections people show us, to interpret how they would like to be photographed and to understand what they are referring to when they describe the sorts of images they would like to have. Thus a researcher's photographic prac-tice (and as such visual research methods) can be guided and informed by local people's photographic expectations *vis-à-vis* portrait photogra-phy. This is one of the benefits of allowing our visual methods to be shaped through our interactions with the people and institutions we encounter during the research process, rather than being preconceived.

Ethnographers often photograph ritual or other cultural activities. Indeed in urban India Banks found much of his photography was at communal ritual events. Sometimes his informants actively 'directed' his photography: at one event his informants insisted that he 'took a pre-posed photograph of the woman who had paid for the feast, ladling a dollop of a rich yoghurt-based dessert on to the tray of one of the feasters' (Banks n.d.). Banks interprets this photographic event to show this collaborative photography was informed by his own and his informants' knowledge:

> It was composed and framed according to my own (largely unconscious) visual aesthetic and is part of my own corpus of documentary images of that feast. But it is also a legitimization and concretization of social facts as my friends saw them: the fact that the feast had a social origin in the agency of one person (the feast donor) as well as by virtue of the religiously and calendrically prescribed fasting period that preceded it; the fact that this was a good feast during which we ate the expensive and highly-valued yoghurt desert. (Banks n.d.)

For Banks, this 'directed' photography became a way of visualizing and reinforcing his existing ethnographic knowledge because 'I "knew" these social facts, because I had been told them on other occasions, but by being directed to capture them on film I was made aware not only of their strength and value but of the power of photography to legitimize them' (Banks n.d.). When researching women and bullfighting in Spain in the 1990s, I attended an evening reception given after a talk by the woman bullfighter Cristina Sanchez. As I was available at the event with my camera, my informants also directed my photography by asking me to photograph them posing in groups with Cristina. Here I became an active collaborator in the production of photographs that followed local conventions in bullfighting culture.

On another occasion I was in the audience of a bullfight with a young woman informant. During the performance she instructed me which

© *Sarah Pink 1993*

Figure 3.2
A group of students from the University Aula Taurina asked me to take their photograph with the woman bullfighter Cristina Sanchez (*centre*). In the photograph they are holding copies of the journal edited by the Aula Taurina, which has my photograph 'The Bullfighter's Braid' on the back cover.

standard stages I should photograph, as well the stages of her personalized narrative of the event, such as when her favourite bullfighter waved to the part of the ring where she and the other members of his supporters' club were sitting. During his performance, she asked for my camera to photograph him performing the kill herself. Most bullfight fans regard the kill as the most important stage of the performance, and thus also the key photographic moment. Through her actions my informant had not only shown me the importance of this, but had also used the camera to express her own knowledge of the bullfight. In these situations my informants had already imagined the photographs they wanted me to take and those they wanted to take themselves: they were constructing them in response to an existing visual culture, the discourses of which they were conversant in. By analysing the context in which the images were taken and the local photographic conventions to which their composition complied, I gained a deeper understanding and a more informed visual representation of the significance of particular social relationships, representations of self, and of stages of the bullfight.

Returning the gaze: ethnographer as photographee

Whereas in some project designs researchers ask informants to photograph for them, in other contexts photography develops through informants' own initiatives. In this section I discuss situations where the ethnographer has become the photographic subject of her or his informant(s) and reflect on what we might learn from these sometimes surprising instances. When working in cultures where most people are owners of cameras and literate in the visual conventions that guide particular categories of photography, being photographed by the people with whom one is researching is probably a common experience amongst ethnographers. Yet it is infrequently discussed. These serendipitous moments when the people who we are learning from take control of the camera can provide striking insights.

My first experience of being photographed by an informant was during my women and bullfighting research in Spain. In 1993 Cristina Sanchez visited Córdoba where I was doing my research. The Director of Museums, who was hosting her day in the city, invited me to accompany them and a local bullfighting journalist during their tour of the town. My role was to photograph their day in Córdoba and the Director often told me what to photograph. When we were all sitting in a bar during the visit he asked for my camera, and photographed me sitting at the table with Cristina. Essentially he had taken the photograph that, according to the standards of the visual culture of bullfighting photography, I should have wanted to have (see Pink 1997a: 102). I connected this photograph to my existing knowledge. I had already studied bullfighting fans' personal photographic collections and historical images of bullfighters and their associates and knew that this was a recurring image composition. In fact, it was similar to the photographs I had already taken, guided perhaps subconsciously by my knowledge of these conventions, of Cristina being interviewed by a local bullfighting journalist. The important point about the Director's photograph was that by situating me within the conventional composition it confirmed for me visually the knowledge that I was already developing from other sources.

Local photographic practices and images that incorporate the ethnographer can tell us about much more than photographic conventions. During his fieldwork in Malaysia in 2003–4 John Postill was photographed with a group of his informants, standing behind a banner. Postill writes:

> It all started when a web forum user opened up a thread on the trouble he was having getting the municipal council to fix a drain that had collapsed outside his backyard. The forum thread grew longer and longer and eventually a group of residents, led by the person who started the thread, decided to take action and organise a demonstration to draw media attention to this issue. Being a

dutiful fieldworker, I joined the demo but tried to keep a low profile. Yet this was a poorly attended demo, and when I was asked to stand behind the only banner to make up the numbers I foolishly obliged. As a result, the following day my portrait appeared in the Chinese-language press, alongside that of the demonstrators. This photograph was the cause of much strife and conflict, both online and offline, as the web portal founder accused the demonstrators of misusing the portal's domain. He felt that the banner in question was not only rude about the municipal council; its author had also tarnished the portal's domain name (USJ.com.my) by displaying it on the banner. He demanded a public apology on the web forum, as well as to the municipal council. (Postill 2005)

Having appeared in the photograph, even though he was not intending to be part of the demonstration, Postill also had to apologise and explain his mistake to the town council. The incident nicely shows how photographic meanings are generated on several different levels. First, the photograph was needed to transform a small demonstration into a reportable reality for the news media. Once digitalized and distributed on-line the photograph took on another meaning as it was used as a form of evidence that the web portal's name had been misused, and by whom. Through this the 'innocent anthropologist' Postill learnt how, identified photographically, he had inadvertently become implicated in this. To explain his appearance in the photograph he needed to refer back to the intentionalities and motives that had informed its moment of production (Postill, personal communication).

In 2005 I found myself in another fieldwork situation where I became the photographic subject. As part of my work about slow living in Aylsham, Norfolk, I am following a series of projects developed under the umbrella of the town's Cittàslow status. One of these is a community garden project that is transforming a piece of disused land in a residential area of the town into a place that local people can comfortably walk through on their way to town, take their young children to play in, and sit and relax in. Supported by a local charitable organization (ACT), the project is managed by a committee of neighbours from the streets that surround the plot of land, chaired by David Gibson. To follow this project as it developed, I first interviewed David. I arrived at the home of David and his wife, Anne, one very rainy morning and was welcomed into their living room. We sat around the table with coffee and biscuits and discussed many things relating to the town and the community garden and David talked me though his file on the project. As part of my research process I am creating portraits of the people I work with, and I photographed David and Anne holding a photograph of the type of path they were proposing to have put down across the garden. As we talked I learnt that David's file was more important than I had first imagined. In it he was meticulously documenting the development process of the community garden project, visually through photographs and garden plans, in written documents and by taking notes on the stages and activities. Part of my research concerns how memories of Cittàslow and its projects are created in the present and for the future. In this case I found

© Sarah Pink 2005

© Sarah Pink 2005

Figure 3.3

As part of my research about a Cittàslow community garden project, I interviewed David Gibson, the chairman of the project committee, and took the above photograph of him with his wife, Anne, in their home. However, through the very act of researching the community garden I myself became subject to David's own process of documenting the project, as he likewise photographed me sitting at the same table for his own records. When we proceeded outside so that I could video David as he showed me the plot of land and explained the plans for it, again my own visual production was balanced by his: the video still below, shows David photographing me.

that as the researcher studying the project I was also a subject of the documentation process. As David put it, it was 'tit for tat'. He photographed me for *his* records. First, sitting at the table during the interview, and later, standing outside in the garden itself, with a jacket and umbrella kindly lent to me by Anne, as I videoed him showing me around the plot in the pouring rain (Figure 3.3). David's documenting work was however not isolated. ACT had also contracted someone to create another layer of documentation to assess the project in terms of the learning opportunities it created. By researching in a context where the visual and written recording and documentation of local events and activities was occurring at a range of different levels, including the local media, it was inevitable that I would myself be documented.

Collectively these examples of the ethnographer being put in the frame remind us that as visual ethnographers we are not the only people who actively use photography to explore, construct and understand other people's experiences and worlds. Indeed, we can learn much by attending to how other people use photography to insert us into their categories, projects and agendas.

Viewing ethnographers' photographs: interviewing with images

In this section I explore the roles photographs may play in interviews or conversations. In Chapters 1 and 2 I argued that visual images are made meaningful through the subjective gaze of the viewer, and that each individual produces these photographic meanings by relating the image to his or her existing personal experience, knowledge and wider cultural discourses. This approach critiques the assumption that 'photographs can be *tools* with which to *obtain* knowledge' (Collier and Collier 1986: 99; second italics are mine) in order to argue that photographs are visual objects through which people reference aspects of their experience and knowledge. Therefore, when photographs become the focus of discussion between ethnographers and informants, certain questions arise. For instance, how do ethnographers and informants situate themselves and each other in relation to the photograph? How does the intersubjectivity between ethnographers, informants and the material/visual images 'complete' the identity of an informant during an interview? How do informants create narratives with and around photographs and ethnographers? It is not simply a matter of asking how informants provide 'information' in 'response' to the content of images. Rather, ethnographers should be interested in how informants use the content of the images as vessels in which to invest meanings and through which to produce and represent their knowledge, self-identities, experiences and emotions.

The term commonly used to refer to photographic interviewing has been the rather problematic 'photo elicitation', which Harper writes: 'is based on the simple idea of inserting a photograph into a research interview' (2002: 13). I do not wish to criticize the method, rather the

© *Sarah Pink 1992*

© *Sarah Pink 1992*

Figure 3.4

During my research in southern Spain, when I attended receptions, still unable to speak
good Spanish, my camera became a means of being occupied, photographing details of
who was present, the sequence of events and taking the photos that people asked for. In
this way I was able to produce a set of images that allowed me to represent the sequence
and participants of the event and to collaborate with some of the subjects of my
photographs to produce images in which they represented particular social relationships.
Once the photographs were developed, I discussed them with certain key informants. This
helped me to learn more about the participants in the event, their social networks and
how they situated themselves in the 'bullfighting world'. When people asked for copies of
certain photographs, both for themselves and to give to other participants in the event,
I was able to learn about their own social networks and the links that an individual may
be trying to forge or strengthen by passing an image of himself or herself with another
participant to that person.

terminology and its implications. Photo *elicitation* implies using photographs to elicit responses from informants, as such to 'draw out' or 'evoke' an 'admission, answer *from* a person' (*Concise Oxford Dictionary* 1982; my italics). This principle was more cogent with earlier uses of the method and understandings of visual meanings employed in visual research in the 1950s and 1960s. For example, researching farming families who were also employed in urban factories, Collier used his photographs of both work locations as reference points in photographic interviews to examine his informants' attitudes to city life, factory work and migration to the city. His work provides a useful example of how his informants talked about the images and of how a photographic research project may evolve over time. Collier's analysis was based on the assumption that 'the facts are in the pictures' (Collier and Collier 1986: 106 [Collier 1967]) and the idea that the ethnographer may elicit knowledge about the visual content from informants. Later, Harper developed an approach that attempted to integrate photo elicitation with the 'new ethnography' that emerged from the postmodern turn by redefining it as 'a model of collaboration in research' (1998a: 35). For Harper, photographs are not simply visual records of reality, but representations that are interpreted in terms of different understandings of reality. When informants view photographs taken by an ethnographer they will actually be engaged in interpreting the ethnographer/photographer's visualization of reality. In a photographic interview, therefore, ethnographer and informant would discuss their different understandings of images, thus collaborating to determine each other's views. Harper suggests further that photographs allow us to produce knowledge unavailable through verbal interviewing: because the brain processes visual and spoken information differently, 'images evoke deeper elements of human consciousness than do words' and 'the photo elicitation interview seems like not simply an interview process that elicits more information but rather one that evokes a different kind of information' (Harper 2002: 13).

Taking a similar approach, Donna Schwartz shows how interviewing with photographs led her to new knowledge. She identifies her photographs of a Waucoma community as representations of her own vision of the physical and social environment. Basing her analysis on the principle that 'the photograph prompts personal narratives generated by the content of the image', she describes how her use of photograph in interviews 'was informed by the unique and contradictory nature of the medium ... photographs elicit multiple perceptions and interpretations' (Schwartz 1992: 13). Photographic interviews can allow ethnographers and informants to discuss images in ways that create a 'bridge' between their different experiences of reality. Photographs can become reference points through which informants and ethnographers represent aspects of their realities to each other.

© *Sarah Pink 1993*

© *Sarah Pink 1993*

Figure 3.5
These photographs of Cristina Sanchez (*above*) and Finito de Córdoba (*below*)
became part of the way I discussed bullfighting during my fieldwork in Spain. Informants
used these photographs to comment on the bullfighters' performance skills and on the
development of my own skills in learning to take the photograph at the 'right' moments
of the bullfight. In doing so, they were able to represent their own expert knowledge of
the bullfight. From these discussions I was able to learn about the knowledge that
was meant to inform appropriate bullfight photography as well as the values and
knowledge that my informants used to inform their commentaries on the images.

In different contexts, ethnographers will inevitably be able to use images as part of interviews in different ways. For instance, during fieldwork in Spain I made another use of my own bullfighting photography. By attempting to learn how to photograph the bullfight myself, I produced photographs that allowed my informants to comment on my knowledge of the bullfight and at the same time express their own (see Figure 3.5). Importantly, when we discuss our own photographs with the people whose lives, values, experiences etc. we are trying to understand, the images create a point at which our intersubjectivities intersect and at which particular types of knowledge can come to the fore as they are employed to give relevant meanings to visual representations.

As digital technologies are increasingly used in ethnography, digital methods of interviewing with images are also developing. Photo-elicitation interviews can be carried out by showing informants digital images on lap-top computer screens. Software to support this by allowing users to record audio commentaries linked to the images has recently been developed and is available at www.anthromethods.net.

Viewing informants' photograph collections: interviewing with images

Conversation is filled with verbal references to images and icons. People use verbal description to visualize particular moralities, activities and versions of social order (or disorder). Sometimes informants refer to absent images (including photographs) or they might introduce material images or objects into a conversation. Indeed ethnographic films often include scenes in which informants show and discuss photographs with the filmmaker. Examples of this can be found in *Photo Wallahs* (MacDougall and MacDougall 1991) and *Faces in the Crowd* (Henley 1994). In the ethnographic literature such examples of people 'talking with photographs' are not frequently described. However, since I have been shown people's personal photograph collections so often during my own research, I am sure it is a common occurrence, and one visual ethnographers would be wise to attend to. As I indicate in this section, attention to the meanings that people create when they combine images and words can create exciting new knowledge. Indeed, what is also curious about this process is that our first interpretations of the images people show us are not necessarily those we leave our interviews with. In this section I focus on examples of when people use their personal photograph collections or albums to communicate about their lives. Then I discuss the related topic of domestic and public displays and exhibitions in a later section.

During my fieldwork, people have often brought or shown me photographs as part of the stories they have been telling me about their lives. During my first fieldwork in Northern Ireland, I sat with a Protestant woman, at the time in her forties, talking at her kitchen table. Long before we had met, she had married a man who had converted his own religion from being a Catholic to becoming a Protestant. He had remained friends with some Catholics, and because of the religious tensions in Northern Ireland this created complications in their social life. His wife was seeking a way to express this religious divide to me and, although she had not been speaking of their wedding at the time, she told me she would show me a wedding photograph. As I waited for her to fetch the photograph I expected to see a 'white wedding' – the couple and the confetti – but she handed me a photograph taken from the back of a church. One side of the photograph was filled with people but the other was empty. She explained how her husband's family could not attend the Protestant service because they were Catholics, so his side of the church was empty. They were waiting outside the church and after the service all went to the reception. It seemed that this beginning had become symbolic of a continuing state of affairs for her. She had not been talking about her wedding, or showing her wedding photos, but they had become a visual reference point in a narrative about other boundaries and the way her life was currently affected by the religious divisions that the photograph symbolized so powerfully for her.

Judith Okely describes how her informants' own photograph collections became important in her research about the 'changing conditions and experience of the aged in rural France' (Okely 1994: 45). When an elderly woman informant in a nursing home led her to her room and took out a box of old photographs Okely 'found a route to her past through images' that stood for 'profound recreations of her past' (1994: 50). For Okely, these images were not merely illustrations of her informant's oral narrative, but were evocative descriptions and comments. She argues that the introduction of the photographs into their conversation enhanced the sensory dimension of the interview: 'A mere tape recording of her speaking in a formalised interview could not have conjured up the greater sense of her past which we mutually created with the aid of visual images' (1994: 50–1). Okely notes that a history related through a series of 'selective images of the past', and captioned by a verbal narrative, is inevitably subjective, selective and fragmented. Nevertheless, she also shows how this collaborative research allowed her and her informant to collaboratively create a version of the past that extended beyond the limitations set by the linearity of a verbal or textual narrative:

> Both of us pieced together the memories from whatever was picked up from the box, and created a synthesised whole. In reacting to the visual images, randomly stored, the woman was freed of linear chronology, any set piece for a life history and a purely verbalized description. The images did some of the work for both of us in ways which adjectives and other vocabulary could not supply. (1994: 51)

Okely emphasizes the need for reflection on how researchers experience informants' photographs. She notes how in her own experience she was 'watching, listening and resonating with the emotions and energy of her living through the photographs' (1994: 50).

When people use photographs to tell stories about their experiences, identities and practices these images become embedded in personally and culturally specific narratives. They might, actually purposefully, and unprompted by the researcher, seek out photographs to employ as part of the narratives that they are also developing verbally.

Handing over the camera: informant-produced images and photo-interviews

In collaborative photographic research it is increasingly common for ethnographers to ask informants to photograph for or with them. Often researchers give informants/collaborators a disposable camera to use and then return to them for processing (other, perhaps digital technologies will be more appropriate in some contexts). Informants' photographs often allow the researcher access to and knowledge about contents they cannot participate in themselves. They might allow routes into children's worlds. For example, in Mizen's research discussed above, children were asked to use disposable cameras to keep photographic diaries of their work contexts. In the photographer Ewald's work, this forms part of a collaborative venture since: '[Ewald] shares control over the process of visually representing children's lives, their stories and their faces', and 'Emphasising how students can communicate their stories with photography, Ewald then asks them to photograph scenes from their lives' (Hyde 2005: 174). Ewald's photographic practice draws from mixed methods, each of which becomes interwoven with others as they combine in the process of the production of knowledge. Working with older people, Suzanne Goopy and David Lloyd (2006) have used informant photography in a project about quality of life amongst ageing Italian Australians. Their informants were asked to photograph 'those places, people, objects and/or situations that lend them identity and express or add to their quality of life' to produce series of snapshots that represent 'a spatial discourse of place and self'. They interviewed their informants about these photo-diaries and then asked them to produce a second photo-diary. The second stage was crucial because Goopy and Lloyd report 'the participants became more intimately involved in creating an amateur auto-ethnography'. The final stage of the research built on these diaries and interviews: the researchers and informants collaborated to produce a composite photographic image from photographs taken by the researchers. This aimed to reflect 'their [the participants'] overall sense of identity and quality of life'. These composite images contribute to the research process by giving 'the participants the opportunity to select and emphasise aspects of their domestic environment' and are part of the final published representations of their understandings of quality of life (see Figure 6.5).

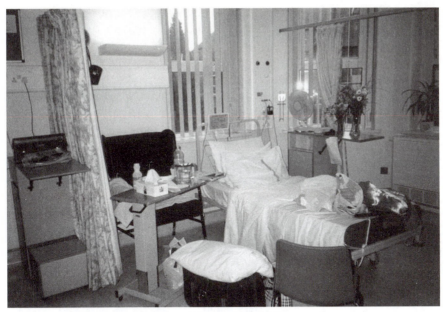

4-bedded Ward. © Alan Radley and Diane Taylor 2001

Figure 3.6

In their research into experiences of hospitalization and recovery, Alan Radley and Diane Taylor asked patients to take their own photographs of the hospital ward. They suggest that to learn about the hospital ward – a space in which patients spend extended periods of time – 'it seems sensible to use a form of record that allows patients to show what matters to them while in hospital'. By asking patients to photograph twelve of 'the objects, spaces and places that they found most significant', Radley and Taylor 'aimed to capture some of the most important features of recovery after surgery'. Although they had not originally planned to be there, the researchers were required to be present when their informants took the photos and in several instances assisted them with this. They later interviewed each patient about the images both during their time on the ward and later once they had returned to their homes. Radley and Taylor argue that, although these photographs could not depict respondents' actual experiences of being in hospital, they did have significant meaning for the patients involved. This meaning was made (was narrated) when participants spoke about *why* and *how* they took the pictures, as well as about what was depicted *in* the pictures. To get closer both to patients' experiences of being on the ward and to understanding the meaning the *act of photographing* had for them, Radley and Taylor explain why it is important for the researcher to be present when participants take photographs. As for informant-directed photography, as I have noted above, when it is possible to access and participate in the context of photographic production this can add significantly to our understandings of the ways they can become meaningful.

Red Roses. © Alan Radley and Diane Taylor 2001

Radley and Taylor's writing (cited above) and images from this research can be found online on the *Visualising Ethnography* website at www.lboro.ac.uk/departments/ss/visualising_ ethnography/

In Chapter 1 I discussed the gendered nature of ethnographic fieldwork. The researchers' gender identity always has implications for how she or he is perceived by and able to interact with informants. In my fieldwork in the masculine context of Spanish bullfighting my role as photographer was an appropriate activity in situations where a foreign woman student might have been out of place. However, as gendered individuals there are usually some environments we cannot access. For example, during Natalie Darko's recent research about men's body anxieties, for much of her fieldwork with a men's rugby union team her identity as a young woman researcher worked to her advantage. The men found it easy to discuss their anxieties and concerns with her, and she could access and compare the different private and public narratives they used to articulate their feelings about their body shapes, injuries and achievements. Darko also photographed during her participant observation and interviewed the men with these images. However, she could not enter or participate in some masculine spaces and practices, such as the men's changing rooms and some of their nights out. Instead, she asked her informants to take photographs for her. By then discussing these images with them she was able to learn much more about their actual practices and their feelings about their bodies (Natalie Darko, personal communication).

In these contexts informants' photographs took researchers into spaces it was difficult for them to enter physically themselves. In other contexts access to other people's understandings and experiences of their environments might be gained not simply by giving them a camera to use on their own, but by accompanying them during the image production process. Alan Radley and Diane Taylor's research with people in hospital wards represented in Figure 3.6. shows the value of the researcher's presence.

In Chapter 1 I discussed Radley, Hodgetts and Cullen's (2005) photographic study of how homeless people survive and make their home in the city. Studies like this, as the authors point out, emphasize materiality and, like Darko's work, also the body. They provide researchers with routes through which to explore in interview how people experience and act in the material as well as social and embodied elements of their environments. When informants take photographs for us the images they produce do not hold intrinsic meanings that we as researchers can extract from them. They do nevertheless have two key values. First, they are derived from photographic moments that were meaningful to the people who took the photographs, and within a particular narrative of events. Secondly, when our informant-photographers discuss these photographs they place them within new narratives and as such make them meaningful again. This second layer of significance presents a rich source of data since there is no singular narrative that might give meaning to a photograph, rather the meanings invested in it and the meanings it is used to evoke are multiple. As such, careful use of the images informants produce for us can greatly benefit ethnographic research. They should be followed up with interviews that seek to understand how the images have meanings on both of these two levels.

Displays, exhibitions and archives: viewing semi-public and public photographs with informants

Viewing photographic displays or exhibitions with informants offers further ways of exploring and creating relationships between visual and verbal knowledge. This may involve visiting public exhibitions, viewing photographs displayed publicly (for example, in schools, clubs, bars, town halls), or simply talking around photographs displayed on the wall or mantelpiece of someone's home. By attending to how people interweave such images with verbal narratives, researchers may learn about how these individuals construct their lives and histories.

When we enter people's 'own' spaces – their homes, work spaces, or other areas they have appropriated for themselves – we usually encounter photographic displays. Anthropological studies of the home demonstrate the importance of attending to the domestic material culture (Gullestad 1993; Miller 1998, 2001; Pink 2004b). This includes photography, which is part of the visual, material and sensory composition of the home *and* a medium though which people represent and communicate about their identities to themselves and others in the semi-public areas of home. Rose Gilroy and Peter Kellett's work in the North of England demonstrates the importance of photographic display for older people in their own homes, and as they move into sheltered housing and nursing homes, where private space becomes increasingly limited (2005). Likewise, in France Okely found her elderly informants drew the photographs they had on display into their conversations with her: 'The selected icons of photos which the aged displayed at institutional bedside or on familiar sideboard in their own home were both cultural and individual presentations' (Okely 1994: 51).

In Spain I discussed individual collections and public displays of images to explore people's visual representation of their 'bullfighting world' and its history, and to see how individuals used these visual representations to situate themselves within that bullfighting world. In photographic displays individuals and groups often used photographs to establish identities and to imply relationships. Most bullfighting bars and clubs owned permanent exhibitions that mapped out a local version of the history of bullfighting. When informants took me to see 'their own' bullfighting bar or club, I was frequently given a guided tour of the bar's photographic display. As I was led through these photographic wall displays, narratives of history, place and kinship were developed as informants emphasized family relationships between different bullfighters, their historical authenticity and their local links. The histories I was told when viewing the images were, as in the case of the box of images that Okely's informant drew her faded prints from, multilinear. The chronological history of bullfighting that my informants outlined was intersected with family histories as links between fathers, sons, nephews and great uncles formed particular routes across the various different photographic maps of the bullfighting world that I was shown. For a bullfighter, it was especially important to be situated in this world by having his photograph included in the exhibition, since inclusion in a display and the social relations involved in achieving this are crucial for a bullfighter's career. The cultural construction of history and the contemporary configuration of the bullfighting world depends on the strategic inclusion and exclusion of photographs of certain people (Pink 1997b: 56). Bullfight *aficionados* used similar strategies in their semi-public displays at home. These included photographs of themselves in amateur performances, or photographed with famous bullfighters, and thus mapped personal versions of the 'bullfighting world' that placed the owner of the exhibition at their centre. I was also invited to the openings of many exhibitions of bullfight photography during my research in Spain. At these events I discussed photographs with informants as we milled around the exhibition spaces. Their comments about the content and style of photographs gave me a better understanding of how different photographic representations fitted with each person's vision of the contemporary and historical world of bullfighting and of how they constructed their own place and identity in that world (see Pink 1997b).

In Spanish bullfighting culture photographic exhibitions pertain to the visual culture of a group. Public photography archives and displays are also often produced with a locality focus, and can contribute to processes through which the identities and histories of towns or other settlements are produced. Làszlò Kürti discusses a community archive project he was involved in setting up in the town of his birth, Lajomizse in Hungary. He found that although the town had been labelled a place without 'serious history', in fact what this 'masked was the fact that there was no written history'. The first project was the creation of a Digital Photo Archive (DPA) that aimed to 'collect, analyse and archive family photographs'. Kürti writes, 'As more and more photographs were offered and scanned into our DPA, the more the town's past began to emerge as unique and colourful'. Analytically this produced two areas of knowledge about the past focusing on 'the moment the picture was taken, and the post-photographic event that the pictures clandestinely suggested' (Kürti 2004: 51). Kürti's detailed analysis of the images that composed the DPA provides an insight into the sorts of academic knowledge that can be derived by studying community archives. As he points out, 'These postcards of a single settlement chronicle the diverse practices, cultural and political commitments that have generalised the past century. They reveal that the visual representation of a community is always suspect to being a momentary snap-shot-like description manipulated both by the makers and users' (2004: 65). In my research about Cittàslow in Aylsham, Norfolk I have also witnessed the role of photography in the constitution of local history, through the production of a digital community archive that is exhibited at public events. As part of carnival in Aylsham in summer 2005 an exhibition of historical photographs sourced from the town's community archive and local people's own collections was presented in the town hall. In one section of the exhibition local people were invited to identify people featured in old photographs by

writing their names on photocopied sheets, thus participating in the
process of the production of this archive of local history. In the main room
of the town hall a series of tables upon which photographs were laid out
covered past carnivals and, more generally, local history (see Introduction,
Figure 2). Here, as I talked with people from the town they pointed out
how their own families, memories and histories were interwoven with this
exhibition.

Absent photographs

In Chapter 1 I noted how sometimes people speak about absent images. They
may describe a famous photograph, a photograph seen in yesterday's
newspaper, a photograph of a child or relative, a photograph that they
hated so much that it was torn up and thrown away, or simply a photograph that is somewhere else. While ethnographers may never actually see some of the photographs informants describe, they provide
interesting examples of how informants visualize certain emotions, values and experiences. It is also important to pay attention to how informants speak about images that they have hidden or thrown away: it is
not only the photographs that people keep that are of interest, but those
that they reject and their reasons for doing so may be of equal interest.

Summary

This chapter has emphasized two dimensions of ethnographic research
with photographic images and technologies: an appreciation of both the
local and academic visual cultures in which ethnographers work and
how researchers may employ photography and photographs in the production of knowledge. Ethnographic image production and discussions
of images both respond and refer to local and academic visual cultures.
Ethnographers should recognize that neither local nor academic visual
and written cultures are superior to the other. As the individual through
which the experience of each is mediated, photographers/ethnographers
should attempt to maintain a reflexive awareness of how the demands of
each inform their work.

Usually the processes of learning about local visual cultures and the
production of one's own images go together. However, in different
projects photographing, collecting and interviewing with/talking about
images will inevitably develop in different ways. The photographic
research methods described above are not intended to be comprehensive,
but to present a series of ideas and examples of existing work and of
the potential for photography in ethnographic research. Variations in the
methods developed in different projects are not just contingent on the cultures in which researchers work, but also on the personal styles of ethnographers and the social relationships in which they are involved. The key

to successful photographic research is an understanding of the social relations and subjective agendas through which they are produced and the discourses through which they are made meaningful.

FURTHER READING

Harper, D. (2002) 'Talking about pictures: a case for photo elicitation', *Visual Studies*, 17 (1): 13–26

Pink, S., Kürti, L. and Afonso, A.I. (eds) (2004) *Working Images*, London: Routledge. (Especially chapters by L. Kürti, G. Orobitg, and O. da Silva and S. Pink)

Radley, A., Hodgetts, D. and Cullen, A. (2005) 'Visualizing homelessness: a study in photography and estrangement', *Journal of Community and Applied Social Psychology*, 15: 273–95

Video in Ethnographic Research

Many ethnographers and their informants produce and view video in their personal lives and professional work. However, until very recently video has been allowed only cursory mention in ethnographic texts on research methods. In the past, visual sociologists largely concentrated on photography, rarely considering the potential of video in the research process (Lomax and Casey 1998: 2). Visual anthropologists became interested in video in the 1980s, applauding new developments in video technology for the convenience, economy, durability and utility they offered. In comparison with film, which was used extensively in anthropological research in the 1970s (see Morphy and Banks 1997: 5), video was cheap and could record for a considerably longer period of time. During this period the potential of video was often harnessed to serve a scientific-realist approach. For example, Collier and Collier saw the idea that a video camera may be left running continuously for several hours as an advantage compared to the relative selectivity imposed by both the cost of film and the need to reload a camera more frequently (1986: 146). However, since the late 1990s researchers from different social science disciplines (such as social anthropology, sociology, queer studies) have begun to engage with video anew and as distinct from ethnographic film. This has meant exploring reflexive uses of video in ethnography, using video not simply to record data, but as a medium through which ethnographic knowledge is created. Simultaneously, technological developments, especially in digital video, invite new practical possibilities for video in research and representation. In Chapter 2 I discussed how particular cameras may be interpreted by video subjects, thus impacting on their strategies of self-representation. It is also worth reflecting on the design of the video technology used and how this affects the researchers' or video makers' strategies. In the 1990s Chris Wright described how the Sony PC7 digital video camera differs from more conventional cameras. In place of a viewfinder, the PC7 has a fold-out mini-TV screen that creates distance between the camera operator's eye and the camera, allowing the camera operator to see both the camera screen and the scene recorded. Thus the camera no longer follows the operator's eye but allows him or her a split vision, and to see and decide what is being recorded in relation to the scene in front of the camera (C. Wright 1998: 18–19). My experiences with a similar model, the Sony PC1E, in 1999, supported this and this design of digital video camera has persisted into the twenty-first century, now being more or less standard across a range of domestic and semi-professional models of the kind used in ethnographic research. Moreover, such technology changes not only the camera operator's view, but also what the video subjects see. Using the open camera screen of the video, the researcher can now maintain better eye contact with video subjects because the camera itself is not hiding his or her face. Video footage can also be viewed 'in the field' on this screen and listened to through the external speaker, with informants or people who have appeared in the video. In comparison with viewing playback though the camera viewfinder with headphones as one would have done using previous analogue technologies, this viewing context also allows researcher and informants to discuss the images during viewing. Video is of course not simply visual – it is an audio-visual medium and sound recording is part of video recording. In many instances the camera's internal microphone will be sufficient for the type of video methods discussed in this chapter. However, to achieve good sound quality, especially when not close up to the source of the sound, researchers might also consider using an external microphone and at times a radio microphone.

Ethnographers should develop a self-conscious approach not only to their relationships with the video subjects but also to how both relate to the camera, and to their different agendas regarding the video technology and recordings. In this chapter I discuss examples of using video cameras of different types over the past fifteen years or so. However, I write with the assumption that most contemporary video ethnographers will be using digital camcorders.

Defining ethnographic video

In the 1990s literature about ethnographic video and filmmaking there developed a tendency to distinguish between 'objective' research film or video footage and 'creative' footage produced for ethnographic filmmaking. This distinction was informed by debates in the 1970s and 1980s about the relationship between cinematography and scientific ethnographic film (see Banks 1992). Some (e.g. Heider 1976) argued that ethnographic film should be objective, unedited, not 'manipulated'; it should be guided by scientific, ethnographic principles, rather than cinematographic intentions. Such footage was intended to be stored as a film archive and screened to anthropological audiences; it was part of a project of recording an objective reality. During the same period others produced more creative, expressive films intended for public consumption. In particular, Robert Gardner 'distanced himself from realism' (see Loizos 1993: 140), producing films that used cinematographic and symbolic techniques that challenged the criteria set by Heider. Collier and Collier applied a similar distinction between 'research' film which 'is made to contain relatively *undisturbed* process and behaviour from which to develop information and concepts' and 'ethnographic' film that 'is usually edited to create a narrative selected by the filmmaker-producer' (Collier and Collier 1986: 152). They dismiss the possibility of using 'ethnographic' film for research purposes, claiming that the selectivity involved in its production makes it invalid as an observational record. These categories persist in recent work (e.g. Barbash and Taylor 1997) that regards research footage as objective data, 'raw material' and a scientific document. In this view creativity is not part of research as the ethnographer's intentionality must be scientific to be 'ethnographic'.

Here I propose three main criticisms of this approach. First, it is usually impossible or inappropriate to video-record people or culture 'undisturbed'; people in a video are always 'people in a video'. Moreover, like any ethnographic representation, research footage is inevitably constructed. Secondly, ethnographic knowledge does not necessarily exist as observable facts. In Chapter 1 I argued that ethnographic knowledge is better understood as originating from fieldwork experiences. Knowledge is produced in conversation and negotiation between informants and researcher, rather than existing as an objective reality that may be recorded and taken home in a note book, camera film or tape. Thirdly, and parallel to my discussion of defining ethnographic photography (Chapter 3), the question of the 'ethnographicness' of video footage does not depend entirely on its content or on the intentionality of the video maker, but its ethnographicness is contextual. In the broadest sense a video is 'ethnographic' when its viewer(s) judge that it represents information of ethnographic interest. Therefore video footage can never be purely 'ethnographic': a video recording that ethnographers see as representing ethnographic knowledge about an event and how it is experienced might, in their informants' eyes, be a video of a birthday party. This broad and contextual definition of ethnographic video invites the possibility for a range of different genres of video to be 'ethnographic'. This includes not only ethnographers' video footage, but (for example) home movies, events videoed by informants for ethnographers, indigenous videos made for self-representation to external bodies and documentary videos made through collaborations between researchers and informants as part of applied research (see Pink 2004a). None of these recordings are essentially ethnographic, but may become so when they are implicated in an ethnographic project.

Ethnographic video and local 'video cultures'

Ethnographers' uses of video benefit from awareness of how informants use and understand video technologies and representations. As Lomax and

Casey noted from their experiences of videoing interactions between midwives and their clients, 'the camera ... is socially significant given both its ability to preserve interaction for re-presentation and participants' awareness of that ability' (1998: 6). However, reflexivity entails more than simply an awareness of how participants' interactions are affected by their 'camera-consciousness'. Rather, we need to firmly situate their self-awareness within the cultural and media contexts in which they live out their everyday lives. Moreover, an ethnographer with a video camera is a person with a video camera, the camera becomes part of its user's identity and an aspect of the way he or she communicates with others. It is not only cultural difference that influences the way video becomes part of a project, but in each situation the camera will impact differently on the relationships researchers develop with other individuals and the social roles they play. An individual ethnographer does not have one single and fixed identity as a video maker, but this will be negotiated and redefined in different contexts. To be reflexive ethnographic video makers need to be aware of how the camera and video footage become an element of the play between themselves and informants, and how these are interwoven into discourses and practices in the research context.

The complexity and variability of this researcher/filmmaker-informant relationship is demonstrated audio-visually in Braun's video essay, *Passing Girl, Riverside: an Essay on Camera Work* (1998), a reflexive text about video as 'a tool for cross-cultural research' (The Royal Anthropological Institute's Ethnographic Film Festival Catalogue 1998). Braun presents footage from three video projects he developed in Ghana, narrated with his reflexive commentary to represent the relationships he formed with the subjects of his research and video making in each project. The first part of the video discusses a short video recording of a young girl who passed by Braun's rooftop vantage point during a street festival. When she noticed that he was filming her, the girl performed to the camera, delighted at his attention, until, realizing that his interest in her had passed, she appears angry and disappointed. In his commentary Braun discusses the intentionality of video maker and subject. Reflecting on the power relationships and related ethical issues that are implied by such uses of the camera, his text provokes questions about the right of the researcher to film under such circumstances. In his next project Braun developed a collaborative relationship with his video subjects, this time members of a Ghanaian theatre company. He made a deal with the company to produce a series of commercial videos that they would sell in local villages. In return, they allowed him to travel with, and make his own documentary about, the group. This example demonstrates how the subjects of video may appropriate a video maker and his technology for their own ends. This entails a rather different power dynamic from that Braun experienced in his fleeting relationship with the young girl. Finally, Braun presents footage shot in the Ghanaian village in which he had lived as a child when his parents were missionary doctors. Here he negotiated his video making on yet another basis. His existing relationship with the local community enabled him to video freely and he shared his images by screening the footage for his subjects. These three examples show nicely how the video practices of one individual researcher can fit into local cultures and specific relationships with individuals in different ways.

Above I have noted how in Braun's second project he participated in producing local visual culture by making commercial videos for his collaborators. In most contexts of contemporary ethnographic research television, film and video form part of local cultural consumption, and often production too. An appreciation of local television and video cultures, and people's interpretations of media narratives and how these inform their understandings of video images, also support the use of video as a research method. I would not propose that media research *must* become a part of ethnographic work with video; each individual project will have its priorities and media may not be one of them. Nevertheless both public and domestic uses of television, video, film and internet are an important dimension of many local cultures and a growing area of ethnographic interest (see, for example, Hughes-Freeland 1997; Askew and Wilk 2002; Ginsburg et al. 2002; Rothenbuhler and Coman 2005). The emergent field of media anthropology (see for example www.philbu.net/media-anthropology/) is developing an interdisciplinary approach linking the concerns of anthropology, sociology and media studies. Within this has developed a method that has been called media ethnography. This approach was earlier formulated as a departure from 'audience studies' and 'reception studies' in media analysis to propose a reflexive ethnography of media reception that focuses on how 'audience creativity' intersects with 'media power' (see Morley 1996: 14). However, media ethnography may now be said to be more generally an ethnographic approach to studying media forms and practices and their meanings within specific cultural contexts, individual narratives and social relations. This includes the possibility of going further than simply doing participant observation with television, video or film audiences and internet users to understand viewers'/users' individual and cultural understandings of media representations by extending this to also cover media practices such as commercial, public and domestic media production. Media ethnography can support ethnographic research with video by helping researchers to understand how their informants' interpretations of video cameras and 'ethnographic' video recordings are informed by meanings they invest more generally in audio-visual media practices and representations.

For example, a project by three visual anthropologists, Manuel Cerezo, Ana Martinez and Penelope Ranera, demonstrates the importance of sensitivity to media narratives and the meanings that informants invest in visual representations of themselves. The researchers were working with African immigrant workers in Spain. Since they had used photography quite extensively in the project, to the pleasure of their informants, they found their informants' reactions to their introduction of the video camera surprising. Its presence displeased them and created moments of tension that were difficult to deal with (Cerezo et al. 1996: 142). Neither did the informants like the images of themselves in the video; while they admired its landscape scenes, they found themselves 'ugly' and 'poor' (1996: 143). The researchers situate these responses in relation to popular culture, pointing out that the immigrants, who work very long hours and have a low economic level, nevertheless return home every evening to watch television or videos. From the informants' viewpoint the video images of themselves on a television screen were images of poverty, they were permanently recorded images and could be seen by anyone (1996: 143). The informants' own gaze on the video images of themselves thus objected to the researchers' 'innocently' filmed video footage. This raised ethical issues that led Cerezo, Martinez and Ranera to argue that visual products like video should not be produced without their protagonists' permission. Their work emphasizes how important reflexivity can be in video research. The researchers' self-reflexivity and discussions with their informants about the video representations revealed how each of them had gazed differently on the video footage. By exploring this they learned both why the video images were problematic and how their informants inter-preted images of themselves with reference to contemporary popular media culture. It is not only our informants' understandings of media representation that should inform our work as ethnographers, but also their understandings of media production practices – in both public and domestic contexts.

From 1999 to 2000 I undertook (with Unilever research) two video ethnography projects that explored aspects of the relationship between self-identity and the home in Britain and Spain. The research involved an in-depth interview of about one hour with each participant, followed by a 'video tour' of his or her home. The video tour entailed my infor-mant showing me around the home while I video-recorded him or her. Guided by prompts, participants led the tour discussing with me aspects of the visual and material home, their feelings about it and treatment of it (further reading about this method can be found in Pink 2004b, Pink 2004c, Pink 2005: ch. 4). As the video tour method developed in the dif-ferent sites and contexts of my fieldwork – that is, in the homes and personal narratives of different individuals – I realized that it was cul-turally embedded in specific ways. First, using a small domestic video camera (as described above) I was introducing a domesticated research technology that already fitted in the home. However, because this was also the 'latest' and smallest of the new domestic digital video cameras at the time, it aroused people's curiosity to hold and examine it. Secondly, all my informants in this research were conversant in video use. They had preconceived ideas about what to expect from and how to behave with a video camera. Although none of my informants had ever experienced a similar research exercise, each of our video recordings could be seen as a performance that had been informed by existing cultural and personal knowledge and experience about how one per-forms and communicates 'on camera'. Finally, the video tours are inter-esting because they show how each informant appropriated the video tour process him or herself by attaching it to a (usually subconsciously) chosen existing cultural narrative. For example, some informants devel-oped the tour by taking the stance used to show a prospective buyer around the home, others used what I have called a '*Hello!* magazine' type narrative to communicate the idea of showing the home in a way that presents a lifestyle, and finally others linked the tour and the way that it encouraged them to reflect on their own personal trajectories to a counselling narrative. As such they were able to comment on both the material home, their embodied experiences of it and their self identities as we toured it. These performances and uses of narratives can be seen as an element of my informants' negotiations with me – since they also used them as mechanisms through which to select what they would and would not show me within the private space of their homes. They did not ever ask me not to video but at the same time took control over what I could and could not access through video (see Pink 2004c).

In contrast to working in domestic space, my experience of video-recording a public event in Northern Ireland in 1990 was very different. In this case I was carrying a large JVC semi-professional camera and was accompanied by a sound recordist with a professional-looking microphone. The video was part of an ethnographic project about migra-tion from Belfast to London. We were to video-record the unveiling cer-emony of a statue of William of Orange, just outside Belfast, and were developing a commentary on this event through interviews with George, the key informant, a migrant from Belfast to London, and interviews that he was leading. Once we had requested permission to film, with our professional-looking equipment we were ushered by the organizers into the enclosure reserved for television and film crews. Our presence with the camera developed various responses from people attending the event. One woman treated us as a source of public information, another interviewee gave well-considered responses to George's questions as if to a TV audience. In this case my collaboration with George involved nego-tiation over the planning and direction of the video. The other infor-mants were in a sense also *his* informants. The ways we worked at the public event were also framed by our interviewees' and the organizers' interpretations of our activities, this being contingent on their own knowledge about video.

Knowledge that situates video technologies and representations locally can benefit ethnographic work and support collaborations with informants in a number of ways. This may include knowledge of local visual media and video culture, about local people's interpretations of video technology, reflexivity about the researcher's own role and infor-mants' understandings of this. It is also useful to explore how video technology is made meaningful locally. This might involve examining the discourses through which video is discussed. For example, is it discussed in relation to notions of, or exhibitions of, wealth or of scientific innovation? In what categories do local people situate video, such as popular culture, art, domestic activity or leisure?

The potential of video as a recording method

The approach I have advocated in the earlier chapters of this book is critical of the realist stance and of methods texts that limit the potential of video to recording focus group discussions and interviews to avoid losing important visual data and cues. Video is undoubtedly good for such visual note-taking, but such uses ought to be qualified with a rejection of the naive assumption that video records an untainted reality in favour of a reflexive approach that accounts for how video can become part of a focus group discussion or interview. This, combined with knowledge about the video or media culture of interviewees or focus group participants, should help the researcher to decide if video would be appropriate for that particular group, and how video could successfully be used in that specific research scenario. For example, when using a video camera to record midwife–client interactions, Lomax and Casey rightly acknowledge that 'the research is not marred by the necessary involvement of the researcher, but conversely, she is a contributor to the constitution of the interaction' (1998: 26). While their use of the tape is realist, they also use it as a device for reflexivity, noting that 'the involvement of the researcher in the interaction can be analysed and understood from the video text. The analysis, in turn, is informative about "normal" consultations; i.e. how midwives organise an overall structure of the visit' (1998: 26).

Video can be used for ethnographic diary-keeping (e.g. Holiday 2001; Chalfen and Rich 2004), note-taking (including surveys of the physical environment, housing, etc.) or recording certain processes and activities. For example, the sociologist Tim Dant, reflecting on his video research about the work practice of car mechanics, comments that 'Because of the capability of capturing the visible and hearable actions and interactions of people going about their ordinary life, it [video] would seem to provide a rich source of data for those social scientists interested in studying local social situations.' He goes on to suggest that 'The flow and pattern of life as it is lived is recorded and retained in the moving picture with sound to become available for close study and multiple replays' (2004: 41). Such uses are perfectly viable, although it is important to keep in mind that video materials of this kind should be treated as *representations* rather than visual facts. Moreover, their analysis should take note of the collaborations and strategies of self-representation that were part of their making. Nevertheless, this is not so much a limitation as an indication of the potential of video for ethnographic research. In this chapter I focus largely on how video ethnography can be much more than visual note-taking, to explore how it is embedded in processes of knowledge production.

Getting started

There is never any single 'right moment' to start using a video camera. In some cases video recording may become an element of a researcher's relationship with his or her informants right from the first meeting. For example, in my video ethnographies of the home in England and Spain video-recording was an unavoidable element of the fieldwork and was agreed with each informant from the outset. I introduced video as a matter of course as part of our interview process. In other projects, however, uses of video are negotiated on different terms. It may even be several months before the ethnographer considers it the 'right moment' to introduce video. Francisco Ferrándiz (whose work I discuss below) did not begin to use video in his research in Venezuela until he was already six months into the fieldwork, and then, as he notes, the 'most complex visual project had to wait a couple of months more' (1998: 26).

Similarly, video work with different informants may start at different times in a project as relationships between ethnographers, technology, images and different individuals develop at different paces and in different ways. For example, when I was shooting my masters degree project (*Home from Home*) in Northern Ireland, the grandmother of George, my key informant, was keen to be video-recorded talking with George in a conversational interview. However, initially, his mother did not want to participate. As the project proceeded, we continued to video-record interviews with various members of the family – an outing that George made with his nieces and some local public ritual events. Every evening we returned to George's parents' home where we were staying and viewed the SVHS footage through their video recorder and television. Although the SVHS images were not perfectly projected through the VHS recorder, we could see and hear enough to know we had the footage we wanted. George's mother also became interested, keen to see her grandchildren and other family members on video. As her interest and confidence in the video making increased, she volunteered to be interviewed.

Getting started is not solely a matter of finding the right moment but also involves technical procedures. This varies according to the equipment used but includes getting the camera out and setting it up, organizing sound recording and lighting. These procedures become bound up in the research process. For example, in their sociological research on midwife–client interaction, Lomax and Casey found that actually starting the video-taping 'became, in our research, a matter of some complexity and analytic interest' because 'even with specific arrangements, it is not possible to enter a person's home and set up camera without becoming interactionally involved' (Lomax and Casey 1998: 7). Similarly, when I interviewed people with video in their homes, I often collaborated with my interviewees to arrange that lights are strategically placed and switched on as we moved around video-recording. Here the technical demands of video-recording became a collaborative issue as both the interviewees and interviewer sought extra sources of indoor lighting.

Video and the production of ethnographic knowledge

When we use video as a research method we are not merely video-recording what people do in order to create visual data for analysis. Rather we are engaging in a *process* through which knowledge is produced. Above I have emphasized the importance of understanding the cultural context in which one uses the camera. In this section I show how there is further variation in terms of what one might achieve through video ethnography. In part this is related to the different social and cultural settings of the different projects discussed below, and in part to the different research agendas video was engaged to support. In each of the projects referred to the researcher has taken a reflexive approach to the discussion of the methodology used in her or his work.

Learning to see
One of the opportunities afforded by doing long-term participant obser-vation with a video camera is that one can learn not just about how other people do things but also become engaged in similar practices oneself. Where the practices one is learning about involve visual evaluation the camera can be an important tool. In Chapter 3 I discussed how I photographed the bullfight in ways that both followed the conventions of existing bullfight photography and under my informants' direction. Then by showing them these images, taking their criticisms of how I had *seen* (photographed) the performance and discussing what they *saw* in my photographs I came closer to understanding their visual knowl-edge about and criteria for evaluating a performance, performer and bull (see Pink 1997a). Through a discussion of her video research about cattle breeding in Northern Italy, Cristina Grasseni has suggested that the visual ethnographer might, by apprenticing her- or himself to their informants, develop what she has called 'skilled vision': the ability to see and thus understand local phenomena in the same way as the people with whom the researcher is working. Grasseni proposes that there is 'a parallel between the process of apprenticeship that a visual ethno-grapher has to undergo, and the process of education of attention that is required of anyone participating in a community of practice'. As such an ethnographer might learn to share 'an aesthetic code' (Grasseni 2004: 28) with her or his informants. In her own research, working with a breed expert Grasseni tried to 'develop an "eye" through an

apprenticeship into looking at cattle'. As part of this process she used her video camera to keep a video diary, from which she showed footage to her hosts to comment on in such a way that this allowed her to compare her own way of seeing with theirs (Grasseni 2004: 17). Grasseni describes how when she first began to tour farms with a breed inspector she 'did not know what to point the camera at, because [she] could not *see* what was going on'. She realised that in order for what she saw to become meaningful she would need to learn 'to share the breeder's vision' (2004: 20). She began to use her video camera under the guidance of an expert who explained to her how to evaluate a cow.

> As a result of his instructions, I started to look at the udders from underneath, lowering the camera to knee-height. I concentrated on the volume of the udder, trying to shoot from under the cow's tail to line up her teats. I also began to frame the cows mainly from behind, keeping the camera high above their backs to show the line of the spine and the width of the shoulders. (2004: 21)

The video camera was important in this exercise, since rather than simply looking at the cow as instructed, Grasseni video-recorded this vision; as she puts it, 'the camera functioned as the catalyst of my attention, tuning my eyes to the visual angles and the ways of framing the cow through the inspector's gaze' (2004: 21). As this example shows, video can be used as part of the process of learning to see as others do, in a directed way. Moreover this produces audio-visual materials that informants can then comment on to produce a further layer of knowledge. Grasseni situates these uses of video in relation to a theoretical understanding of vision. She argues that the idea of participant observation should be reformulated as not simply imitating what other people do, but (drawing from ideas of ecology) as a way of learning about how people's shared visions (or understandings) 'co-evolve' (2004: 28–9).

Collaboratively representing everyday experiences

In other projects long-term fieldwork may not be a possibility, either due to the timescale allowed for the research or the nature of the subject. My own 'Cleaning, homes and lifestyles' project (developed with Unilever Research in 1999) was an exploratory applied video ethnography study that examined the relationship between people's self-identities, values, moralities, knowledge about housework, and the actual housework practices they engaged in, products they used and how they used them. We hoped to learn what domestic cleaning and the products used for it meant to people within the wider contexts of their lifestyles, homes and self-identities. I had six months to complete the research from beginning to the final report and presentation. There was no time for the immersion in my research participants' lives that forms part of long-term participant observation. This was for two reasons. First, I needed to complete the fieldwork within three months. Secondly, I was to study the relationships between 40 individuals, their lifestyles, homes and cleaning and the fieldwork was to take place in their homes. Short of living with each of them for several months I would be unable to participate in their everyday lives for extended periods.

For this study I developed a collaborative method, called the 'video tour', to achieve an in-depth understanding of the social and material worlds people live in (see Pink 2004b). Therefore I only had one meeting with each informant in which we collaboratively set out to explore their homes using the video camera. Whereas Grasseni sought to learn the 'way of seeing' of cattle experts, and as such be able, using the camera, to imitate their practices herself, my approach was to ask my informants to show me their homes and to describe their practices to me on video both verbally and through embodied performance (see Pink 2004b, 2005). My meeting with each research participant lasted between two and four hours. The research meeting involved two tasks. First, a tape-recorded interview covering areas including their self-identities, everyday lives, usual cleaning practices, moralities and values concerning dirt and cleanliness, knowledge about cleaning and definitions of clean and dirty etc. The interview was structured by my checklist, but was focused on allowing the research participant to talk and explain these areas her- or himself. It was a collaborative interview in that we worked together to enable the research participant to define these areas of their lives. Secondly, the video tour followed. This was a collaborative exercise that involved each research participant working with me to represent her or his experience of everyday life in the home and the routine practices this involved. Whereas in long-term fieldwork we would wait for events to unfold over a period of time, here we did not have that luxury. Instead we had one hour of video tape on which to represent the research participant's life in her or his home. Therefore we very consciously worked within a constrained time period to explore and represent the home and to discuss the human and material relationships, sensations, identities, emotions, memories, creativity and activity associated with the research participant's life there. This included participants giving demonstrations of how everyday domestic activities were performed. They used their whole bodies as well as words to show me what their lives and experiences were like in their homes as I probed and guided the 'tour' according to the objectives of the study.

Through this research I aimed to produce, with my informant, shared understandings of their past experiences and current practices. To do so I had to depend on our collaborations and to work with them to help them draw out, reconstruct and represent the relevant experiences in a way that was meaningful to them, and to me. This produced a set of interview transcripts and recordings and videotapes. Their content, which was at one level my audio-visual representation of the research experience, included descriptions and discussions of informants' past experiences, demonstrations of how things are done, or of what has happened in a past situation, and explanations of knowledge and meaning, values and moralities. The other layer of knowledge was based on my own first hand experience of the contexts in which the research participants lived and experienced, gained through the video tour. Whereas to produce the knowledge represented on video my informants used their whole bodies, to understand the research context I also used my own. This type of video ethnography does not provide access to the level of experience and shared knowledge that might be produced through the type of involvement in people's lives permitted by long-term fieldwork. But it does allow us to explore collaboratively, and intensively, the visual and other sensory knowledge and experience that form part of people's everyday lives.

Handing over the camera: spontaneous video

In Chapter 3 I discussed instances where informants have taken the camera into their own hands either to provide the researcher with photographs of him- or herself, or knowing that the researcher will give them copies, to produce the images of an event or activity that they want to have themselves. An interesting example of how this might also work in the context of video ethnography is demonstrated in Francisco Ferrándiz's work with Venezuelan spirit cults (1996, 1998). In this case also we see how video can provide a route to visual and sensory knowledge and, interestingly, how the camera itself was appropriated within a culturally specific activity. Situating the role of video in his fieldwork in relation to the cult's existing relationship with, and experience of, media representation, Ferrándiz pays particular attention to the way the video-recording developed through the intersubjectivity between himself and his informants. In some instances the video became a catalyst that helped create the context in which it was used, as in the case of a ceremony that was organized by his informants as part of the event of videoing it. However, of particular interest is that when Ferrándiz began shooting video, six months into his fieldwork, the informants with whom he was closely collaborating also took the camera to shoot footage themselves, each of them creating 'completely different visual itineraries of the same place' (Ferrándiz 1998: 27).

Ferrándiz takes his analysis further than merely the question of how different people created different video narratives of the same context. He forms continuities between the video making and the ritual activities in which his informants were involved; the visual practices of video-recording and the ritual practices coincided as people moved in and out of trance and in front of and behind the camera's viewfinder as the ceremony proceeded. In this research the video camera became part of the material culture of the ritual and its recording capacity an aspect of the ritual activity. Therefore Ferrándiz was able to learn about ritual practices both by observing the ritual uses of the camera itself and by analysing and discussing the video recordings that these uses produced.

Informants' video diaries

Above I have discussed a case where informants took the camera themselves. In other work, similar in ways to the photographic studies discussed in Chapter 3, researchers have given video cameras to informants, asking them to film their own lives. This use of video has a long history since Sol Worth and John Adair's (1966) 'Navajo Film Themselves' project which had as its main objective 'to ask the Navajo to show "us" (acknowledged researchers) how they saw themselves and their surroundings, or even better how they wanted to show themselves and their selves to outsiders' (Chalfen and Rich 2004: 19). Richard Chalfen (a visual anthropologist) and Michael Rich (a medical researcher) comment that the principle of handing the (now video) camera over to the research participants has been applied in a large number of studies across a wide range of disciplines. But, they note, few of these projects have been written up as academic studies (see Chalfen and Rich 2004: 19–20). One exception is Ruth Holliday's work on the performance of queer identities (2004).

Chalfen and Rich's own study was produced in the context of applied medical anthropology. Chalfen and Rich have developed a method called Video Intervention/Prevention Assessment (VIA) by which 'Young patients were instructed to follow a specified protocol to "teach your clinician about your illness" by using consumer model videocams in their homes, neighbourhoods, schools, work, church and events of their own selection. They could also make a series of diaristic "personal monologues"' (2004: 17). This means that 'VIA asks young people who share a medical diagnosis, such as asthma, obesity … to create a visual illness narrative, documenting their experiences, perceptions, issues and needs on video.' Developed in the form of video-taped diaries, these recordings represent the experience of illness from the patient's perspective. They provide a route through which clinicians, assisted by the analysis developed by the research team, might access patients' knowledge and understandings of their illnesses (2004: 18). This is seen as a way of creating better understanding and communication between clinicians and patients in a context where each may understand the illness in different ways. As such, Chalfen and Rich refer to this method as offering a form of cultural brokerage (2004: 20–2) (which is characteristic of applied visual anthropology work more generally).

As is often the case in applied visual anthropological studies, in this work it is not only the results of the research that impact on the lives of the participants, but also for the process becomes empowering (see below). Chalfen and Rich note that (in the case of a study of asthma sufferers) '[t]he process of self-examination had resulted in quantifiable improvements in patients' asthma status, possibly because of the cognitive dissonance between what they observed themselves to be doing and what they knew they should be doing' (2004: 23).

Collaborative/participatory video and the empowerment of participants

As some of the examples discussed above have shown, ethnographic video production may become interwoven with local video cultures. Such work is by nature collaborative in the sense that it involves the active participation of the informants in the processes by which knowledge is produced. It is indeed, as Banks (2001) has also pointed out, hard to imagine visual research that is not collaborative; however, there are of course different ways and towards different ends that video ethnographers and informants work together. One way to consider the question of collaboration is by asking what the various motives for participation in a video ethnography might be. In Chapter 2 I raised Engelbrecht's question: for whom do we make ethnographic films? Engelbrecht refers to documentaries that are edited and screened to anthropological and other audiences. But the question also applies to research footage: for whom do we shoot this footage when we collaborate with individuals and groups who also have an interest in the footage? Such collaboration results in ethnographers working with informants and participating in 'their' video culture, as well referring to other video cultures (for instance, video conventions in ethnographers' personal lives as well as in their academic discipline). Here I discuss two collaborative video projects that have produced research footage that was guided by the intentionalities of both researchers and informants, and also responded to the demands of academic and informants' video cultures. The idea of video as a medium that can be used to empower otherwise disenfranchised people has been developed in work on participatory development (e.g. White 2003). As the examples below show, this can also be applied to the use of video in ethnographic research that also serves academic ends (see also Pink 2004a, 2005: ch. 5).

Barnes, Taylor-Brown and Weiner (1997) have described a project to produce video tapes in which HIV-positive mothers recorded messages that would be viewed by their children after the mothers' deaths. The researchers' intention was to use 'the concept of "eternal mothering"' to provide 'a framework to study the interactive aspects of mothering and the significance of impending maternal death from a stigmatising illness' (1997: 7). They collaborated with each mother to produce a video document that she felt would represent her appropriately to her children once she was dead. Barnes, Taylor-Brown and Weiner follow Chaplin (1994) in attempting 'to replace the sociology *of* a topic with a sociology that emphasises less distance between verbal analysis and visual representation as data' (Barnes et al. 1997: 10), thus reducing the distance between the researcher and the subject.

Conscious of the positivist tradition that has informed their discipline, Barnes, Taylor-Brown and Weiner weigh up the 'experimental' restraints of their project, concluding that it offers limited opportunity for triangulation and noting how the presence of the camera and researcher may have affected the 'reality' recorded. However they argue that these limits are outweighed by the quality of the self-representation and narrative created by the mothers as 'the method offers the spontaneity and vividness of an uninterrupted stream of information from the individual, as the mother is allowed to talk without researcher intrusion in the form of questions' (Barnes et al. 1997: 13). The project departs from a scientific experimental stance by applying the feminist approach advocated by Chaplin (1994), whereby the knowledge is produced not about but for women, and the women themselves are situated 'at the centre of the production of knowledge' (Barnes et al. 1997: 13). They write, 'We acknowledge that there is no one single interpretation of social action that can claim to be definitive', and follow Chaplin's point that such representations do not convey singular meanings, but that '[i]n post-positivist and feminist philosophy the study offers a range of suggestions and an opportunity to construct a constellation of meanings about mothering' (1997: 14). They realize that they are dealing with:

> What mothers, within the contexts of their social worlds, select to represent of themselves to their children in permanent, structured, visual form, is interrelated to their attitudes about how mothers care for and protect their children, how their impending death from AIDS influenced their mothering and how stigmatisation from AIDS may be transferred from them to their children ... their self-presentation. (1997: 21)

They saw this video tape as an empowering visual medium: it 'offers women, minorities, HIV-infected people, and other marginalised groups, an opportunity to reproduce and understand their world as opposed to the dominant representation depicted in the mass media' (1997: 27). Here the collaborative video research was situated in a particular cultural use of video that the mothers found appropriate to develop. Through it the researchers assisted the mothers in producing cultural documents that allowed them to develop simultaneously a sociological understanding of self-representation and experiences of mothering.

Contemporary visual ethnographers are working in contexts where power relations are complex. They involve not only the relations between researcher and informant but also with other institutions and individuals. The example above shows how collaborations with informants have contributed to their empowerment in more personal situations; in other projects ethnographers have used video in collaborative work to create both academic knowledge and to empower people who have lived through political conflict. Drawing Jean Rouch's notion of a 'shared anthropology', the visual anthropologist Carlos Flores discusses his collaborative video work with Maya Q'eqchi filmmakers in post-war Guatemala. Flores shows how a community-based video project he developed collaboratively with local Q'eqchi people simultaneously 'provided important ethnographic insights about an indigenous group and its transformations' and 'provided the communities with new mechanisms for sociocultural reconstruction and awareness after an intensely traumatic and violent period of civil war' (2004: 31).

Attaching himself to and initially adopting a participant-observer stance in an existing NGO video project, Flores began to learn that existing practices clashed with his own expectations of indigenous video: they seemed to represent a development agenda rather than focusing on traditional indigenous practices or the recent history of conflict, and were made in Spanish rather than local languages (2004: 35). When, in the next stage of his involvement, he began to contribute his own filmmaking skills and ideas, he encouraged them to take up these other themes, focusing on planting rituals in one video and conflict in another. As Flores's article shows, such collaborative work both opens up possibilities and is constrained in what it can achieve (2004: 39). His work also reveals that (like other work in applied visual anthropology – see Pink 2004a, 2005: ch. 5) it is not simply the final film document that is important, but rather the collaborative processes by which it is produced: it is through these processes that both new levels of engagement in thematic issues and of self awareness are achieved by participants and ethnographic knowledge is produced.

Viewing footage with informants: interviewing with/talking around video

Showing video footage to informants can also become part of a research project. In the examples discussed below this ranges from a formal video-recorded interview, during which the informant viewed and commented on video footage of an event in which he had participated, to much more casual screenings in which informants have become involved out of personal interest rather than by request. Whatever the context, the purpose of this method should not be simply to use video images to elicit responses from informants or to extract information *about* the images. Rather, viewing video with informants should also be seen as 'media ethnography'. This combines ethnographers actively discussing video images with informants and examining how they situate themselves as viewers of the footage. This means asking questions such as: How do informants' commentaries on video footage relate it to other aspects of their video/media culture? And what discourses do they refer to in their comments and discussions of the footage?

While studying at the Granada Centre at the University of Manchester, I collaborated with a fellow MA student to make a video about a Jewish family Passover meal. After shooting footage of the family meal, we asked our key informant to view and comment on this footage in an interview that was also video-recorded. This interview was held in his living room, where he sat by the video player, with a purposefully arranged array of family photographs and icons in the background behind his head. On viewing the 'ethnographic video' of the meal, our informant began to reflect on a range of related topics that were of ethnographic interest and served to contextualize the participants and the ceremony in religious, historical and kinship terms. In other instances interviewing or talking with video can become incidental to the project. When I was shooting the Belfast-based part of *Home from Home,* George and I viewed the footage in his family's living room most evenings. Other family members became keen to view and comment on these screenings of interviews and activities in which George and relatives were involved. I was able to learn more generally from their comments on the themes we were exploring in the video, part of which was concerned with why George had left to live in London and their views on this.

In some cases informants' responses to video can be surprising and may even change the direction of the research. Janet Hoskins describes how her research developed in tandem with her use of video in a project originally intended to be a study of ritual communication in the Indonesian island of Sumba. Hoskins screened video footage of past ritual events to the villagers who had participated in these activities. Treating the footage as a visual record of the rituals, she proposed to ask her informants specific questions about their activities. Their answers were to be used as data for her wider project that aimed to resolve cognitive problems concerning the sociology of knowledge and this distribution outside an inner circle of specialists (Hoskins 1993: 81). However, once she began to screen the video footage to her Sumbanese audience, she was struck by 'the feelings of discomfort, shock and sorrow' they expressed. Her research changed direction 'to explore issues relating to the filmic distribution of time' and 'the emotional responses to images of dead persons' (1993: 78). Situating her analysis of the responses to the film in terms of her knowledge of Sumbanese culture, Hoskins began to develop research about 'cultural perceptions of time' (1993: 80). Her video images of people who were now dead had accidentally disrupted the temporal and emotional process of mourning the dead that was so important to her informants.

Editing, distributing and viewing video footage with his informants was also an aspect of Ferrándiz's project in Venezuela (described above). Ferrándiz produced a tape when his informants asked to see copies of the video. He edited the footage to include expressive imagery by using slow motion to represent some trance sequences. The video was widely viewed and well received in the shanty town where Ferrándiz was working. The slow motion sections were to the satisfaction of his informants: 'it is important to stress the success of the use of slow motion, which seemed to embody with more accuracy the emotionality and fuzziness of the temporality experienced during the ceremonies, somewhere in the scales of trance, as opposed to the times where real time was used' (Ferrándiz 1998: 30). Viewing the video produced with informants can help researchers to work out what are and are not appropriate representations of individuals, their culture and experiences. These processes are represented audio-visually in Zemirah Moffat's reflexive ethnographic film *Mirror Mirror*. As part of the process of researching and making the film, Moffat involved the participants in a series of feedback sessions in different contexts: viewing footage of themselves individually on a laptop; viewing a rough-cut of parts of the film projected onto a stage that the participants usually use for performances in a bar;

Figure 4.1

Zemirah Moffat's film *Mirror Mirror* explores queer identities in London. Embedded in the research and film making process is her collaborative and reflexive approach that accounts for both her own identity and part in the film and how the subjects of the film wish to represent themselves. As part of this she screened her footage to them in various contexts and edited their responses into the film itself.

'Why ask Josephine?' © Zemirah Moffat 2006

In this scene the people represented in the film comment on a rough-cut they have viewed with Zem at the university. Their conversation, referring to the scene below, in which Zem cheekily asks Josephine if she likes her penis, is as follows:

Lazlo:	It's really interesting, yeh because except for that moment, you're not playing with any of the tropes of gender questions.
Zem:	Hope I've avoided them.
Lazlo:	So it's curious, because you know everybody has the same prurient interests and everybody wants to know but that's not what you've been doing in the film so does it make sense, I mean especially without this information that she said you could ask her anything? Then there'd be a set-up for it, if we knew she'd given up control and you could ask her anything, and this is what you being perverse, basically, had decided to ask her, then I get it.
Maria:	Yes!
Josephine:	But I'd like this conversation to be cut in. (*all laugh*)

'Do you like your penis?' © Zemirah Moffat 2006

Here Zem makes herself a co-subject of the film.

and then viewing and commenting on a rough-cut projected onto a screen in a university seminar room. In this case the participants, conversant about their own identities and active discussants of the process of representation and the extent to which the film was achieving its aims, continue to negotiate the way they are portrayed throughout the whole visual ethnographic and filmmaking process.

Ethnographic uses of digital video

Technological innovations usually create or inspire new possibilities. Above I have noted how using digital cameras has changed ethnographers' perspectives on what is being filmed. Digital technology has also opened new possibilities for how video is used in research and representation and in creating continuities between these stages. I discuss this further in Chapter 8. Here I briefly consider how video, combined with other digital technologies, might be used in the research process. Above I have already noted how Zemirah Moffatt has screened her video tapes to the participants in her film video as part of the process of creating the film. Their comments have been fed back into the shooting and editing. However, little has been written about uses of digital video and other technologies as part of fieldwork. One example is a digital video research project designed by Fischer and Zeitlyn that has a brief similar to Hoskins's (see above) original research aims. Entitled 'Mambila Nggwun – the construction and deployment of multiple meanings in ritual', their research intends to use digitized video recordings of ritual to 'produce specific models of how collective representations of a specific socio-cultural ritual event are structured and distributed between participants and observers, and how these are accessed and used by people to solve problems in the present' (www.lucy.ukc.ac.uk/dz/ Nggwun/nggwun_1.html). In order 'to capture the many perspectives that contribute to the [ritual] event' the researchers use video in two ways: first, in existing fieldwork they have 'videoed segments of the event from as many points of view as possible, filming under the advisement [sic] of indigenous consultants'; secondly, they propose to 'select segments of this video ... under the advisement [sic] of indigenous consultants, to prepare computer-based multimedia documents as an elicitation device for a range of participants and observers' (Fischer and Zeitlyn n.d.). Fischer and Zeitlyn's collaborative use of digital technology allows this project to stand out from most existing ethnographic research with video. This creates new possibilities for the representation, organization and analysis of visual materials with the collaboration of informants in the field, as well as for the post-fieldwork organization and interpretation of materials (see Chapter 5).

Summary

In this chapter I have suggested a reflexive approach to video in ethnographic research that focuses on the question of how knowledge is produced through the relationship between the researcher and the subject of ethnographic video, the technologies used, and local and academic visual cultures. Recently, uses of video in ethnographic research have developed in tandem with new technologies, innovations and theoretical perspectives. Shifts from a realist approach to video as 'objective' reality to the idea of video as representation shaped by specific standpoints of its producers and viewers have encouraged the development of collaborative approaches to the production and interpretation of video images. The introduction of digital video and computer-based techniques seems particularly appropriate for the application of these methods and is forming the basis of future development in video research.

FURTHER READING

Grasseni, C. (2004) 'Video and ethnographic knowledge: skilled vision in the practice of breeding', in S. Pink, L. Kürti and A.I. Afonso (eds), *Working Images*, London: Routledge. (A useful methodological perspective on vision and seeing in ethnography and an example of using video in research)

Grimshaw, A. and Ravetz, A. (2004) *Visualizing Anthropology*, Bristol: Intellect. (Contains a set of case studies of uses of video and other media that link visual anthropological and arts practice)

Pink, S. (2004) *Applied Visual Anthropology*, a guest edited issue of *Visual Anthropology Review*, 20 (1). (The articles by Chalfen and Flores discussed in this chapter are to be found in this text and in Pink 2007)

Pink, S. (2005) *The Future of Visual Anthropology: Engaging the Senses*, London: Routledge, ch. 5. (A chapter about applied visual anthropology and its role in the future of visual anthropology. Discusses case studies from the public, private and NGO sector)

Pink, S. (ed.) (2007) *Visual Interventions*, Oxford: Berghahn. (An edited volume containing a series of case studies of video uses in applied anthropological research)

5

Classifying and Interpreting Photographic and Video Materials

The ambiguity of visual images and the subjectivity of their producers and viewers have been central concerns of Chapters 1–4. In this chapter I take a similar approach to academic interpretation, analysis and categorization of ethnographic photography and video. The academic meanings that ethnographers give to visual images are also arbitrary and are constructed in relation to particular methodological and theoretical agendas. Individual researchers classify and give meanings to ethnographic images in relation to the academic culture or discipline with which they identify their work. Moreover, ethnographers are themselves subjective readers of ethnographic images and their personal experiences and aspirations also inform the meanings they invest in photographs and video. A reflexive approach to classifying, analysing and interpreting visual research materials recognizes both the constructedness of social science categories and the politics of researchers' personal and academic agendas.

There are points in most research projects when ethnographers need either to use an existing method of organizing, categorizing and interpreting the visual materials they have accumulated, or to invent their own. While visual sociologists and anthropologists have obviously developed their own ways of ordering and analysing ethnographic photographs and video, until recently little has been written on the storage and analysis of qualitative visual research materials. More recently, however, several factors have contributed to the development of a more extensive literature. First, an increasing number of software packages for qualitative data archiving and analysis now also accommodate digital photographs and video. Secondly the use of digital still photography and video itself encourages electronic archiving practices. As the user downloads or captures images directly onto their computer, archiving options are often presented by the software used and, at any rate, files need to be labelled and stored for identification. Thirdly, software for storing, logging and manipulating images is immediately available at no great cost; often a version is supplied with a new computer. Finally, a growing interest in visual methods and their analysis along with (especially in the UK) moves from the research funding councils to scrutinize existing and develop innovative methodologies, has encouraged researchers to investigate and to reflect and report more fully on their archiving and analytical practices. In this chapter I discuss approaches to archiving and analysing visual research materials and examples from recent projects.

Analysis: a stage or a practice?

In some ethnographic research projects the distinction between field-work and analysis appears clearly defined. In traditional ethnographic narratives this is usually achieved either spatially or temporally as researchers return from a fieldwork location to the place where analysis will take place, or when project schedules dictate that the fieldwork period is over and analysis and writing up must begin. However, as most texts on research methods emphasize, analysis actually continues throughout the whole process of ethnographic research (see Burgess 1984: 166; Hammersley and Atkinson 1995: 205): 'It begins from the moment a fieldworker selects a problem to study and ends with the last word in the report or the ethnography' (Fetterman 1998: 92). Recently, ethnographers have begun to account for the constructedness of distinctions between ethnographic fieldwork site, home and academic institution, arguing that interdependencies and continuities, as well as differences between these different times and location, be recognized (see Chapter 1). Sometimes ethnographers do research at home or write up their work while still in the field (see Amit 2000). A strictly conventional fieldwork narrative whereby researchers go to the field, get the images and then take them home to analyse them is not always appropriate or possible. Research and analysis may be conducted in the same or different locations or time-periods and researchers may develop insights into the relationship between research experiences, theoretical concepts or comparative examples at any point in the process of doing ethnography. Given the multiplicity of forms the relationship between research and analysis may take, researchers should be aware of how these two elements interlink in any single project. For visual research this means scrutinizing the relationship between meanings given to photographs and video during fieldwork, and academic meanings later invested in the same images.

Like other items of material culture, visual images have their own biographies (see Appadurai 1986). When they move from one context to another they are, in a sense, transformed; although their content remains unaltered, in the new context 'the conditions in which they are viewed are different' (Morphy and Banks 1997: 16). This also applies to the biographies of images that travel through the research process. Photographs and video images are interpreted in different ways and by different individuals at different points in ethnographic research, analysis and representation. Images first produced, discussed and made meaningful during fieldwork will be given new significance in academic culture where they are 'separated from the world of action in which they were meaningful and placed in a world in which they will be interrogated and interpreted from a multiplicity of different perspectives' (Morphy and Banks 1997: 16). Analysis is not a simple matter of interpreting the visual content of photographs and video, but also involves examining how different producers and viewers of images give subjective meanings to their content and form.

I intend to outline an approach, rather than describe a method for visual analysis. Therefore the principles discussed in the first sections of this chapter refer to ethnographic video and photographs. However, the two media do offer different possibilities for ethnographic analysis. These are discussed in the final sections.

Images and words: the end of hierarchies

The modern project of ethnography was largely 'to translate the visual into words' (C. Wright 1998: 20). This approach, which formed the basis of scientific approaches to visual research, assumes that while ethnographic information may be recorded visually, ethnographic knowledge is produced through the translation and abstraction of this data into written text. For example, Collier and Collier see analysis as a distinct stage of research at which the visual is decoded into the verbal through a process analogous to the translation of art to science or subjectivity to objectivity. This 'involves abstraction of the visual evidence so we can intellectually define what we have recorded and what the visual evidence reveals' (Collier and Collier, 1986: 169–70). Through this procedure, they assert that images may become 'the basis for *systematic knowledge*' (original italics). However, images can only ever be 'primary evidence' that has an 'independent authority' and 'authenticity', but that 'may often have no place in the final product of the research, except as occasional illustrations' (1986: 170).

Here I outline a different approach that begins with the premise that the purpose of analysis is not to translate visual evidence into verbal knowledge, but to explore the relationship between visual and other (including verbal) knowledge. It recognizes that different types of visual and written representations bear varied relations to theory: some might be informed by theory, others might advance theoretical argument. This subsequently opens a space for visual images in ethnographic representation (see Chapters 6–8). In practice, this implies an analytical process of making meaningful links between different research experiences and materials such as photography, video, field diaries, more formal ethnographic writing, local written or visual texts, visual and other objects. These different media represent different types of knowledge that may be understood in relation to one another. For example, when I analyse my visual and written materials from my research about slow living, I find different types of written and visual knowledge about particular themes of the research are represented in my diaries, notes, video recordings, audio recordings and transcripts, and photography. During fieldwork I use each of these media to represent the various stories of the research in different ways. Each medium evokes different elements of my fieldwork experience. Therefore the photographs do not simply illustrate the field notes, and the video is not simply evidence of conversation, interviews or actions. Rather, images and words contextualize each other, forming not a complete record of the research but a set of different representations and strands of it.

Working with visual and verbal fieldwork materials in this way does not constitute a new method. Rather it is more a case of making explicit the ways that many researchers already find that visual and other data become interwoven in their projects. Some anthropologists have developed reflexive texts that interrogate the process by which the knowledge represented in written or visual work was produced (see Chapters 6–8). One good example is Peter Biella's discussion of how he produced his hypermedia text *Masaai Interactive* (n.d.). Here fieldwork and interpretive processes are made explicit through a series of layered notes that show how Biella's work with the fieldwork materials developed (see Biella 1997 and Chapter 8 where ethnographic hypermedia practice is discussed in more detail).

The idea that subjective experience can be translated into objective knowledge is itself problematic for reflexive ethnography. Therefore an analysis that simply produces written academic knowledge from visual data has little relevance. Instead, ethnographers need to articulate the experiences and contexts from which their field notes, video recordings, photographs and other materials were produced, their sociological or anthropological understanding of these ethnographic contexts, and their relevance to wider academic debates.

Content and context (1): the realist approach

The relationship between the context in which images are produced and their visual content is important for any analysis of ethnographic photography or video. However, different theoretical and methodological approaches view this relationship quite differently. Here I compare two approaches. The scientific-realist approach seeks to regulate the context in which images are produced in order that their content should comprise reliable visual evidence of complete contexts and processes. In contrast, a

Interwoven fieldwork materials in multiple media in a 'slow city'. © Sarah Pink 2005

Figure 5.1

When researching carnival in Aylsham, a town with Cittàslow status, the first event that helped me to understand what was happening was the Carnival Subcommittee meeting held in the Town Hall. In my notes I wrote how I realized that 'Carnival committee draws together a range of people, their networks and resources to produce a multifaceted event'. I also highlighted what was to become a theme in my research as I wrote how people were coming together and collaborating under the umbrella of this cittàslow event. These observations, as well as listening to discussions about how and where different components of carnival should be placed, alerted me to the social and sensory elements of carnival. The themes continued through my audio-recorded interviews with Mo the Town Clerk (*bottom left*) and Sue the Aylsham Partnership Officer (*bottom right*), as they elaborated on the history, official regulations and dramas of producing carnival.

At carnival I photographed and videoed. My images were guided by events as they occurred and by the interviews and notes I had already made. I was keen to photograph aspects of carnival I knew were significant for slow living, such as an ice-cream vendor chosen because he produced his ice-cream locally. I was also especially interested in the activities of a group of teenagers who were fund-raising for a trip to Italy to cook at a slow food festival. As part of my carnival research I videoed the cake stalls and kitchen and spoke with those involved. I wanted to get a sense of both the busy kitchen and the excitement at having raised the funding themselves. The research I did at carnival itself linked with my next interviews with two of the teenagers who had prepared and sold cakes at the event, Katy and Amy. Here they discussed with me their experiences of and feelings about carnival and my interview transcripts thus produced a further layer of data as they situated individual experiences, narratives and memories within the wider context of the event.

reflexive approach argues that it is impossible to record complete processes, activities or sets of relationships visually, and demands that attention be paid to the contexts in which images are produced.

Realist approaches to images in ethnography assumed the object of analysis would be the image itself or its content. The context of image production was thought to be important in two ways. First, contextualizing information provided knowledge about the activities, individuals and objects represented in the images' content. Secondly, by regulating contexts in which images were produced, the representativeness of their content could be ensured. These procedures were thought to create the conditions for a reliable analysis because, as Collier and Collier insisted, '[t]he significance of what we find in analysis is shaped by the context established by systematic recording during fieldwork'. This approach demanded that, to be 'responsibly' analysed, visual evidence must be 'contextually complete and sequentially organised' (Collier and Collier 1986: 163). Such approaches have two fundamental problems. First, their assumption that the context may be completed (and closed). Secondly, the idea that the sequence determined by series of photographs or video produced by the ethnographer represents *the* relevant narrative of events or *the* key set of actors.

An examination of how the realist approach was applied to visually recording technology demonstrates its strengths and limitations. Collier and Collier's approach to visual documentation of technology was based on the idea that 'when we record all the relationships of a technology we have, in many circumstances, recorded one whole view of a culture' (1986: 65). Their case study discusses an Andean Otavalo weaver. Through photographing the weaver and discussing the quality and content of the photographs with him, they were able to record the Otavalo weaving process. He became their guide, helping them to document photographically the work and technology of other weavers. They describe the work as 'an acted out interview stimulated by the feedback of photographs', arguing that 'if the subjects of a study have the initiative of organising and informally directing the fieldworker's observation, the result can be a very complete and authentic record' (1986: 73–4). This method clearly allowed the researchers to develop a close collaboration with their informant and thorough ethnographic knowledge about Otavalo culture and weaving. They produced a series of images that were informed by and represented local knowledge about weaving. The case study presents a good example of collaboration in action. My criticism is of their claim that this technique allows ethnographers to 'record one whole view of a culture'. In Chapter 1 I introduced Clifford's (1986) argument that ethnographic truths are only ever partial and incomplete. Collier and Collier's method actually consists in isolating the key elements of a process; they suggest that '[a] process must be photographed so exact steps can be isolated. It is by this systematic observation that a technology can be conceived functionally' (Collier and

Collier's 1986: 69). One could argue that a series of photographs that record a process represent only one standpoint on weaving technology and, moreover, in isolating this technological process, decontextualize it from other important elements of weaving. In short, rather than being complete the visual record is inevitably partial. Isolating the stages of a generalized version of a technological process in this way can provide an abstract or ideal model of that process. Nevertheless, this cannot be a complete or authentic record. Rather, it is a representation of weaving, and is inevitably partial. Even if the context of visually recording such a process is regulated, the content and chronology of the images will not necessarily represent a reliable, complete and truthful account. Therefore analysis of their visual content would not be an objective analysis of a truthful visual record, but one (academic) gaze interpreting a subjective (even if collaborative) visual narrative.

Scientific approaches to social research, informed (like realist approaches to documentary photography) by a notion of visual truth, tended to categorize and interpret images in terms of their content and chronology. The contrasting approach I outline in the next section is instead based on three assumptions. First, that as it is impossible to photograph or video an objective and true visual record of any process, event or activity, analysis will never be of a complete authentic record. Secondly, rather than being a place for *controlling* visual content, the context of image production should be analysed reflexively to examine how visual content is informed by the subjectivities and intentions of the individuals involved (see Chapters 3 and 4). Thirdly, analysis should focus not only on the content of images, but on the meanings that different individuals give to those images in different contexts.

Initially, however, it is useful to interrogate further the possibilities for realist approaches to images within ethnography. Ethnographers do not necessarily need to completely abandon realist uses of photography or video. For example, to represent what something or someone looked like, or to document an event or process that has occurred. Such images can be usefully treated as (inevitably subjective and framed) records of what actually happened and of the visual and material detail that can be found in any one context or activity. For example, the photographic stills of the woman bullfighter Cristina Sanchez performing shown in Figure 3.1 work on different levels. First, they represent part of the process of a bullfight. Secondly, they document a sequence where Cristina was tossed into the air and then recovered. They are an, albeit subjectively framed and selected, set of images of a real event. Simultaneously the reality that is invested in these images varies immensely according to who is viewing. As the Cardiff University Hypermedia and Qualitative Research team also report, in their work they found that 'We utilised both approaches – finding it necessary to treat our video footage both as realist records (which we coded qualitatively according to broad content themes) and as narratives shaped and generated by the researcher's interactions with specific fieldwork contexts' (www.cf.ac.uk/socsi/hyper/p02/findings.html). Indeed, both historically (e.g. John Collier's (1973) visual study of education in Alaska) and recently (e.g. Rich, Lamola, Gordon and Chalfen's (2000) video work on health issues) in large-scale multidisciplinary and team-based projects using visual anthropology methods, realist approaches to coding complex visual data offer a crucial means of managing and sharing data and triangulating findings. Realist uses of visual images in research are not absolutely incompatible with approaches that recognize the contingency of visual meanings. Nevertheless, it is important to keep in mind that even the reality the researcher him- or herself sees in the image is framed by her or his own culturally and individually specific subjectivity.

Content and context (2): local and ethnographic meanings

Ethnographers usually re-think the meanings of photographic and video materials discussed and/or produced during fieldwork in terms of academic discourses. They therefore give them new significance that diverges from the meanings invested in them by informants, and from meanings assumed by ethnographers themselves at other stages of the project.

For example, in 1994 I returned to the United Kingdom after two years' fieldwork in Spain. I brought with me photographs I had taken, printed and discussed with informants, and video footage I was yet to view on a colour monitor. These visual representations were as important as my field diaries and other bits and pieces of local material culture that I had packed in my suitcases. Yet they also bore their own specific relationship to the fieldwork context. Unlike the field diaries, their visual content had been (or was yet to be) shared and discussed with my informants. Now extracted from their Spanish contexts, these images, memories, experiences and artefacts had already become re-situated within my personal narrative, as well as having moved to a new physical location where they would inevitably be made meaningful in relation to new objects, gazes and commentaries. They had been extracted from the cultural context where they were produced, to be viewed and discussed in the context of my personal life and the academic world in the United Kingdom. Meanwhile, in Spain copies of some of these very photographs and video tapes remained in the collections of my informants and friends. In these contexts these still and moving images no doubt continue to be invested with different meanings, taking on a life that departs from the context in which I was present. Maybe they were used to talk about me and how I had photographed or video-recorded them, to discuss the event during which the image had been taken, or as realist representations of their subjects.

However, while the images I had taken home were given new academic and other meanings in new UK contexts, these meanings did not replace the others previously invested in them during fieldwork. Rather, the images can be thought of as visual spaces in which a number of different meanings may be invested. As such they are used to represent or refer to diverse persons, activities and emotions that may not obviously or directly form part of the visible content of the image. Indeed, social scientists often complain that photographs alone do not represent, for example, emotions, social relations, relations of power and exploitation, but need to be contextualized with verbal discourse or other knowledge in order to invoke such experiences. To analyse images, then, it is more useful to examine how people's uses and definitions of the visible content and form of photographs or video sequences attach them to particular ideologies, worldviews, histories and identities.

In Chapters 3 and 4 I discussed how informants may talk with or around photographs and video. For example, in her Waucoma photographic interviews (see Chapter 3), Schwartz sought to make her photographs sociologically meaningful by exploring the meanings local people invested in them. Here the sociological significance of the photographs was not that they documented a particular social 'fact', or that their content comprised 'ethnographic information'. Rather, the differences in Schwartz's informants' responses 'offered evidence of the negotiability of photographic meanings, undermining the pictures' authority as "truth"' (Schwartz 1992: 15). This led her to interpret the photographs as images that were used to say a variety of different things and as keys to understanding diversity within local culture. Through this collaborative process Schwartz's informants taught her 'how to interpret images of their lives' (1992: 15). Schwartz's sociological interpretation was thus rooted in the research process – it regarded the images as subjectively and plurally defined, rather than having one single ethnographic meaning or status.

Similarly, in Spain the anthropological meanings I gave my photographs were informed by meanings that informants gave to these images. For example, one photograph, 'The Bullfighter's Braid', became a focus of attention during the research. The photograph was published in a local newspaper and won a regional photography prize. Several informants and bullfighting clubs asked for copies. This gave me the opportunity to discuss the photograph and its content with a range of different people who I found fitted it into different narratives. Some discussed it in terms of art and its artistic value. One informant commented on its 'natural', unconstructed and 'authentic' appearance. Others used it to publicize a forthcoming event. Through my exploration of the different local meanings the photograph was given, I began to invest my own anthropological meanings in it. When I interpreted the photograph in relation to the conventions of the photographic culture of bullfighting I saw it as an ambiguous image that both imitated and challenged

The Bullfighter's Braid. © Sarah Pink 1993

Figure 5.2

This photograph of Cristina Sanchez became central to my research. During the research it was exhibited on local television, formed part of the collections of local bars, as well as of local people who had asked for copies. It was also published in a local newspaper (Pink 1993). Once returned to the United Kingdom it was exhibited in an ethnographic photography exhibition, published in book chapters and journal articles and was used for the front cover of my book (Pink 1997a). Not only was the image published in different places, but also it was defined in different ways and given new meanings as it travelled between these different contexts.

the gendered iconography of 'traditional' bullfight photography. While it copied a standard composition in bullfight photography, the conventional symbolism was broken as the bullfighter's hair braid was long, blonde and feminine, rather than the short, thin, coiled braid of the male performer (see Pink 1997b). When I analysed this ambiguous symbolism together with people's comments on the photography, I linked this to gender theory. Building on different local meanings given to the photograph, I added meanings derived, first, from my understanding of local oral and visual discourses on 'tradition' and, secondly, from anthropological theories of gender. For me, 'The Bullfighter's Braid' is laden with local and academic meanings; the photograph itself represents the point at which these different meanings intersect, thus linking the contexts of research and analysis.

Images we can't 'take home'

Analysing ethnographic images does not only imply analysis of images ethnographers take themselves and then take home. In Chapter 3 I described Okely's research with elderly people (see Okely 1994). During these interviews Okely's informants showed her their photographs and these images formed part of Okely's experience of their memories and histories. The photographs Okely describes comprise part of her ethnographic knowledge and are indispensable to her discussion and analysis. However, Okely does not mention having the photographs copied or taking them away for analysis.

In Spain I researched the career of Antoñita, a woman ex-bullfighter (see Pink 1997a). Similarly, Antoñita showed me her collection of snapshots that documented moments of development and success in her short career and she lent me a video of her performances that I viewed with a group of her friends. It did not feel appropriate to ask for copies of the prints and tapes. However, these images and her uses of them to criticize her performances and reminisce about old acquaintances and events were central to my analysis of her career and how she represented herself in relation to other individuals, institutions and activities in the local bullfighting world. I also took notes on the event of viewing the video and how Antoñita's friends had used it to discuss her performance, skills and career. My analysis was not only of the visual content of video text, but also of how my informants used it to speak about the woman bullfighter.

In these projects the visual content of the Spanish bullfighting video were relevant to my analysis. However, it was less important to copy these images to take home and subject them to a systematic analysis than it was to analyse how they were used to represent and discuss the themes of my research. It is not only images that cannot be removed from some research locales. The field notes, diaries and images that do accompany researchers home should always be understood in connection with those representations and experiences that it is impossible to transfer spatially or temporally in any tangible form.

Organizing images: the issue of the archive

Just as research methods are usually shaped by the project they serve and are frequently developed during fieldwork, categorizing research materials is often a task that researchers develop for themselves in connection with their particular research materials. While there is no set method for organizing ethnographic images, the systems researchers develop for categorizing images should be informed by appropriate theoretical and ethical principles. Here I outline the implications of ethnographic archives and classification systems and argue for a reflexive approach to this aspect of ethnographic work.

Archives and visual classification systems have been characterized as objectifying systems, imposed on the weak by the powerful. The political agendas that informed the classificatory work of visual anthropologists and sociologists in the 1970s and 1980s doubtless differed from those of colonialism and state order (see also Chapter 3). Nevertheless, both modern social science and the institutions of modern states have participated in a 'project' that has used photography to 'map humankind', 'to define humankind, as individuals, as types or genres of humankind, and as a species' (Lury 1998: 41). This realist approach to photography catalogued and defined visual records according to their content. A critique of this practice and the power relations that it entailed highlights some problems associated with the concept of the archive. Sekula's (1989) critique of Victorian photographic archives highlights the repressive potential of portrait photography. Sekula discusses how photographs were used to record systematically the characteristics of criminals' faces, arguing that 'photography came to establish and delimit the terrain of the *other,* to define both the *generalized look* – the typology – and the *contingent instance* of deviance and social pathology' (Sekula 1989: 345; original italics). Anthropologists have similarly taken issue with repressive uses of photography during the colonial period. Edwards (1992) discusses the importance of situating colonial photographs of people from 'other' cultures in relation to the ideologies and intentions of their producers. She points out that '[t]he power relations of the colonial situation were not only those of overt oppression, but also of insidious, unequal relationships which permeated all aspects of cultural confrontation' (Edwards 1992: 4). Hence, regarding colonial photography as symbolic of this power relationship that was 'sustained through a controlling knowledge which appropriated the "reality" of other cultures into ordered structure' (1992: 6).

This realist approach to cataloguing and ordering images of individuals from other cultures was a means of objectifying and categorizing 'the other', an exercise that implied hierarchy and the oppression that was part and parcel of colonialism. The critique of colonial photography illustrates not only the repressive potential of image archives, but also the difference between scientific-realist and reflexive approaches to photography. The colonial system categorized images according to their content and validated their authenticity in terms of the context in which they were produced (for example, this sometimes involved using a grid-type background against which physical characteristics could be measured). The critical analysis of colonial photographs lends them new meaning by reconstructing the social relations and intentions through which they were produced and therefore transforming their symbolic potential. Previously, colonial photographs were seen as scientific evidence of cultural difference and hierarchy; a critical analysis re-situates them as symbols of a 'controlling knowledge', domination and inequality (see Edwards 1992).

By revealing this agenda, the critical approach disempowers the archive as a controlling mechanism. Moreover, by redefining its contents as individual images with situated meanings (rather than a body of scientific evidence) it challenges the idea of the archive as a coherent 'whole' and suggests that the connections between images are constructed rather than 'given' or 'natural'. As I argue below, connections constructed between and among photographs and other visual and verbal materials are key to the production of academic meanings. Archives are important in the disciplines that use ethnography and should continue to have a role. Not all archives are 'oppressive'; for example, appropriate ethnographic photography and film archives exist in European and US institutions (such as the ethnographic film archive at IWF Knowledge and Media, Goettingen, and the Royal Anthropological Institute's photographic archive), forming valuable resources for researchers. However, ethnographers should take a responsible and ethical approach to the potential of archives to create knowledge. As curators, they should not underestimate the power of archives to 'play an important function in the creation of knowledge' (Price and Wells 1997: 36). This is just as important in the organization of images from individual ethnographic research projects as it is for large collections, since when their power to create knowledge is used to validate one particular vision of social order and reality archives can become repressive and hierarchical.

There is always some tension between different ways of ordering reality through visual images. For example, when ethnographers organize fieldwork photographs they have to contemplate differences between their own personal and academic ways of ordering reality and the orders by which local people construct their worlds and histories visually. Below I suggest some ways this may be resolved, arguing that this tension should be represented in the way images are organized; it may in fact be a creative tension.

Sequential organization and the 'authentic narrative': whose order is it?

Collier and Collier have insisted that to be analysed correctly the spatial and temporal order in which images were recorded must be maintained. If not, they warn that 'reconstructive ordering of the photographs can inadvertently confuse the actual sequence of occurrence' (1986: 180). This approach argues that there is only one authentic visual narrative, and that the chronological linear sequence by which images are produced forms the narrative that represents their true meaning, to which all other sequences or meanings must be subordinate. While recordings of temporal chronologies of events and activities are important research materials, they do not necessarily represent either an undisturbe or 'complete reality'. Moreover, a linear visual chronology may not consistently represent the way in which reality was experienced or conceptualized by all the individuals involved. Narratives and sequences are not necessarily fixed. The order in which events and activities are experienced may change, and the orders in which they are remembered and spoken about may differ from the chronological order in which they happened. For instance, certain aspects of an event or specific individuals may be prioritized in certain cultural discourses and individual memories and representations. Therefore a visual representation of an event inflexibly ordered by its temporal chronology may represent the participants' experience of the event less than it stands for the ethnographer's view of the event's structure.

For example, in Spain I showed three women informants my photographs of a bullfight we had attended together. I had kept (and numbered) the photographs in the order in which the printers returned them. However, they soon became reorganized as my informants prioritized and selected images that represented the event for them. For example, they categorized the images into those of their favourite bullfighter, of themselves and photographs they found aesthetically pleasing but not of documentary significance. Their reorganization of my photographs represented aspects of their experience of the bullfight, centring on their own participation and their favourite bullfighter's performance. Key images showed him waving to the part of the arena where we sat and highlights of his performance. For my analysis, the temporal sequence in which I took the photographs was less important than my informants' comments on, and arrangement of, them, for this was the moment where their knowledge intersected with my photographs. In my analysis these photographs became visual representations of local and personal knowledge and understandings of a specific bullfight and of particular individuals. Ordered temporally and photographed as a systematic record of the procedure of the event on *my* terms rather than on my informants' terms, the set of images would have been little more than a representation of particular performers working to the usual format of the bullfight.

While I have suggested the original shooting order should not be the dominant narrative of any visual representation, it should not be abandoned as it will help situate the images temporally and spatially within the research process. It is useful to keep note of the shooting order to describe the formal structure of events and activities and reflect on how ethnographers structure visual narratives. However, this is not the only or the most authentic version or narrative. Other edited or reorganized versions of my visual narrative of the bullfight also represented knowledge and experience of the performance and were equally ethnographically rich. This applies not only to visual recordings of events and performances, but also to other activities and procedures. While it is useful to record visually the process and sequence of activities, the ways people structure and experience the reality of those activities may not be encapsulated in the temporal sequence photographed.

Thematic organization and multiple categories: dealing with diverse photographic meanings

The meanings of visual images may be determined exclusively by neither the temporal sequences in which they were shot nor by categories based solely on their content. The same image may simultaneously be given different meanings in different (but often interconnected) situations, each of which has ethnographic significance. Any system of ordering and storing images should account for their ambiguity of meaning and fickle adherence to categories. This means developing ways of categorizing images that acknowledge the arbitrary nature of their interconnected meanings and are not dominated by content-based typologies or temporally determined sequences. Below, by interrogating just one photograph, I demonstrate that to place an image in a single category denies the richness of its potential for facilitating and communicating ethnographic understandings. This example discusses how a single photograph taken during fieldwork in Spain was invested with ethnographic meanings that drew together other resources of knowledge about the photograph's subject and her culture. While the image alone reveals nothing, it is given ethnographic meaning when linked to other types of knowledge through my analysis.

The photograph in Figure 5.3. was taken in 1992 in the afternoon during *feria* in Córdoba. Encarni, my friend and informant, had dressed up in her *traje corto* especially to meet me for the afternoon, show me around the *feria*, and have a drink. She also wanted to show me her outfit because she thought seeing it would be interesting for me and useful for my research. We were engaged in two different leisure activities. Mine was vacation and tourist leisure, and in part my photography was structured by this. Her leisure was *feria* and time with a friend. Simultaneously our professional agendas were intertwined: one theme of the outing was my anthropological research; another was her chance to practise the spoken English that she needed to do well in her exams. When we planned to meet she mentioned that I should take my camera to photograph her *traje corto*. This portrait was one of three photographs that we took. It was taken in the *casetta* (temporary open-air bar) of the Finito de Córdoba bullfighting club.

When I analysed the photograph and considered how it could represent 'ethnographic knowledge' I reflected on the context of its production. The afternoon was a special occasion, or at least not a normal occasion, for various reasons. First, we were in *feria* – a context some anthropologists would say is distinct from 'everyday' time. In this sense it was a 'classic' context for an anthropological photograph. Secondly, we were in a bullfighting club's *casetta*. Encarni does not usually spend her afternoons drinking in bullfighting club *casettas* or in the clubs themselves. She took me to the *casetta* because she thought it was the kind of place I should be researching. Thirdly, the occasion was a photographic

© *Sarah Pink 1992*

Figure 5.3

This photograph of Encarni became the subject of my other informants' discussions about the image of a 'traditional woman', it became part of her family and personal photograph collection and it also became a reference point in my own academic work, at a conference and in my book, as shown here (Pink 1997a: 74, Figure 10). The original caption to the photograph was as follows:

> Encarni is an English teacher in a FE college in Spain. She has no interest in bullfight-ing and does not lead what she considers to be a 'traditional' lifestyle. However she is interested in some traditional music and dance and dresses in her *traje corto* for the *feria*. One day during *feria* she dressed in her *traje* so that I may see her 'tradi-tional' costume and photograph her. Most other informants who saw this image remarked that she looked like a 'typical', 'traditional' *Cordobesa*.

moment: it was worth taking a photo because Encarni was wearing her *traje corto*. When someone dresses up in a *traje corto* or gipsy dress it is quite normal that a friend or relative should photograph them. In this sense the photograph simply documents a conventional photographic moment.

These aspects of the context helped me to think through how mine and Encarni's intentions had intersected to represent themes of anthropological visual interest, local visual conventions and personal objectives. This enabled me to associate certain anthropological and local meanings to the photographs. However, once the photograph was printed, it was invested with new meanings in Córdoba. These interpretations helped me to link the photograph to other aspects of my research, each time making it more heavily laden with meanings.

The photographs were originally taken as slides. I had two copies of this one printed and gave one to Encarni. A couple of days later she asked me if she could also have a copy for her mother; the photograph had already begun to travel. Leisure is a key theme in family photography (see Chalfen 1987; Slater 1995), thus the photograph fitted into the family collection. While the 'photographic moment' was not a family event, dressing up at home in the *traje corto* was. The photograph was also in my 'research' slide collection (ready for a seminar presentation at the university the following year). A print was in my 'personal' collection of photos of friends and parties I had enjoyed in Spain. During my fieldwork this photograph album also became part of my research. Some Spanish friends who flicked through this album of friends, parties and trips said Encarni looked very traditional, very '*Cordobesa*'. Wearing her *traje corto* she represented the beautiful, 'traditional' Córdoban woman. My mother, who met Encarni when she visited England with me and stayed with my parents, recognized her friend. Later in England the photograph had further adventures. In my PhD thesis I used the photograph to visualize one of the paradoxes of the notion of 'tradition' in Córdoban identity. Encarni had dressed as a traditional woman for *feria* and other informants had used the photograph to identify her as representing local traditional femininity. However, Encarni did not describe herself as 'traditional'. She has two university degrees and is an English teacher. She said she had learnt a lot about local traditions by helping with my research.

This analysis of the photograph was informed by my understandings of a number of other visual and verbal, individual and cultural, narratives, discourses and practices. The focus of the analysis was not so much the content of the photograph, but how the content was given meanings relevant to my project. For example, the photograph of Encarni could be fitted into a temporal sequence of a series of photographs that I took of the *feria* that day, or a series of photographic portraits of 'traditional' costumes. In my book I used it to represent knowledge about changing gender roles and identities in contemporary

Andalusia (see Chapter 6). In the future the same photograph may take on further ethnographic meanings.

The multiple ways that just one image may be significant implies that classifying sets of hundreds of photographs or hours of video footage would develop as a complex web of cross-referenced themes and images. For some projects it will be worthwhile to develop systems of codifying images. However, this can be time-consuming and the extent to which images can and need to be formally managed in this way may depend on the sheer quantity of images, commentaries and themes involved. In some projects images can be managed more intuitively. In my own experience, I have found that during fieldwork particular images and sequences of images become the focus of informants' attention and these have tended also to become the main images in my analysis.

Rather than proposing a formula for organizing ethnographic images, my intention is to offer a series of suggestions from which to begin working. Any system of organizing and storing ethnographic images should situate them in relation to the multiple meanings and themes of the research. Therefore, for example, the photograph of Encarni would be linked to themes of discourses on family photography, traditional iconography and festivals, and this would connect with a range of other visual and printed materials and notes from field notes, photography, video and local documents. It would entail a way of attempting to map the interconnecting elements of discourse and experience to which each image may refer when used in a specific context. A codifying system would also need to account for how any one image may later be invested with new meanings as the project develops and researchers make new interpretations and connections between visual, verbal and written materials.

Organizing video footage

Above I suggested how ethnographic photographs may be organized and connected to other elements of ethnographic and theoretical enquiry during analysis. Some of these general principles also apply to video.

First, in Chapter 4 I described some video production scenarios, emphasizing the collaborative element of video making and the intersubjectivity between the video makers and informants. These social and wider contexts of video production should be accounted for. Secondly, the different meanings informants and ethnographers invested in the video footage at different times and the discourses to which these meanings are linked should be considered. In Chapter 4 I discussed 'talking with video' and a 'media ethnography' approach to informants' viewing practices. Different people interpret the same footage differently, giving their own meanings to its content. As my discussions of 'The Bullfighter's Braid' and the portrait of Encarni suggest, local interpretations of images are of equal interest to ethnographers as the visual and verbal content of video. Thirdly, relationships between video footage and other research materials and experiences (including memories, diaries, photographs, notes and artifacts) provide important insights as each medium may represent interrelated but different types of knowledge about the same theme.

Video also differs from photography in that it communicates different types of knowledge and information and has different potentials for representation. Video communicates through moving rather than still images, includes sound, and the information is represented lineally on video (although electronic logging can enable one to identify key sections for analysis). Categorizing and analysing analogue video materials can be more costly, cumbersome and time-consuming than it is with photographs. It involves more technology (including recorders and players), possibly tape transfer to different formats for viewing and transcriptions of verbal dialogue. However supposing that most researchers will now be using digital video these processes have become much less expensive and do not normally require extra technical support.

The specific research methods and visual technologies appropriate to each project vary (see Chapters 1 and 2). Video therefore plays diverse roles in different projects (see Chapter 4). Correspondingly, there is not *one* process or method for categorizing or analysing ethnographic video that every researcher may follow. Rather, this varies according to researchers' objectives, the content of the tapes and the meanings attached to them. In some cases video recordings are treated as realist representations of specific interactions or activities; in others they are used as symbolic representations, evocative of (for instance) emotions, experiences, power relations or inequalities. In some projects they fulfil both roles simultaneously. First, I briefly describe conventional treatments of video tape, logging visual data and transcribing verbal data, suggesting their implications and proposing appropriate uses.

Above I criticized analytical processes that translate visual images into printed words. Logging and transcribing certainly involve representing visual and verbal representations in printed form. As such they could also be said to define video footage. I am not recommending that printed transcripts and verbal descriptions replace video footage, but that logging and transcription are used to map visual and verbal knowledge otherwise only accessible lineally, to make it more easily available. This should identify and categorize different parts of the tape according to their content and/or the diverse meanings that can be invested in them, and in relation to the contexts and relationships of their production.

Different projects require that video is logged to different degrees of formality. Especially when there is a limited amount of footage, it may be possible simply to work with these materials visually, without documenting their contents verbally. However, in many cases detailed documentation of visual and verbal knowledge represented on the tapes may facilitate easier access. This is especially the case for projects that involve data-sharing (e.g. Rich et al. 2000: 158–60). For close scrutiny of video tapes this could include producing time-coded log tables with information on camera angles and distances, spoken narrative and visual content. If footage includes significant verbal dialogue or interviews, then these may be transcribed. Ethnographers who are interested in the subtleties of conversation and communication among the subjects of the video (and between the subjects of the video and the video maker) may find that a log of the visual and verbal narratives of such interactions is useful for analysis. Visual logs and written transcripts provide easily accessible versions of the content of tapes, if they are also time coded, so that images can be easily located for reviewing. Using different approaches to the same materials can also be helpful. For example, the Cardiff University Hypermedia and Qualitative Research team note that from their own experiences of working with ethnographic video

> (t)he multimodality of video footage means that its meaning is produced on a number of levels. We found that coding of video was most useful on the level of categorizing footage very broadly into general themes. For more ethnographically attuned analysis, editing the video material into narrative-governed relationships and scenes produced deeper insights into the interactions between filmed participants (and with the researcher and camera). (www.cf.ac.uk/socsi/hyper/p02/findings.html)

Close scrutiny of video tapes should also account for links between the content of the video and other aspects of the ethnography (such as photographs, field diaries and notes). For example, in Figure 3.3 I discuss my experience of interviewing David and Anne Gibson during my research about a community garden project. As part of the research about this project I interviewed and photographed David and Anne, and David took me on a video tour of the garden site. I have also been to steering group meetings and interviewed the people responsible for managing the project at other levels. Within this research the video sequence plays a vital role because it enables me to connect the sensory and material dimensions of the garden to the administrative, bureaucratic and even emotional narratives that are drawn out more strongly in the interviews, committee meetings and chats that informed my prior knowledge of it. Simultaneously, without the context provided by these other materials, the video footage of David showing me the garden would be unable to evoke the context of the meetings, the sentiments of 'community' and coming together that were discussed in the interview, and the sets of visual and written printed documentation that are integral to the process by which it is being transformed from a disused site to a community garden. It is often by making connections between different sets of visual and written research materials that a deeper understanding of the materials is possible. Visual methods are rarely used in isolation from other methods and, correspondingly, visual materials should be analysed in relation to other research texts.

The specific categories used to organize video footage in any one project also depend on how researchers intend to use video to represent their work. If footage is to be edited into a documentary video or a series of short clips, scenes may be categorized because of their ability to communicate on the terms of video editing conventions, their aesthetic appeal, and the quality of sound recording. A different basis for selection and categorization might be established if the footage is to be organized thematically for a hypermedia representation or screened unedited as part of a conference presentation (see Chapters 7 and 8).

Computer-assisted qualitative data analysis software and visual ethnography

In the past visual ethnographers have had little use for computer-assisted qualitative data analysis software (CAQDAS). This software works on the principle that the data is coded by the researcher according to sets of categories that can assist in both data retrieval and, to a limited extent, analysis. More recent versions of CAQDAS have begun to accommodate also video and photographic materials. Nevertheless, at the time of writing, on-line reports on their suitability for working with ethnographic materials are not very encouraging, although the Cardiff University Hypermedia and Qualitative Research Website suggests that 'As dedicated [CAQDAS] programs develop it seems likely that they will include better media handling and extra hypertext functionality' (www.cf.ac.uk/socsi/hyper/p02/examplarsl.html). Drawing from work developed in three projects since 1997 this website provides a useful online resource on hypermedia ethnography. Contributors to the projects are Paul Atkinson, Amanda Coffey, Bella Dicks, Bruce Mason, Emma Renold, Bambo Sayinka and Matthew Williams. Before investing in CAQDAS I would recommend ethnographers to assess how important such technologies might be for their own projects. If such processing of data coding and analysis have not been part of one's existing work practices using other forms of research materials then it may be unlikely that they will be useful in supporting visual research. However, for researchers who find these computer-aided methods of analysis helpful, the choice would lie between the new software available. There is a growing literature of expert opinion that can aid these choices and readers should seek the most up-to-date information about the available products at the time they are considering using them. As Christine Barry has advised, 'Not every piece of software will be relevant to every task and researchers will often be able to achieve their ends using non-technology solutions or simple word processing cut and paste.' Barry encourages potential users of CAQDAS to get to know the different programs and their capacities, so that they will know when it might be appropriate to use them. She emphasizes that such software should not be used as a matter of principle but advises that 'the individual researcher' should 'take responsibility for deciding how useful the software will be for them, which package they should use, and how they will integrate this into their existing analysis methods' (Barry 1998: 2.11–2.12). Barry describes how qualitative data analysis software has been criticised by some researchers as providing only a simplistic analysis or not allowing researchers to gain a good overview of their materials, eventually only viewing them in the snippets they have been divided up into for the sake of creating data categories for the analysis procedures that will be undertaken with the software. Such views, Barry argues, are based on misunderstandings of how qualitative researchers ought to be using qualitative data analysis software, pointing out that 'In my own research, I use Nudist as just one tool in my analysis armory, as it only helps me to do part of the work of analysis', and other methods are used to complement this (Barry 1998: 2.7). Rich et al.'s video study of the experiences of chronic asthma sufferers provides an example of how the use of one CAQDAS program, Atlas-ti, has been integrated into mixed methods of analysis and logging of video materials (2000: 159).

Amanda Coffey, Beverley Holbrook and Paul Atkinson (1996), and Bella Dicks, Bruce Mason, Coffey and Atkinson (2005) have suggested that CAQDAS with a hypermedia component might be useful for ethnographers as a multilinear device that can include visual images and written text, and function as an analytical as well as representational device. However, widespread use of this software to bridge the gap between research, analysis and representation is yet to develop. As Dicks and Mason noted in 1998, there are some key differences in the ways sociologists and anthropologists have approached hypertext, pointing out that 'applications of hypermedia tend to divide into those which see it primarily as a tool for the presentation of knowledge which is already – to some extent – codified and defined (educational packages, graphic design presentations, and those applications that see it as an aid for the accumulation of knowledge about a subject that exists only as "data" (CAQDAS approaches)'. As they rightly noted, 'this divide is reflected in recent academic writing on hypertextual ethnography: whilst anthropological commentaries have focused on its promise for integrating film and field notes in the presentation of ethnographies (Seaman and Williams, 1992; Howard, 1988), sociologists have concentrated on its potential for enabling more sophisticated approaches to data analysis (Weaver and Atkinson 1994, 1995; Coffey et al. 1996)'; a dichotomy that has been perpetuated by the commercially available hypermedia software, which does not provide opportunities for both analysis and coding *and* hypermedia presentation in the same program. The Cardiff University Hypermedia and Qualitative Research team have since then been working on a series of digital ethnography projects that explore (amongst other things) ways of archiving, coding, hyperlinking and representing visual and other digital ethnographic materials (see www.cf.ac.uk/socsi/hyper/index.html). They suggest that digital coding and hyperlinking are distinct activities. The former involves the classification of segments of data whereas the latter specifies the relationship between pieces of data and coding would precede hyperlinking (www.cf.ac.uk/socsi/hyper/p02/findings.html). Both practices thus create meanings in different ways: the first categorizes research materials in terms of its content, the second in terms of their relationships to others. In their book *Qualitative Research and Hypermedia* (Dicks et al. 2005), the research team reflect on how they selected CAQDAS and other hypermedia software to analyse sociological multimedia data. Their work is a useful case study of the digital production, analysis and storage of visual and other materials within a specific project.

Generally, visual anthropologists have been less enthusiastic about using CAQDAS, myself included, and have specialized in the production of hypermedia in ethnographic representation (e.g. Biella, Chagnon and Seaman 1997: CD; Ruby 2004: CD, 2005: CD; see also Pink 2005: chs 4 and 6). The initial engagement required by the software in terms of learning its structure and analytical and coding systems implies a large investment of time. Personally, working with relatively small amounts of data that I have produced myself and know my way around well, I have not felt that it is worth either investing the time needed to learn how to work with such software or that the complex systems of coding and organization of materials that it offers is necessary for my materials. However, as I have noted above, larger-scale projects (e.g. Dicks et al. 2005; Rich et al. 2000) involving several staff who share greater quantities of data benefit more from these technologies. Researchers who decide against using CAQDAS, however, still have options for digital data storage and analysis. Barry (1998) has noted how using the cut and paste functions of a word processor can serve well for the analysis of interview transcripts (see above). Similar work can also be done with digitized photography and video footage using software such as QuickTime Pro or Adobe Premier for video and an image editor such as PhotoShop for photographs. In my research about slow living I have found that my digital video can be captured, named, annotated, in some cases edited into representational narratives, and stored in files for easy access using Adobe Premier. Still photographs likewise are archived automatically by Adobe PhotoShop. Once categorized and stored digitally in this way, such materials can be interlinked and accessed through hyperlinks created in word processing, visual or web page software. Just as I am completing this book new software for digital visual ethnographic research, archiving and analysis is becoming available online at www.anthromethods.net.Whatever the system used, computer-aided storage and analysis is useful since it allows us to combine images and words on the same screen and create links between them.

Summary

I have suggested a departure from the idea that analysing ethnographic video and photographs entails translating systematically recorded and contextualized visual evidence into written words. Instead, a reflexive approach to analysis should concentrate on how the content of visual images is the result of the specific context of their production and on the diversity of ways that video and photographs are interpreted. Photographs and video may be treated as realist representations of the reality of fieldwork contexts as ethnographers understand them (as in the realist tradition in documentary photography); but they are always representations of the subjective standpoints of the image producer and other viewers, including informants. This has implications for how visual archives and categories are conceived and demands that researchers pay attention to the interlinkages between visual and other (verbal, written) knowledge. This approach to visual meanings has implications for how photography and video are used in ethnographic representation.

FURTHER READING

Dicks, B., Mason, B., Coffey, A. and Atkinson, P. (2005) *Qualitative Research and Hypermedia: Ethnography for the Digital Age*, London: Sage

Rich, M., Lamola, S., Gordon, J. and Chalfen, R. (2000) 'Video intervention/prevention assessment: a patient-centered methodology for understanding the adolescent illness experience' *Journal of Adolescent Health*, 27 (3): 155–65. Available on-line at www.viaproject.org/VIAMethod.pdf (accessed 12 November 2004). (Discusses the analysis of video materials in an interdisciplinary team)

Part 3
Visual Images and Technologies

The production of ethnographic text, whether an undergraduate dissertation, MPhil or PhD thesis, or an ethnographic monograph or article, is usually referred to as 'writing up'. In Chapter 5 I criticized the related analytical practice of converting fieldwork experience, notes and images into written words. In Chapters 6–8 I question this dominance of written words in ethnographic representation. I suggest that representation of ethnographic knowledge is not just a matter of producing words, but one of situating images, sometimes in relation to written words, but also in relation to other images, spoken words and other sounds. Part 3 therefore discusses the potential of photography and video for ethnographic representation in printed, video and hypermedia text.

In Part 2 I focused on the social relations, personal standpoints, cultural discourses and social science theories through which images are produced and given meaning in ethnographic research. Part 3 builds on this by exploring how these elements of ethnographic image production can inform their subsequent uses for ethnographic representation.

In Chapter 5 I criticized approaches that treat ethnographic photographs as a mere 'supplement to the notes' (Hastrup 1992: 13) and analysis as the translation of images into words. Such approaches have a correspondingly problematic perspective on the potential of images for ethnographic representation (see Taylor 1996: 67). One example is Hastrup's argument that 'writing may encompass the images produced by films, but not the other way round' (1992: 21), thus seeing written text and images as hierarchically related. She claimed that written text is capable of invoking a degree of reflexivity and self-conscious knowledge that the iconographic visual communication of ethnographic film, which must be 'taken at face-value', cannot achieve (1992: 20–1). While Hastrup was right that the written word can communicate in ways images cannot, the idea that this implies a hierarchical relationship unduly privileges written words over images. I suggest an approach to the visual in ethnographic representation that acknowledges the interrelationship between the visual, the verbal and the written in ethnographic experience, social relations and cultural practices and sees this as a basis for its potential for reflexive ethnographic representation. The idea that written text inspires reflexive reading, while visual text does not, also underestimates the potential of photography and video for ethnographic representation and is challenged by the practical and theoretical work of visual ethnographers (e.g. Biella 1994; MacDougall 1997). Instead, the key differences between visual and written texts are, first, their capacities to evoke other people's experience in different ways, and second, the ways and extents to which they can engage with academic theoretical debates (see Pink 2005).

While different media certainly communicate in different ways, the medium of representation used does not alone determine its reception. Viewers and audiences of ethnographic images are also interpreters of text, and by acknowledging their agency we can understand better how ethnographic knowledge is received. This understanding may in turn inform how ethnographers construct their texts. For example, for film this implies regarding 'film as *experience* – and as such never completely controlled by filmmakers, subjects or viewers' (Mermin 1997: 49; original italics). Mermin suggests that film narrative should be understood 'as a means by which filmmakers begin to supervise and direct their viewers' experiences of reading and creating meaning from their films' (1997: 49); (see Chapter 7). Similarly, as I argue in Chapter 6, photography is not necessarily taken at face value but is experienced by viewers. Therefore, an ethnographer's role would be to inspire viewers to question self-consciously the content and meanings of their photographic representations. In constructing written and visual texts, ethnographers are concerned not simply with producing different forms of representation and knowledge, but also with what their readers, viewers and audiences will do with these representations. As James, Hockey and Dawson remind us, 'representations, once made, are open to re-representation, misrepresentation and appropriation' (1997: 13). One concern for contemporary authors of ethnographic representations should be how to create texts that will be engaged with self-consciously and reflexively and not taken 'at face value' as written ethnographic facts and visual illustrations or evidence. This issue is addressed for each medium discussed in Chapters 6–8.

The agency of readers/viewers to make ethnographic representations meaningful on their own terms also raises ethical issues. As James, Hockey and Dawson warn, 'once we have committed to words on paper, or to visual representation through film, we may at one and the same time lose control yet be haunted by our representations of others' (1997: 13). Similarly, from their ethnographic film making experience, Barbash and Taylor predict that '[e]thical problems will arise despite your best intentions. They may even emerge after your film is finished and in distribution' (Barbash and Taylor 1997: 49). New textual strategies give rise to new ethical concerns and in Chapters 6–8 I discuss ethical issues specific to the use of each medium.

Montage, multivocality and democratic texts

In Chapters 1 and 2 I argued that academic and local epistemologies and knowledge are equally 'truthful' and the former should not be regarded as superior to the latter. Correspondingly, in Chapters 3 and 4 I proposed an approach to photography and video in ethnographic research that accounts for the different ways researchers, informants and others experience and understand the realities in which they live. This diversity of worldviews, narratives and understandings of reality that ethnographers encounter during fieldwork therefore forms the basis of ethnographic knowledge, and some would argue that it should also be represented without translating these local voices into the authoritative voice of social science. During the 1990s several scholars began to consider how the many voices, or multivocality, of ethnographic experience can be integrated into the design of ethnographic representations.

Some (e.g. Kulick 1995) have challenged the usefulness of seeing ethnography in terms of a linear narrative that represents the ethnographic experience as one in which ethnographers go to the field, get the data and then go home to analyse and write it up (see Chapters 1 and 5). Similar criticisms have been made of ethnographic representation for failing to recognize the multiple and simultaneous realities in which people live and participate, the intersubjectivity between ethnographers and their informants, and the different voices, perspectives and temporal and spatial locations that ethnography involves. In 1995 Marcus argued that, to resolve this, ethnographic text should be constructed according to a principle of montage to create ethnographic representations that incorporate the multilinearity of ethnographic research and everyday lives (see Marcus 1995: 41). In contrast to the linear narratives of a conventional ethnographic text, a montage text would recognize that sets of diverse worldviews exist simultaneously and would represent these without necessarily translating them into the academic terms of a social science. In Marcus's words, '[s]imultaneity in ethnographic description' replaces 'discovery of unknown subjects or cultural worlds' (1995: 44). Marcus thus called for a type of written text that would not confer hierarchical superiority on academic discourses and knowledge above the discourses and knowledge of local individuals and cultures (I make a parallel argument for a non-hierarchical relationship between written and visual text here). He argued that while it is important to maintain an academic 'objectifying discourse about processes and structure' (1995: 48), this should not be privileged above representations of other discourses. Instead, Marcus insisted that a simultaneous and non-hierarchical representation of different local, personal, academic and other epistemologies, each coherent in themselves, should be developed within the same text. Therefore, ethnographic text becomes a context where ethnographers/ authors can create or represent continuities between these 'diverse worlds, voices or experiences', and describe or imply points in the research at which they met or collided. Some of the projects I discuss in Chapters 6–8 have attempted to develop montage texts in practice.

One earlier text that remains an excellent example is Paul Stoller's book *Sensuous Scholarship* (1997), which demonstrates how representations of diverse realities might coherently intersect in the same text. Stoller proposes a 'sensuous scholarship' that accounts for how ethnographic knowledge is created not just through the observation of visible phenomena, but through other sensory experiences, such as physical pain and taste. For Stoller, the 'flexible agency of the sensuous scholar is key'. This combines the 'sensible and intelligible, denotative and evocative' and the 'ability to make intellectual leaps to bridge gaps forged by the illusion of disparateness' (1997: xviii); in his terms, 'to tack between the analytical and the sensible' (1997: xv). A flexible representation 'underscores the linkages of experience and reality, imagination and reason, difference and commonality' (1997: 92). To achieve this, he combines a range of different textual styles, including a mystical Sufi story, poetry, autobiographical accounts, academic writing, photographs and a discussion of both performance and ethnographic film.

Text that allows academic, local and individual narratives to co-exist, implying no hierarchical relationship between either the discourses that are represented or their medium of representation, certainly offers a temptingly democratic model. However, it should not be used naively or without caution. As James, Hockey and Dawson have warned, the question of how to represent multivocality should not be approached in isolation from a consideration of its political and ethical implications. While the ideals and intentions of multivocality are important, the question of 'whether such democratic representations are in the end possible, or even desirable, remains' (James et al. 1997: 12). Moreover, Josephides has questioned the possibility of a democratic multivocality, as 'letting the people speak for themselves, or allowing them agency as actors with their own theoretical perspectives still may not escape the suspicion that the ethnographer is using them for her own ends' (Josephides 1997: 29). She questions whether ethnographers' strategies, apparently intended to bring the reader closer to the informants' subjectivity, really only constitute ethnographers' uses of informants' words to make their own points. Textual practices that are designed to give the subjects of the research a voice (such as printing, recording, or keying in *their* stories, perspectives, words, narratives or photographs) may constitute only a new textual construction in which the narrative of the ethnographer is just as dominant and those of the subjects subordinate. Issues surrounding multivocality and democratic representations raise many questions that are equally important for printed text, photography, video and multimedia. These questions will be raised in the discussions of the implications of different media for the construction and interpretation of ethnographic text.

The following three chapters cover visual representations of ethnography using printed text, video and hypermedia. These have not been selected because they are superior to other media, but because in my experience they are the media with which students of ethnography have most opportunity to work. Photographic exhibitions, poster presentations, slide shows and other visual representations are also valuable ways to communicate ethnographic knowledge. Each of the media discussed here has had a different historical relationship to ethnographic research and representation. The structure of each chapter therefore differs slightly to situate uses of the medium in relation to particular discourses and practices.

6

Ethnographic Photography and Printed Text

Printed text as a medium for ethnographic representation

This chapter explores uses of photography in printed ethnographic publications. Photographs usually form part of texts that are also made up of written words and possibly other visual depictions. In many existing publications photography has been incorporated into a structure already established for written ethnography. Therefore, first, I briefly discuss ethnographic writing before focusing on the potential of photography for the printed text medium.

In the Introduction I discussed the implications of Clifford's (1986) comparison of ethnographic writing to fiction. Contemporary ethnographers have largely incorporated an understanding of ethnographic text as a subjective, but hopefully loyal, representation of culture and experience into their work. Subsequently, comment on the constructedness of ethnographic text has become an almost mandatory passage in ethnographic methods textbooks published since the last decade of the twentieth century. This has involved an insistence that careful attention is paid to the literary nature of ethnographic writing, and how ethnographers convince their readers of the authenticity and authority of their accounts. Modern ethnographic writing has been criticized for its tendency to describe the people studied in abstract and generalizing terms, and in the ethnographer's dominant and objectifying voice. Instead, it has been suggested that informants' voices should also be allowed a place in ethnographic text, and that ethnographers should write reflexively in order to acknowledge the subjectivity and experiences on which their writing is based. It is usually now taken for granted that ethnographic texts cannot communicate *the truth* about any one culture or society, but are inevitably, like any other visual or verbal narrative or image, representations.

In the 1990s this attention to the qualities of written text as a medium led to a large literature that discussed these issues in detail from theoretical perspectives (e.g. Clifford and Marcus 1986; James et al. 1997; Nencel and Pels 1991; Stoller 1997) and in methodology texts (e.g. Ellen 1984; Hammersley and Atkinson 1995; Walsh 1998). In some of these the importance of reflexivity for both reading and writing ethnographic text is rightly stressed (e.g. Back 1998). In response, some ethnographic writers developed experimental texts that explore the possibilities of alternative uses of narrative, structure and textual strategy (e.g. Stoller 1997; Tyler 1991), and attempt to produce representations that take readers closer to the perspectives and experiences of the subjects of their research (see Josephides 1997). However, since then, no alternative written ethnographies stand out as landmarks of changing styles in ethnographic representation. If anything the contemporary ethnographic monograph appears to have maintained a conventional format, tempered by an increased reflexive awareness on the part of most authors. As part of this some ethnographers have also become increasingly disposed to using photographs in their publications. This, coupled with the new technology that has reduced the cost of printing photographs which has increased publishers' willingness to include images, opens new opportunities for photographic representation in ethnography. In this chapter I suggest an approach to combining photographic and written text that responds to the demands of the reflexive ethnography outlined above. I do not aim to advocate an abrupt break with contemporary forms of ethnographic representation, but to demonstrate how the incorporation of photography may create enhanced meanings and argumentation and thus shift ethnographic representational practices more subtly.

Photography and claims to ethnographic authority

The introduction to *Writing Culture* (probably the best-known critical text on ethnographic representation) begins with a passage in which Clifford describes the photograph featured on the book's cover. In this photograph, he tells us, 'the ethnographer hovers at the edge of the frame – faceless, almost extraterrestrial, a hand that writes' (1986: 1). Clifford does not discuss the reality of the specific ethnographic experience represented in the photograph, but uses his written words to invest meanings, relevant to the theme of the book, in the photograph. After this brief demonstration of the ambiguity and arbitrariness of photographic meaning, and the potential of photographs for producing 'fictional' accounts, the contributors to *Writing Culture* do not return to the role of images in creating the 'ethnographic fictions' and partial truths of ethnographic writing (see Clifford 1986: 19). However in the 1990s other anthropologists began to examine how photography has been used to create particular types of ethnographic knowledge in existing texts. Much of this work focused on historical texts. For example, Edwards's two edited collections (1992, 1997b) interrogate (mainly) colonial uses of photographic representation (see Chapter 3). John Hutynk's

(1990) analysis of Evans-Pritchard's use of photographs in his Nuer texts likewise reveals the power relations and classificatory schemas in which uses of photographs were embedded (see also Pink 2005: ch. 2). Below I discuss how others have analysed how photographs are situated in twentieth-century ethnographies to comment on the implications of this for the production of ethnographic meanings and understanding other cultures.

Deconstruction of how ethnographers/authors go about convincing their readers of the authenticity of their representations has been central to discussions of ethnographic writing. This has included a critical perspective on how grammatical tenses have been used to situate the subjects of research temporally within ethnographic texts (e.g. Fabian 1983; Pratt 1986). Conventionally, ethnography is written largely in the present tense, the 'ethnographic present', and some research methods texts (e.g. Fetterman 1998: 124) recommend this to students. However, Pratt (drawing on Fabian 1983: 33) has critically deconstructed the use of the 'ethnographic present', arguing that 'the famous "ethnographic present" locates the other in a time order different from that of the speaking subject', thus abstracting and objectifying the 'other' (Pratt 1986: 33). In contrast, descriptions of the research experience locate 'both self and other in the same temporal order', usually represented in the form of personal subjective narrative and written in the past tense. This inserts 'into the ethnographic text the authority of the personal experience out of which the ethnography was made' (1986: 33). Thus writing in the present tense has abstracted and objectified the subjects of research, while writing in the past tense has constituted the ethnographer's claim to authority and authenticity. John Davis has interrogated ethnographic uses of photography in a similar way. Drawing on Barthes's comment that the claim of the photographer is that he or she 'had to be there', he points out that in ethnographic texts photographs are often used in the past tense, as the ethnographer's proof that 'I was there' (Davis 1992: 209). As such, photographs have been used to support ethnographers' strategic claims of authenticity and authority to speak as a person with first-hand experience of the ethnographic situation, and as a source of privileged knowledge. Stanley Brandes has noted a similar use of photographic portraits in his analysis of photography in existing ethnographies of Spain. Here, in Julian Pitt-Rivers's (1954) and Irwin Press's (1979) ethnographies, photographic portraits have been used to represent 'evidence' of 'considerable trust between subject and photographer' and to contribute 'to the authenticity of the anthropological study' (Brandes 1997: 10). In this way photographs were part of a strategy to convince the reader and to position the ethnographer as an authoritative voice within the text.

Davis points out that, as part of another textual strategy, ethnographers often situate photographs and maps in the present tense to indicate that 'these kinds of artefact ... are permanent and continuous.

Anyone can see them and comment appropriately in the present tense' (Davis 1992: 208). In this way photographs are incorporated in what has been called the 'literary illusion' of the 'ethnographic present' that represents 'a slice of life – a motionless image' (see Fetterman 1998: 124–5), thus becoming part of an objectifying practice. Often it may be appropriate that students follow the convention that David Fetterman suggests, of using the 'ethnographic present' for the sake of 'linguistic convenience'. However, as Mary Louise Pratt (1986: 33) and Davis (1992: 214) have shown, in fact, ethnographers tend to mix past and present tenses in their writings to particular effect.

When a photograph is situated in the present tense and is treated as a realist representation, a particular relationship between the text, the image and the ethnographic context is constructed. The specificity of the photographic moment, set in the past, is lost and instead the photograph is situated in a continuous present. It becomes a photograph that could be taken any time, a generalized representation of an activity or type of person. Such uses tend to present images as evidence of an objective reality that exists independently of the text, yet can be brought into it through the image. In contrast, by situating a photograph in the past, the content of the image may be interpreted as the product of a specific 'photographic moment'. This approach, which allows ethnographers to locate photographs within the research reflexively, can be seen in the relationship between the photograph and caption developed in my book *Women and Bullfighting*. For example, on one image page (Pink 1997a: 102) two photographs show two different uses of photography in ethnographic representation. The first photograph, taken of me with the woman bullfighter by an informant, indeed provides evidence of my presence when she came to the city I was living in. However, it is intended to function differently from the more traditional 'I was there claim' of an ethnographer photographed in the field with his or her informants. Instead, it is intended to represent the process by which my knowledge about local photographic collections and aspirations is linked to representations of self-identity in the bullfighting world (as discussed in Chapter 3). To achieve this, it is captioned in a way that refers reflexively to the 'photographic moment' as: 'This photograph of me with Cristina Sanchez was taken when an informant requested my camera to provide me with an appropriate visual image'. The second photograph, of the woman bullfighter signing a photograph for one of her fans, is presented as a realist image, captioned in the ethnographic present as 'Cristina Sanchez signing a copy of "The Bullfighter's Braid" that had been reproduced on the back cover of a bullfighting journal ...'. It is a specific image of something that actually happened, and that refers to the relationship of my own photograph 'The Bullfighter's Braid' to the local context of my research. It is simultaneously intended to be an example of a common local practice – the autographing of photographs by local celebrities. Other good examples of uses of photography that are situated temporally in terms of the moment and context in which they were produced are found in David Sutton's excellent ethnographic monograph on food and memory and Greece. Here, for example, Sutton situates a series of three photographs taken by the anthropologist Vassiliki Yiakoumaki at an EU-sponsored seminar on cooking in Greece. He then uses the visual content of the images as a reference point through which to highlight themes and issues related to his research (Sutton 2001: 62–3).

Images and written text: captions, narratives

Historical and contemporary uses of photographs in sociological and anthropological texts have tended to use captions or references in a main body of written text to situate photographs (for a detailed review, see Chaplin 1994: 197–274). Below I discuss how the relationship between word and image contributes to the production of ethnographic meanings.

In existing ethnographies photographic captions have tended to make photographic meaning contingent on written text. In Elizabeth Chaplin's interpretation this subordinates photography to the written word since when a photograph is captioned by text, 'it loses its autonomy as a photograph and thus any claim to make a contribution in its own right' (Chaplin 1994: 207). As Chaplin concedes, captioning is not always inappropriate: used correctly photographs and words can work together to produce the desired ethnographic meanings. However, in other contexts photographs need more autonomy. Chaplin proposes that to achieve this, photographs should be separated from written text (1994: 207). As an example of this, Chaplin cites Gregory Bateson and Margaret Mead's *Balinese Character* (1942), in which a series of images are printed on one side of a page and the extended captions are printed opposite. This arrangement creates a subtle separation of image and text, thus allowing some autonomy to the images and permitting the viewer to interpret them in relation to one another rather than connecting each image primarily with its written caption.

Different ways of combining written words and photographs in ethnographic texts are informed by particular theories of photographic meaning. For example, a realist approach to photography would be associated with a text that uses photographs as evidence, to support and illustrate written points. For example, as Chaplin (1994: 232) shows, while making innovative uses of word and image in Bateson and Mead's *Balinese Character* (1942) and in Goffman's *Gender Advertisements* (1979), photographs are treated as ethnographic evidence and displayed in terms of 'scientific categories'. Brandes's (1997) survey of photography in the ethnographies of Spain during the period 1954 to 1988 shows how photographs were used to illustrate abstract versions of social and cultural life of towns and villages that were often given false names and of informants whose identities were 'hidden'. For example, Brandes claims that the photographs in Pitt-Rivers's *The People of the Sierra* (1954) both distance the village from 'reader's direct experience' (1997: 7) and 'impart an image of the Other' living in a 'rural, poor, religious, super-stitious, technologically-backward Spain' (1997: 8). Brandes argues that Pitt-Rivers's use of photography created a problematically primitivizing representation of rural Spain. In the 1990s as publishing technology developed, uses of captioned images as evidence and illustration became increasingly frequent. However, realist uses are not always inappropriate. For example, the contributors to Cohen, Wilk and Stoeltje's (1996) ethno-graphic collection on beauty pageants illustrated their chapters with photographs of women participating in these and related events, and Penny Harvey's (1996) monograph about EXPO 1992 in Spain contained 13 captioned images of EXPO architecture taken mainly by the author. Therefore these realist uses of photography as illustration and to imply aspects of the reality of human experience are not out of place. However, as viewers of ethnographic images we must remember not to take them as absolute truths. They are in fact subjective representations. At the beginning of the twenty-first century some interesting new uses of pho-tographs are being developed alongside ethnographic writing. One example is the work of David Sutton (2001), mentioned above and in Figure 6.1.

In the past most social scientific uses of ethnographic photography to represent generalized cultural characteristics and specific categories of activity, or artefacts, overlooked its wider potential for ethnographic representation. This was due, first, to a lack of engagement with pho-tography as a medium and, secondly, to a neglect of the role of readers/viewers in the construction of ethnographic meanings. As indicated above, recent work has begun to engage with these questions further. In the following sections I elaborate on this with reference to discussions of the potential of different types of photography for ethnographic representation and case studies from recent projects.

Images, words and readers

Above I discussed the strategies authors use to make images meaning-ful within texts. This discussion would be incomplete without a consid-eration of how photographs might be interpreted by readers/viewers. If contemporary ethnographers are to create texts that readers/viewers will engage with and experience reflexively and self-consciously, they need to present images in ways that encourage or inspire readers to reflect on the meanings they give to texts themselves. As Barndt sug-gested, '[a]s viewers, too, we are invited to acknowledge our own loca-tions and subjective responses to these images as generative tools' (Barndt 1997: 31). Different forms of representation imply non-conventional

Agonistic shopping from an itinerant vegetable seller
Kalymnos, 1996. © David Sutton 2001

Figure 6.1

In his book *Remembrance of Repasts* (2001), David Sutton makes different uses of photography, using captions to infer both realist notions of 'what really happens', as well as to reflexively imply the specificity of the moments in which photographs were taken. In the page reproduced above (2001: 22), the series of three photographs are captioned in a realist sense and represent the experience of a common everyday practice. In doing so they create a physical closeness to the subject, but through the generalization of the caption they suggest that they represent what 'agonistic shopping' is usually like.

practices of reading ethnography and innovative uses of photography in printed text will also make new demands on readers/viewers.

Texts that explicitly challenge conventional scientific formats because they are constructed in novel ways or contain subjective prose or images invite new ways of viewing/reading. Some of the best examples of this are still found in the work of John Berger and Jean Mohr (see also Chaplin 1994). Their series of uncaptioned images show how photographic narratives can emphasize the ambiguity of visual meanings, giving viewers/readers greater scope to self-consciously develop their own interpretations of photographs (see especially *Another Way of Telling*, Berger and Mohr 1982). For instance, in *A Fortunate Man* (Berger and Mohr 1967), visual and written narratives are interwoven in the text but do not explicitly cross-reference one another. The photographs form a visual narrative or story that may be interpreted in relation to the written text, but are not illustrations of it nor explicitly captioned by it. Berger and Mohr's work is not ethnographic, in the sense that they do not intentionally and explicitly work to the academic agenda of ethnographic research or representation. Nevertheless, their texts demonstrate the potential of photography for ethnographic representation. In *Another Way of Telling*, they address the question of viewers' participation in the creation of knowledge and meaning from text, seeing photographs as 'a meeting place where the interests of the photographer, the photographed, the viewer and those who are using the photograph are often contradictory' (1982: 7). The photo-essay 'If each time' (in *Another Way of Telling*) is both an exploration in photographic theory and an exercise in offering agency to the viewer. The authors' introduction emphasizes the ambiguity of the images as well as the viewers' role in interpreting them:

> We are far from wanting to mystify. Yet it is impossible for us to give a verbal key or storyline to this sequence of photographs. To do so would be to impose a single verbal meaning upon appearances and thus to inhibit or deny their own language. (1982: 133, original italics)

As they note, 'There is no single "correct" interpretation of this sequence of images.' Here Berger and Mohr beg that readers take a self-conscious and reflexive approach to inventing their own storylines or interpretations of the photographic narrative, and are aware that theirs is one 'single' understanding, among many possible others. Berger and Mohr emphasize that the photographs are 'ambiguous', and ought not to be taken at 'face-value'. If this approach is applied to photographs published in ethnographic texts, it invites readers/viewers of photographic representations to participate in producing ethnographic meanings. Berger and Mohr's texts present a strong contrast to conventional social scientific texts in their uses of words and images. However, some social scientists have recognized the value of learning from such examples.

In the 1990s Elizabeth Edwards suggested that ethnographers respond to the possibilities and challenges of photography by looking 'across the boundaries' of the disciplines that 'traditionally' use ethnography to engage with photographic theory (Edwards 1997a: 53). This, Edwards proposed, would be similar to 'literary awareness' in ethnographic writing where 'creative texts expressive of culture, such as novels, diaries, short stories and autobiography', have been incorporated alongside more conventional 'objective' texts. She argued that, similarly, two categories of photography may be used in ethnographic text: on the one hand, 'creative' or 'expressive' photography (which parallels the use of novels, diaries, short stories and autobiography) and on the other, 'realist' images, that treat photography as 'the documenting tool' (which parallels 'objective' written text). Used within the same text, these categories of photography 'might be complementary rather than mutually exclusive' (1997a: 57). These uses of photography in ethnographic representation would challenge the approach 'in which photographic contribution to scientific knowledge depended on the accumulation of visual facts' (1997a: 57) and 'the photograph is intended to function as a *record* rather than an *interpretation*' (Wright 1999: 41; original italics). Edwards's ideas suggested a new potential for photography in ethnographic representation. Her approach also implied a non-hierarchical use of different types of image and knowledge within the same text, in this case the two categories of 'realist' and 'expressive' photography. As opposed to realist photography, expressive photography (like Berger and Mohr's photographs) exploits the potential of the medium 'to question, arouse curiosity, tell in different voices or see through different eyes' (Edwards 1997a: 54). It breaks the conventions of realist ethnographic photography by, for example, ambiguously representing fragments and details, and acknowledging the constructedness of images. Like expressionism in documentary photography, it 'aims to present a subjective reality' and 'the symbolic value of the image may be more important than straightforward denotation' (T. Wright 1999: 44). Edwards argued that such photography has a place in ethnographic representation because, 'there are components of culture which require a more evocative, multidimensional, even ambiguous expression than the realist documentary paradigm permits' (Edwards 1997a: 54). She indicated how expressive and realist photographs may work together, as metaphors for different types of knowledge. Expressive photographs, she suggested, are hard to comprehend since '[t]hey do not slip easily into preconceived notions of reading culture' (1997a: 69) and because 'expressive' imagery belies 'the *inevitability* of not comprehending everything' – it challenges the claim to authority and 'truth' that is embedded in the 'realist' approach (Edwards 1997a: 75; original italics). Therefore, by begging that readers/viewers do not take photographs 'at face value', expressive photography would encourage a self-conscious and reflexive approach to viewing and producing meaning from photographs. If expressive photographs are published alongside realist photographs in ethnographic text, they may question readers'/viewers' assumptions about the truthfulness and completeness of the realist photographs, and in doing so challenge conventional ways of reading/viewing realist images.

Edwards's approach demonstrated well how different types of photograph, situated in relation to written text and other images, might represent different types of ethnographic knowledge, invoke diverse aspects of experience and address particular issues and questions. Nevertheless, as yet few ethnographers have developed such publication projects. One recent exception is the work of the photographer John Perivolaris, who has worked closely with a Moroccan migrant to Spain (Youseff) to represent the migrant experience. Pervolaris's photographic exhibition *Migrados* combines images that refer to a range of different genres. Wide-framed realist photographs, such as his images of migrants' living spaces and travelling on the Mediterranean Highway, are implicated as documents of typical migrant spaces and activities as they unfold. Close-ups of material forms and culture – discarded shoes, a glove, a boot-print – refer to the imprints that migrants leave on the environment and the artefacts they cast off through their migration narrative (Figure 6.2). Combined with Perivolaris's captions, these images function in a way similar to that Edwards describes for the work of Elizabeth Williams because they 'remain true to photographic integrity in using the interplay between the realist and the expressive to communicate about culture and to allude to wider issues' (Edwards 1997a: 65). Others of Perivolaris's images are staged, in collaboration with Youseff (see Figure 1.2), representing a shared construction of migrant realities and practices which contrasts with the form of intersubjectivity implied by his portraits of migrants.

The ways readers/viewers make meanings with novel combinations of written and visual texts have not as yet been researched. Perivolaris's online exhibition of his *Migrados* project has a comments facility that, at the time of writing, has started to generate an interesting dialogue. This presents a useful way of learning about others' responses to our texts. Although it is impossible to know how such an individual and personal activity as reading is actually experienced by others, it is useful to attempt to anticipate (and test with examples) how readers may construct meaning from texts. This includes considering the type of readers/viewers texts aim to address and the discourses (academic and otherwise) and other texts to which their interpretations of it are likely to refer.

Experimenting with photographs and words

Above I noted how ethnographers and publishers are becoming increasingly willing to include photographs in printed academic texts. Nevertheless, even now, in the twenty-first century, it is still not

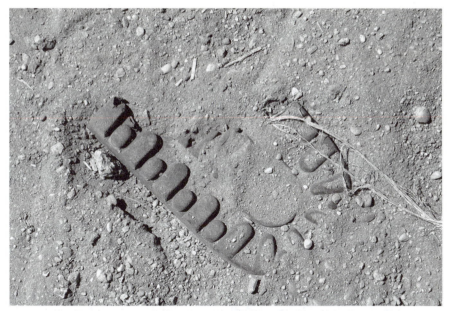

Bootprint, Campohermoso, Almería, Spain, August 2003. © John Perivolaris 2003.

Worker's Glove, Roquetas de Mar, August 2003. © John Perivolaris.

Figure 6.2
Photographs from John Perivolaris's *Migrados* project. More examples of
Perivolaris's work can be viewed in his on-line exhibition at www.flickr.com/
photos/dr_ john2005/.

unusual to find an ethnographic monograph or edited collection that contains no photographs at all. Moreover, those ethnographic texts that do include photographs tend to have a dominant written narrative at their core and to use photographs mainly as evidence or illustration. While some ethnographers have experimented with novel arrangements of images and text, most contemporary ethnographic representation does not confer equal importance or space to photographic and written text. In this section I discuss uses of photographs in ethnographic texts where written words form the dominant narrative. There are multiple ways that ethnographic texts could be constructed with different arrangements of photographs and words, and it would be impossible to cover all of these possibilities here. Here I discuss just some of these. It will be in the practice of researchers and students of ethnography who build on existing work to produce their own visual and written representations that further uses are developed.

In the Introduction to Part 3, I introduced the principle of montage as a model for ethnographic representation. Marcus's vision of a non-hierarchical text (1995) implies a tempting model for creating printed ethnographic representations that do not privilege the 'truth' of written academic text over other representations of knowledge. Such text would imply no hierarchy of ethnographic value between photographs and words, nor hierarchies within these categories. Therefore, just as local written and spoken narratives would be given equal (but different) authority to those of the ethnographer, photographic representations of knowledge produced by both ethnographers or informants, and expressive and realist uses of photography, would all be treated as having equal, although different, authority. Montage is still seen as experimental ethnographic text. However, it does offer a model that is an alternative to conventional ethnographic text. Most existing experimental texts tend to fall somewhere between the two extremes of montage and conventional ethnography, drawing from both, but making a commitment to neither. In this way they maintain sufficient continuity with existing forms of representation to allow their authors to participate in existing written theoretical academic debates, while also departing from and criticizing conventional narratives.

The academic journal *Visual Studies* (formerly *Visual Sociology*) regularly publishes articles with a high content of photographs. These take a variety of forms, such as photo-essays with various different contents and arrangements of photographs and text, captioned photographs, and use photography in a variety of ways. Many articles that have been published in *Visual Studies* (*Visual Sociology*) are informed by scientific and realist approaches to ethnography and photography (e.g. Pauwels 1996; Reiger 1996). However (especially more recently), others develop visual and textual narratives that combine realist approaches to photography with an acknowledgement of the arbitrariness of photographic meanings. An earlier example is Deborah Barndt's (1997) essay which combines her own documentary photography with commercial images, interview transcripts, academic discussions of globalization, and descriptive and reflexive passages. In one section of her text she inter-links photographs and an interview transcript produced on the same day of her research to form a photo-essay in which interview transcripts caption corresponding photographs. In doing so Barndt uses the words of a Mexican tomato worker, Teresa, and the photographs to construct a story related to themes of women's labour and globalization. While Teresa's voice is represented in the text, it becomes one narrative inter-linked with others that is used for the purposes of the researcher's wider project. However, this photo-essay itself becomes a sub-narrative in the author's wider, layered story as she later describes how her other infor-mant, Susan, a Canadian cashier who sells the tomatoes, made the representations of Teresa meaningful in terms of her own reality. Barndt's essay takes a step towards multivocality.

A more recent innovative essay is Rod Coover's discussion of using digital media in cross-cultural work (see also Chapter 8). Here Coover reflects on his own hypermedia practice, drawing from his *Cultures in Webs* CD-ROM (2003). Rather than simply supporting his written dis-cussion with separate web page captures, as has become a convention in social science writing about hypermedia representations (see for example Pink 2005: ch. 6; and this book Chapter 8), Coover has used the designs from the hypermedia pages of *Cultures in Webs* as the basis for the page layout of his article. In doing so he aims to evoke 'the hyper-media reading experience by interweaving photographs, texts, interview excerpts and proverbs to suggest how relationships between visual and verbal referents evolve in the cultural imaginary' (Coover 2004b: 7). His conventional written academic narrative is embedded within, and thus both framed by and part of, the multimedia context. In creating this montage Coover succeeds in subverting the relationship between images and words to some degree because whereas usually in academic text images, quotations, proverbs etc. are set in an academic written frame, here the relationship is reversed.

In the articles discussed above visual images and written texts are laid out alongside each other according to different narratives throughout the text. In others written and visual parts of the text are separated to produce related narratives (e.g. Goldfine and Goldfine 2003; Harper et al. 2005). In the example discussed here, the written text precedes the photographic text. Douglas Harper, Caroline Knowles and Pauline Leonard's essay (2005) focuses on the biographical experiences of Jack, who is an elderly British war veteran living with his Chinese wife in Hong Kong. The first part of the text describes his everyday life and biographical experiences of being a prisoner of war in Japanese camps, showing how the former is still shaped by the latter. This is followed by a series of seven photographs taken by Harper that, by showing Jack at his everyday work at the World War II Veterans' Association and in the war cemetery that he often visits, represent the material signifiers of his everyday practices and memories.

There are of course many different ways in which photographs may be set within written texts, and vice versa. In the current context of social scientific thesis presentation and academic publishing it is still likely to be the former combination that dominates. However, even when cost limits the number of images that may be included in a written text, photographs may still be used in novel and provoking ways. In my monograph *Women and Bullfighting* (Pink, 1997a), wherever possible I tried to use photographs to represent more than simply their content. For example, I captioned images of a bullfighter performing with written details of the technical equipment I had used to take the photograph in order to present my photographs as representations of what amateur photographers may achieve under those circumstances (1997a: 97–8). Other images were captioned in a realist stance (see 1997a: 102) and sometimes I made explicit references between images and the main written text. In one case (1997a: 74), I treat the photograph of Encarni (see Chapter 5) as a realist representation, but its extended caption reflects on the subjectivity of both the context of its production and of the gazes of other informants who spoke about it. The caption aims to provoke readers to question their interpretations of the photograph and recognize the different ways in which the photograph, and the 'traditional' symbols it represents, may be interpreted. Later in the book (1997a: 173–5) I created a short visual narrative with three captioned photographs. These represented different aspects of the relationship between bullfighting and the media that were not explicitly addressed in the written text, leaving readers/viewers to reflect on the relationship between these and the written narrative.

As these examples indicate, realist uses of photographs can provide an important layer of knowledge in ethnographic texts. When considering the meanings they imply it is useful to analyse their relationship to other narratives and forms of representation in any one text. For example, Paul Stoller's book *Sensuous Scholarship* (1997) is presented to the reader as an experimental and reflexive ethnographic text. However, here Stoller uses photographs in a realist stance, as documentary evidence and illustration of his written descriptions, simply captioned as, for example, 'Hauka Spirit Possession, Tillaberi, Niger, 1977' (1997: 50) or 'A medium possessed by the Hauka, Istambula, Tilaberi, Niger 1984' (1997: 54). Given the context Stoller creates in his text, his realist use of images does not necessarily have a problematically 'objectifying' effect. Embedded in a reflexive written text, these images, overtly realist, provide yet another 'register'. The photographs indeed objectify individuals' performances into generalized roles and actions. Nevertheless, as Marcus (1995) has pointed out, an objectifying discourse is not necessarily out of place in a montage-style text. The reflexive narratives that co-exist in Stoller's written text challenge the reduction of individual subjective experience to objectifying captions and imply to the reader who is really engaging with

© Sarah Pink 1997

Figure 6.3
This is one of three photographs that are set alongside the text of a chapter in
Women and Bullfighting (Pink 1997a: 173–5, Figure 12). They are not treated as
illustrations of events, activities or objects described in the text, but are intended
to make separate but related comments on the role of the media in the 'world of
bullfighting'. The original caption was as follows:

> Media attention is not solely directed at performances. Both *aficicionado* and anti-
> bullfighting meetings … (see Figure 22) become 'media events'. In this image a *Canal
> Sur* television cameraman prepares for a reception in the *Museu Taurino* (1992) whilst
> the speakers stand by a painting of the deceased bullfighter *Manolete*.

the text that the captions represent just one interpretation. In this sense
the expressive text serves to fracture (Edwards 1997a: 75) the objectifying
potential of the photographs, thus positioning them as just one visual perspective, and not a universal truth.

The photo-essay in ethnography

The photo-essay, although a relatively well-known genre, is infrequently
used for ethnographic representation. The main exceptions include articles
published in journals such as *Visual Sociology* (now *Visual Studies*) (e.g.
Bergamaschi and Francesconi 1996; Gold 1995; Harper 1994; Nuemann
1992; Suchar 1993; Van Mierlo 1994). More recently electronic photo-
essays have been published (discussed in more detail in Chapter 8). For
example Rod Coover's 'Practice' narrative on his *Cultures in Webs* (2003)
CD ROM and Ricabeth Steiger's *En Route* (2000: CD) published both on CD
and in print in *Visual Sociology*. In part this dearth of photo-essays in social
science publishing could be related to the objection that photographic

essays cannot represent data in a sufficiently objective way. In the past visual sociologists responded to this by arguing that visual essays can be adapted to the need for objective ethnographic representation. For example, John Grady defined the visual essay as 'a statement about human affairs that purports to represent reality', while attempting to avoid subjectivity and ensure validity (Grady 1991: 27, quoted in Simoni 1996: 75). While Grady's approach provides a solution for scientific sociology, as I emphasize throughout this book, subjectivity cannot really be avoided. A contemporary explanation for the limited ways that photographs are used in ethnographic texts is that most social scientists have few resources to guide them in developing innovative uses of images. They tend to resort therefore to conventional formats of inserting photographs into texts that are framed and dominated by written words. Moreover, since much of what social scientists want to say, and much of their participation in existing debates in their disciplines, is still a word-based activity, some may also have little motivation. Nevertheless as the work discussed in this section demonstrates, the photo-essay has much to contribute as another option in the repertoire of social science representation.

Photographs and written text cannot be expected to represent the same information in the same way. If photographs are thought of as a substitute for written words, and expected to achieve the same ends, then a comparison of the two is bound to conclude that written words do the job better. Rather, photo-essays are appropriate for representing certain types of ethnographic knowledge. Therefore, the definition of a photo-essay I use here is not one of solely photographs, but an essay (book, article or other text) that is composed predominantly of photographs. Sometimes the photographs are captioned or will be accompanied by other short texts. Some books or articles are divided into two sections – one photographic, one written – each representing ethnographic knowledge in ways to which the two media best lend themselves. This interpretation of the photographic essay invokes the question of what written words can express that photographs cannot, and vice versa. Some have argued that ethnographic photo-essays (and film) cannot offer structural, theoretical or critical analysis. Certainly, photographs cannot represent social structures, words spoken in interpersonal interactions or conventional theoretical and critical responses to existing academic discourses in the *same* way that written texts can. Nevertheless, photographs can be used in realist or expressive modes to represent, for example, the corporeal experience and facial expressions of people interacting with one another or their material environment, or people who stand for institutions and occupy particular places in power structures. They can also be used to create direct comparisons, and thus evoke difference. For example, in an article that has a written text followed by a photo-essay, Rebecca Goldfine and Olivia Goldfine (2003) compare two neighbours, one of whom is a hunter and the other an animal rights campaigner. The visual component of this text places side by side photographs that represent comparable aspects of their lives and serve to emphasize their differences. For instance, in one pair of photographs the hunter stands opposite his wall-mounted stuffed deer's head, while the animal rights campaigner holds her living cat in her arms (203: 104–5). Photographs may also be used as critical representations, either with or without written text. Chaplin cites Pollock's (1988) photo-essay of portraits of women to suggest that 'image-text presentations can make an important contribution to critique' (Chaplin 1994: 97). Schwartz's (1993) Minneapolis Superbowl project is another example of a critical visual essay. In this project Schwartz and other ethnographic photographers worked as 'participant observers' with a team of press photographers. Their project was to produce critical photographic representations that would 'examine the manufacture of the appearance of reality' presented through the iconography of the Superbowl – itself a 'repackaged visual event' (1993: 23). By using novel camera angles they produced photographs whose content represented 'conventional' aspects of Superbowl iconography arranged in 'unconventional' ways. By 'representing representation itself' (Schwartz 1993: 33) in this way, the photographs represent the Superbowl iconography from alternative, and critical, perspectives, making explicit power relations that were not implied in conventional Superbowl photography. Their photographs are supported by provoking captions and a reflexive text about the context in which they were taken. Thus the photographs form the dominant part of the critique of the way the Superbowl spectacle was manufactured.

Other photo-essays might play on the montage principle noted above. In Chapter 3 I introduced Suzanne Goopy and David Lloyd's photographic research about the quality of life of ageing Italo-Australians. I noted there that, based on photographs already produced by their research participants and on interviews with them, the researchers and participants then collaborated to create a photomontage that represented the key elements that they associated with quality of life. To represent this work visually Suzanne Goopy, David Lloyd, William Hatherell and Angela Blakely have developed a series of plates that use text of varying font sizes to represent the words of their informants, and both single and composite photographs (see Figures 6.4 and 6.5).

Photographs can be used to create representations that express experiences and ideas in ways written words cannot. This is not to say that one medium is superior to the other, but to seek the most appropriate way to represent different aspects of ethnographic experience and theoretical and critical ideas. Perhaps most importantly, this means being prepared to explore how photography can make a significant contribution to this.

Ethical issues in photographic representation

In Chapter 2 I outlined some standard conventions for respecting informants' rights to anonymity and for demonstrating a commitment to protect their identities and interests. I suggested that the idea of protecting one's informants is sometimes overly paternalistic and that by adopting a collaborative approach, whereby the subjects of the

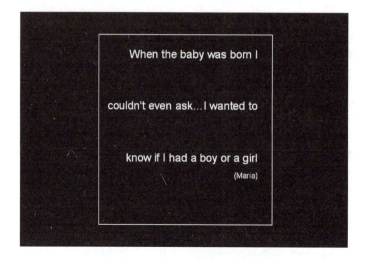

When the baby was born I

couldn't even ask...I wanted to

know if I had a boy or a girl

(Maria)

Figure 6.4

Suzanne Goopy, David Lloyd and Angela Blakely have developed an innovative series of images based on visual ethnographic research about quality of life, with older Italo-Australians. Here a quotation from a participant in the ethnography is placed next to a photograph taken to evoke meanings that emphasize how biographical and emotional sentiments can be invested in everyday practices and objects.

Figure 6.5

Here in another example from the work of Suzanne Goopy and her colleagues (see Figure 6.4.) composite images map the domestic space of their Italo-Australian participants, drawing attention to elements of the material environment and social relationships that are important to their self-identities and quality of life. One of a series of composite photographs by Angela Blakely and David Lloyd photography participate in producing and selecting the photographs that represent them, some of these issues may be avoided. Most of the examples discussed in this chapter reflect this approach. Nevertheless, whatever the role of informants in the photographic production and representation, ethnographers/authors, in negotiation with publishers, are usually responsible for final editorial decisions relating to those photographs. These decisions should be informed not solely by the willingness of informants/subjects for their photographs to be published, but also by ethnographers' knowledge of the social, cultural and political contexts in which the published photographs will be viewed and interpreted. As James, Hockey and Dawson stress, ethnographers should not only take an academic approach to ethnographic texts that acknowledges they are constructed 'fictions' or 'partial truths', but should also recognize that their representations can have political implications, and may be appropriated and used by policy-makers or other powerful bodies (James et al. 1997: 12). When ethnographers use photographs to make academic points they should also consider the personal, social and political implications of the publication of these images for their subjects.

When ethical considerations rule out using some photographs, specific visual representations of ethnographic knowledge or theoretical ideas have to be sacrificed or expressed in other ways. Particularly when working with children, researchers might find they are unable to publish photographs. In other cases the intimate nature of the research topic, or issues related to the status of the research participants, or to relationships they are involved in, will mean that they do not want to be identified. In some cases identities can be concealed. Perivolaris has used this strategy in some of his *Migrados* photographs where the identities of the people he has photographed are obscured since they face away from the camera (see Figure 1.2). Another way of protecting research subjects from public exposure while still using images of them in academic publications is by digitally blurring or covering their faces. Lomax and Casey (1998) and Dant and Bowles (2003) have successfully used this technique to publish video stills that guarantee a certain amount of anonymity. However, this practice is uncommon in ethnographic work and is difficult to reconcile with the idea of using photography *because of* its specificity.

This book focuses mainly on publishing ethnographers' own photographs, but other people's photographs may also help support academic points. In the United Kingdom, ethnographers (like artists) usually own copyright to photographs they have produced themselves. However, if a photograph's copyright is owned by someone else (possibly an individual or, in the case of historical photographs taken by deceased academics, sometimes an archive or other organization), their written permission and sometimes a fee is required for its publication. As regards publishing photographs of other people, the situation is less clear. Fetterman stated that '[a]n individual's verbal permission is usually sufficient to take a picture. Written permission, however, is necessary to publish or display that picture in a public forum' (1998: 67). In my experience, including when photographs of me have been published, written consent was not required. While for Fetterman this might be a moral requirement, it is not always required by publishers, therefore the ultimate decision often lies in the hands of the ethnographer who possesses the photograph. In contexts where it is culturally appropriate, the use of consent forms throughout the research and representation process (see Chapter 2) can clarify this. Copyright law can also vary in different countries. While publishers can normally advise on this, ethnographers may wish to inform themselves on both copyright of their own photographs and that of other people. The UK Copyright Service (www.copyrightservice.co.uk/) is a good starting point for this.

Summary

In this chapter I have proposed a reflexive approach to constructing texts that combine photographs and words. Authors of ethnography should pay careful attention to the theoretical issues, experiential knowledge and textual strategies that inform their practices of representation. This demands attention to captioning and use of tense, and awareness of how different textual strategies imply particular meanings within texts. Meanings do not, however, reside solely in texts, but ethnographic texts are interpreted and given meanings by readers on *their own* terms. Ethnographers should therefore consider how their texts will be situated and made meaningful in terms of other discourses and other texts. Novel textual strategies that combine photographs and written words to use reflexive subjective or expressive texts or images alongside objectifying, realist texts may challenge conventional approaches. To read or create such texts reflexively ethnographers should account for how photographs interact with, cross-reference and produce meaning in relation to other elements in the text, and how these connections are given meaning by discourses and gazes that exist outside the text.

FURTHER READING

Bateson, G. and Mead, M. (1942) *Balinese Character: A Photographic Analysis*, New York: New York Academy of the Sciences.

Pink, S. (1997) *Women and Bullfighting*, Oxford: Berg. (An ethnographic monograph that uses photographs in a range of different realist and expressive ways)

Sutton, D. (2001) *Remembrance of Repasts*, Oxford: Berg. (An ethnographic monograph that demonstrates an effective use of photography in relation to written text)

Visual Studies (formerly *Visual Sociology*). (This journal publishes essays with visual images and photo-essays and is worth checking regularly for new work in addition to the examples discussed in this chapter)

7

Video in Ethnographic Representation

Video and representation

In Chapter 4 I argued that video is not simply a data collecting tool but a technology that participates in the negotiation of social relationships and a medium through which ethnographic knowledge is produced. Here I discuss how video may subsequently be used to represent ethnographic knowledge.

Anthropological filmmakers have led the way in using moving images for ethnographic representation, conventionally producing edited ethnographic documentary films or videos. Successful ethnographic documentaries are screened at ethnographic film festivals, are used for teaching or are broadcast on television. This remains the practice of most visual anthropologists and the aspiration of many postgraduates. However, this chapter is not a hands-on guide to ethnographic video production; Masters degree programmes across the world provide practical training in camera, sound and editing skills, as well as ethnographic film theory. Ethnographic documentary production is a vast and detailed topic and is covered in depth in other texts (e.g. Barbash and Taylor 1997) written by practitioners with years of ethnographic filmmaking experience. Such existing texts are excellent sources of reference and I do not repeat their work here. Rather, drawing from the well-established field of anthropological film criticism and theory as well as recent commentaries on the use of video in ethnographic work, I take a different focus. Not all students and researchers who use video in their research aspire to produce ethnographic documentaries, or have video footage of the appropriate technical or visual format or quality to do so. Here I explore other possible uses of video in ethnographic representation, including using video footage and stills in conference presentations and/or printed text.

Defining 'ethnographic video'

Crawford (1992: 74) listed 'Ethnographic *footage*' as the first of seven categories of ethnographic film, the others being: research films (for academic audiences); ethnographic documentaries; ethnographic television documentaries; education and information films; other non-fiction films; and fiction films. Here I use the term 'ethnographic video', similarly in its broadest sense, to refer to any video footage that is of ethnographic interest or is used to represent ethnographic knowledge. From this perspective ethnographic video does not need to conform to specific film styles or conventions. Rather, it becomes ethnographic when it is used as such. Therefore video representations of any length or style that are used to represent ethnographic knowledge may be referred to as ethnographic video. While video (or film), such as fiction, home movies or television documentaries, may be used ethnographically and might be ethnographic in that they are of interest to ethnographers (see Crawford 1992: 74), they are not discussed here. This chapter is about how video footage shot as part of ethnographic research might be used to represent knowledge about that research to mainly academic audiences.

Debates about the definition of ethnographic film/video have concentrated on documentary film production. However, knowledge of the historical and contemporary theoretical perspectives that have informed these discourses is also relevant to other uses of video in ethnographic representation. Early ethnographic film theory and practice suggested ethnographic film should represent whole cultures and, to ensure its scientific value, ethnographic film styles should (among other things) avoid close-ups and attempt to film whole contexts, activities and action, as well as be minimally edited and use only original synchronous sound (e.g. Heider 1976). These approaches intended to avoid subjectivity and specificity and insisted that ethnographic concerns should be prioritized above cinematic strategies. In the 1980s, responses to these initial approaches suggested new theoretical perspectives that put new demands on film styles. For example, Rollwagen argued that anthropological film should be informed by existing anthropological theory and structured according to anthropological demands (1988). Ruby, one of the first visual anthropologists to engage with notions of reflexivity, in the early 1980s, argued for a reflexive approach to ethnographic filmmaking that would break down the art/science dichotomy that had dominated social science (1982). Then, by the 1990s, David MacDougall (e.g. 1997) had proposed that ethnographic documentary film should be used to challenge objectifying approaches in anthropology to emphasize the experiential and individual nature of social life and develop its potential to represent individuals and specific aspects of experience. This currently dominant approach informs a style of filmmaking that focuses on individuals rather than whole cultures and the subjectivities of both filmmakers and subjects are appreciated. Since the late 1990s, when high quality digital video, smaller cameras and editing on a standard PC or laptop computer became available, further shifts in the practice of and approaches to ethnographic documentary making have emerged. David MacDougall (2001) has drawn from his own experiences of using digital video to make his *Doon School* films in India to comment on how both the filmmaking process and the sorts of films that he can produce have departed from those associated with the older technologies. As MacDougall (2005: 121–3) and Ruby (2000) have both indicated, freed from the obligations derived from making films financed by television broadcast companies, digital ethnographic documentary makers can work alone and in closer collaboration with film subjects, to follow serendipitous narratives during video fieldwork and represent topics of issues that serve both the academic discipline and the film subjects (rather than the agendas of broadcast television).

The history of and debates over ethnographic film have been well rehearsed (e.g. Crawford and Turton 1992; Devereaux and Hillman 1995; Grimshaw 2001; Heider 1976; Henley 2000, 2004; Loizos 1993; MacDougall 1998, 2005; Morphy and Banks 1997; Pink 2005; Rollwagen 1988; Ruby 2000). A detailed analysis of them is not my concern, but is a necessary background for any aspiring ethnographic documentary maker. Knowledge of the history of ethnographic filmmaking is not only important for understanding how theories inform ethnographic documentary styles. Rather, as Peter Loizos has pointed out, 'there are several contexts in which the question of classification becomes practically important' (Loizos 1993: 8). These include seeking funding for film production, eligibility of films to compete in ethnographic film festivals (and how they are classified by film prize judges) and acquisition and use of films by educational institutions and libraries. Not only film/video makers' own definitions, but also other people's classifications of ethnographic films determine how they are eventually used and interpreted. If an ethnographic documentary video is produced for dissemination in academic or popular circles (at film festivals, as a teaching resource, or television documentary) the video's style, technical specifications and image quality must conform to the demands of those audiences and institutions.

The relationship between video research and video representation

In Chapter 4 I discussed how researchers may combine video with still photography, tape-recording, note- taking and other methods in projects in which video making was not the main objective. Then, in Chapter 5, I suggested how video materials might be analysed alongside and in relation to other research materials. In this chapter I follow these uses through by focusing on how such video recordings, which are already interlinked with other ethnographic media, may be integrated into ethnographic representation.

In Chapter 4 I described how during the twentieth century a distinction between research footage and cinematic footage associated the former with science and the latter with art, thus arguing that the former should have no role in representation. Here I suggest that these categories of ethnographic film and research footage, and corresponding roles proposed for them, should be re-thought. Some have rightly argued that the same footage may participate in more than one category. For instance, Crawford defines 'Ethnographic *footage* ... [as] ... unedited film material, which may be used in its unedited form for research purposes or eventually be edited into a film' (1992: 74). However, subsequent approaches treated research and documentary footage as two distinct types shot with different intentions. Barbash and Taylor argue that while documentary footage, shot with an intentionally creative narrative, would be edited into ethnographic film, 'the essential point of research footage is that it be as unselective and unstructured as possible – in other words that it provide less *discourse about* social life than an *objective record* of it' (Barbash and Taylor 1997: 78). In research, '[t]he camera is deployed as an impartial instrument in the service of science, fixing all that is fleeting for infinite future analysis' (1997: 78). In this scenario research footage has no place in ethnographic representation; it would be 'translated into words' in the way I criticized in Chapter 5. According to Barbash and Taylor, it would be unsuitable for finished films since good observational documentary differs from research footage as 'in its pursuit of objectivity, research filming tends to lack that engagement with human affairs that makes them, to their participants, real. The desire to be impartial tends to make the filming unselective, and so the footage may seem unstructured to anyone not already in the know' (1997: 78).

Barbash and Taylor are right to insist that ethnographic documentary footage is selectively and carefully shot to correspond with structural and stylistic demands of documentary making. However, by using an art/science dichotomy to associate artistic, subjective and selective creativity with representation, and scientific, objective and systematic recording with research, they not only ignore the inevitable subjectivity research involves but by defining research footage so narrowly rule out its potential for ethnographic representation. They delimit video research and video representation as two essentially different projects and in doing so restrict the potential of video representations for reflexive engagement with the research context. The relationship between video research and video representation needs to be explored in terms that go beyond this either/or focus on the production of ethnographic videos or the translation of video recordings into verbal knowledge. This point has two main implications.

First, it seeks to bridge the gap between using video as an exploratory and subjective fieldwork tool and the practice of ethnographic documentary video making. David MacDougall's discussions of the making of his *Doon School* films show how this might be achieved within documentary making practice (2005: 120–44). Rather than simply making a film he 'began to think about a long-term study of the school using a video camera as a means of inquiry'. Through this process, he produced a series of five related films, which had not been pre-planned (2005: 122). Other visual anthropologists have started to draw from ethnographic filmmaking styles as part of their methodology for exploring other people's everyday realities as part of research. For example, Jayasinhji Jhala has used a method based on David MacDougall's camera work in his film *Lorang's Way* (1979) that follows the film subject as she/he walks through his dwelling area showing it to the filmmaker and talking to camera (Jhala 2004: 62). In my own video tour method I use a similar technique, which also draws from established ethnographic documentary making practice and was based on my MA training in observational documentary at the Granada Centre for Visual Anthropology (Manchester, UK). Ethnographic video research and representation are starting to share methodology and practice in a way that suggests they can no longer be viably thought of as a binary pair in the way Barbash and Taylor present them.

Secondly, however, some visual anthropologists have started to suggest that ethnographic documentary making is not always the best academic use of ethnographic video footage (e.g. Ruby 2004; Pink 2005). Following on from this, similar to the point I made for photography in Chapter 4, I suggest here we start thinking about how different types of expressive or realist video footage might work together in relation to each other and other forms of text in video or multimedia productions. In Chapter 8 I follow this through further with reference to the use of video in ethnographic hypermedia texts.

The methods I suggested in Chapter 4 aim to produce research video that is not objective recording, but subjective text, often produced collaboratively with informants. It is never impartial and not necessarily unstructured and usually *does* engage with human experience and individual concerns. A reflexive approach to using research video in representation involves situating video footage in the research process to understand how knowledge was produced through video-recording, exploring, for instance, the relationship between video recordings and other verbal, written or photographic knowledge produced during the research. By examining how different visual and written materials give meaning to one another, researchers may find some video footage is best used as realist recording, while other sequences communicate expressively.

The ways ethnographers intend to represent their research inevitably inform how they approach their projects, the technologies used, their relationships with informants and the experiences and knowledge they produce. These relationships, technologies and experiences might also be reflected in their representations. When video plays a key role in the research it seems appropriate to incorporate video in its representation. This does not necessarily mean editing a documentary ethnographic video, but, for example, using video clips, stills or transcripts in conference presentations or hypermedia texts, or with written descriptions in printed publications. Below I suggest some ways in which researchers may experiment with ethnographic video representations. First, however, I discuss video as a medium for ethnographic representation, its difference from and similarities to other media and the theories attached to its use.

Video, other media and reflexive text

As Edwards has argued for photography (see Chapter 6), use of video for ethnographic representation should be informed by an understanding of the nature of video as a medium, and the type of knowledge it best represents. In the existing twentieth-century literature there was virtually no discussion of video in ethnographic representation. However, visual anthropologists did engage with related issues in an extensive debate about the relationship between written text and ethnographic film which form a relevant background for discussing ethnographic uses of video. More recent work in visual anthropology practice also offers important insights into the potential of video in representation (e.g. in Pink et al. 2004; Grimshaw and Ravetz 2004; MacDougall 2005; Pink 2005).

There has been no absolute agreement over the purpose and nature of ethnographic uses of moving images. Historically, approaches to this have shifted with new theoretical ideas. In the 1970s and 1980s film-makers like Paul Heider and Jack Rollwagen (although in different ways) argued that ethnographic films should respond to the same scientific criteria applied to ethnographic writing (see above). Working in the scientific and realist paradigm of the time, they selected corresponding bases upon which to compare film and text. However, during the 1980s and 1990s the art/science distinction that had made ethnographic film so problematic was increasingly dissolved. During this period the demand for reflexivity in ethnographic writing increased (see Chapters 1 and 6) and some ethnographers began to characterize their representations as inevitably selective constructions, partial truths and ultimately literary works – fictions. It was argued that the scientific objectivity that had been assumed for written text, and that artistic film could not achieve, was in fact unattainable. Written text was therefore potentially equally as subjective and artistic as film. Jay Ruby suggested that reflexivity also had a place in film, arguing that anthropological filmmakers should ensure their audiences were made aware of the differences between reality and film as a constructed representation. He proposed that more artistic, expressive forms had a space in anthropology (Ruby 1982: 130) and that 'since film allows us to tell stories with pictures, its potential becomes enhanced within a reflexive and narrative anthropology' (1982: 131; see also Ruby 2000). By this time, reflexivity had begun to develop in ethnographic filmmaking (especially in Jean Rouch's and David and Judith MacDougall's films), during a period of technical and epistemological innovation which enabled 'the filmmakers to be increasingly explicit about how the films were made, and the whys and for-whoms of their making' (Loizos 1993: 171).

New bases for comparing film and text developed as the art/science dichotomy was challenged and they were seen as equally selective, constructed representations rather than objective realist texts. However, new differences between film and written text were also emphasized, maybe most importantly because they have different potentials for representing human experience and a different relationship to the 'reality' of ethnographic situations. However, during the 1990s anthropologists still differed in their conclusions about where these differences lie. For instance, Hastrup argued that the reflexivity that helps contextualize meanings and differences in ethnographic writing cannot be achieved in ethnographic film because the iconographic visual communication of film is 'taken at face-value' and cannot invoke the degree of reflexivity and self-conscious knowledge that written text does (Hastrup 1992: 21). In contrast, the ethnographic films and theoretical written work of MacDougall demonstrated that reflexivity is not a unique characteristic of written text, but may also be represented in film. Other visual anthropologists compared anthropological film and text on a different basis. Barbash and Taylor claimed ethnographic writing is not concerned so much with reflexivity since 'anthropological texts tend to be ... (although of course by no means exclusively) concerned with non-intuitive abstractions like social structure or population statistics', whereas '[f]ilm is a quintessentially phenomenological medium, and it may have a different orientation to social life than anthropological monographs. It has a unique capacity to evoke human experience, what it feels like to actually be-in-the world' (1997: 74–5). Leslie Devereaux similarly argued that 'the camera's special virtue ... is its direct relation to the personal and the particular', pointing out that whether or not ethnographic film can represent 'reality', its 'ties to the specific' cannot be denied. In contrast he suggests that 'academic writing, flees the particular and takes hold of the abstract, that enemy of experience'; that '[t]he expository project, extrapolating from the particular, sticking close to explaining, is not impossible in documentary film. But sticking with the particular, sticking close to experience, is, if anything, more possible in anthropological film than in writing' (Devereaux and Hillman 1995: 71–2).

Moving images and written text certainly bear different relationships to experience and the particular and represent these differently. However Barbash and Taylor's and Devereaux's almost binary distinctions seem to ignore that many ethnographers have written texts that go beyond structures and statistics to contend with subjectivity and the evocation of experience (see Chapter 6) (see also Pink 2005). I would also dispute the idea that the abstract has to be the 'enemy' (Devereaux and Hillman, 1995) of experience. It would seem more reasonable to suggest that the particular and abstract are in fact interdependent ways of representing experience and making it culturally meaningful. A possibly more fruitful way forward is to consider what ethnographers are using video and written representations to achieve. To examine this I look briefly at a currently dominant issue in ethnographic representation: the relationship between the specific and the general and the question of how to represent other people's experiences.

Coping with the relationship between the specificity of human experience and the social scientific practice of producing generalizations is fundamental to academic work. In the 1990s MacDougall's comparison of ethnographic film and writing focused on how anthropologists have struggled with the 'problem of the individual'. The individual, he wrote, had been the 'raw unit of anthropological study' but ironically had not conventionally been an acceptable element of ethnographic representation. MacDougall suggested that while 'ethnographic writing can more easily elide' this contradiction, in ethnographic film the individual 'is sometimes felt to claim altogether too much of their [ethnographic filmmakers'] attention' (1995: 220–1). Therefore, written text can subdue the individual, whereas film cannot. While conventionally ethnographic texts in the twentieth century tended to the abstract, ethnographers are now writing an increasing number of texts that have both incorporated the drive towards reflexivity of the 1980s and 1990s and also seek new ways to come closer to individual experience and the specific in social life (see Chapter 6). A good example is Robert Desjarlais's (2003) monograph that analyses the biographical experiences of two ageing Yolmo Buddhists in Nepal.

The individual is in fact now a current concern for some ethnographic writers as well as for filmmakers. Nevertheless, moving images and written words do have the potential to specialize in different elements of the general and specific and thus represent different types of ethnographic experience and theory. They should not therefore be expected to represent these themes in the same way, as their differences in fact allow ethnographers to broach key issues in different ways. In common, moving-image and written representations form part of ethnographers' projects to represent relationships between different elements (individual, specific, abstract, general, between theory and experience). Ethnographic filmmakers have claimed that video has a special potential to represent the inevitably embodied and multisensory experience of ethnographic fieldwork and evoke other people's sensory experience to an audience/reader. MacDougall suggests video would support this since the audio-visual medium allows us to produce new understandings of '"sensory" knowledge' concerning 'how people perceive their material environment and interact with it' (2005: 269). Grimshaw asks how 'If one of the foundational principles of anthropological knowledge is experience, understanding emerging from the sensory immersion of "being there", how can it be given form that does not involve translating it into a different register?' (2004: 23). She suggests that observational cinema (the dominant style in ethnographic documentary), if rethought as a subjective art form and following Taussig (1993) as 'a very particular form of mimetic practice' (2004: 26) could achieve this.

The direct and immediate audio-visual representation of video is capable of evoking empathetic response in audiences in ways writing cannot. Nevertheless, this does not mean written prose cannot also evoke other people's sensory embodied experiences to readers. In written ethnography this can be achieved in ways that are culturally situated and theoretically framed (Pink 2005). Video and writing play different and complementary roles in ethnographic representation. But *both* are involved in representing individual experience.

There is, however, as yet no cross-disciplinary consensus about how video might participate in academic discourse. For example, Grimshaw (2004) suggests arts practice as a radical way forward for ethnographic video representation. In contrast, the visual sociologist Luc Pauwels, in his analysis of a video article, develops a quite different approach, which he says is 'scientifically informed'. This 'refers to the idea that the construction of the visual product in both its form and content should be guided by and subjected to insights and practices that are expected from any scientific endeavor' (2002: 152). As I have noted earlier in this book, in the twentieth century it was art/science dichotomies that plagued uses of the visual in the social sciences and led many to reject it. The present context of innovation is, however, not one where these old debates are being repeated, but rather seems to be one where different academics are seeking different ways to integrate video into their work. My own view is that we need to seek ways to make ethnographic video representations both accessible and relevant to academic debate. There seems to me to be little point in producing ethnographic video that will only be viewed by other ethnographic documentary makers at film festivals.

Below I suggest a reflexive approach that takes advantage of the different ways video, photography and written text can represent sensory embodied ethnographic experience, theory and critique. By combining media and practices in this way it is possible to produce texts and presentations that draw from both arts practice and conventional social science practice. As such, researchers can represent their work by juxtaposing different types of knowledge, subjectivity, epistemology, experience and voice in ways that complement one another. However, the types of creative innovation and reflexivity that this type of representation implies do not exist only within the text. In Chapter 6 I noted how new types of text demand new forms of readership. Therefore, first, I discuss video and reflexive viewing.

Ethnographic video audiences

While there is an existing literature on ethnographic film audiences, to my knowledge audience responses to ethnographic video footage have not been systematically analysed (with the exception of screening video for informants, see Chapter 4). Until recently, little was known about the viewing practices of ethnographic documentary film audiences. However, since the 1990s ethnographic research into how audiences interpret ethnographic documentary (e.g. Martinez 1992) has developed in tandem with new approaches to studying audiences in media studies (e.g. Morley 1996).

These disciplines have also converged in the 'media ethnography' method (see Crawford and Hafsteinnson 1996), which takes an ethnographic approach to studying audiences. It has been argued that audience research is a moral issue and is part of ethnographers' duty to protect their informants. Even if informants agree to footage of them being presented publicly, they may not understand the full implications of such public exposure. As Braun points out in his video *Passing Girl, Riverside: An Essay on Camera Work* (1998), when a Ghanaian village chief agreed to Braun showing video images of his village in North America, did he really understand the implications of this? Consent is one thing, the extent to which it is really informed, or by what it is informed, is another.

Ethnographic texts, be they books, videos or photographs, are not usually released for public consumption without some consideration of how they communicate. It is advisable to research audience responses to video representation before disseminating it in the public domain. Documentary video makers normally show rough-cuts of their work to various viewers. This may offer professional guidance on the content, stylistic and technical matters before a final edit, as well as examples of viewers' responses. As I suggested in Chapter 4, when possible, rough-cuts may also be shown to ethnographic video subjects for their comments and approval before the final version is cut (see also Figure 4.1). Sometimes informants can anticipate how certain other viewers may interpret the video and can comment on this. However, it is difficult to predict precisely how video texts will be made meaningful, as once they are available in a public domain they are subject to diverse (mis)understandings.

Visual anthropologists now pay serious attention to the politics of ethnographic film representation and spectatorship. In a series of essays (1990, 1992, 1996), based on his research with ethnographic film audiences, Wilton Martinez has shown how individuals' readings of ethnographic films are embedded in complex sets of existing power relations and cultural narratives that conventional ethnographic film narratives and pedagogical strategies do not challenge. Martinez has followed Baudry's (1996) suggestion that ethnographic film viewers are presented with at least two subject positions – 'those constructed by the film(maker) on the one hand, and by the represented subjects on the other' (1996: 74) – therefore demonstrating that individuals' actual viewing practices depend on how the relationship between these different subject positions is constructed *in* the film text, and in viewers' *own* interactions with these subject positions. However, Martinez criticizes conventional ethnographic filmmakers for assuming a subject position for their viewers that is part of an objectifying and disempowering approach to ethnographic representation. Martinez's research indicates that even when filmmakers intend to situate the viewer in a position that challenges ethnocentric and racist ideas, these aims are often not achieved as 'mostly conventional ethnographic films help reinforce students' ethnocentric beliefs' (1996: 77–8). Martinez's critique has alarming implications for ethnographic filmmakers and has been widely referenced.

Nevertheless, Jay Ruby has since pointed out a more recent study by Sam Pack (1999, in Ruby 2000). Pack suggested that ethnographic film and media content serve to mutually reinforce exoticizing interpretations of ethnographic film subjects. He suggests that rather than students having poor viewing skills this might be countered by attention to pedagogical strategies (see Ruby 2000: 191–2). In fact, it would seem reasonable to assume that while teachers can give some guidance, both the direction provided by the filmmaker's narrative and the viewer's existing value meet in the production of people's interpretations of ethnographic film. Indeed, MacDougall has also highlighted the complexity of viewers' relationships to film. Drawing from the ideas of film critics, he points out the multiplicity of ways that film may act on viewers: 'the conventions of filming and editing do not simply direct us to different visual points of view in a film but orchestrate a set of overlapping codes of position, narrative, metaphor and moral attitude' (1995: 223). MacDougall also emphasizes the specificity of the relationships individuals develop with texts:

> Our reading of a film, and our feelings about it, are at every moment the result of how we experience the complex fields this orchestration creates – partly dependent again upon who we are and what we bring to the film. This complexity extends to our relationship to different modes of cinematic address. (1995: 223)

These points can be applied not only to documentary ethnographic film, but also to other types of video representation. Differently constructed videos will both act on and be acted on by different viewers in their own individual ways.

Viewers' interpretations of films depend not only on the subjective relationships individuals develop with film texts, but also on the circumstances of viewing, including the interactions between audience members and the intersubjectivity among viewers. For example, when I screened part of *The Women Who Smile* (Lydall and Head 1990) to a group of second-year sociology students, their interpretations of the film were framed by their individual readings as well as the viewing context and how they negotiated these meanings with fellow students. I introduced *The Women Who Smile* as an 'ethnographic' documentary and asked them to view the film thinking about what made it of ethnographic, rather than purely documentary, interest, and what specific information of sociological interest it contained. I told them that after the film they would discuss these themes in groups and then present their ideas to the class. Therefore the viewing context itself was constructed: the group was to view a film that I had defined as ethnographic, consider its elements of ethnographic interest as individuals, and then share that information with a group of three or four others with whom they had previously worked. Predictably, the students gave the film sociological meanings; they identified the film as being about kinship, ritual, economic activity and gender roles. We also discussed how members of a popular television audience with no access to the academic categories the students had used might have seen the film as documentary rather than as an ethnographic film. The group suggested that a TV audience may have empathized with themes such as motherhood by creating continuities and differences between their own personal experiences and those of women represented in the film.

Once people begin to discuss their different interpretations and experiences of film it becomes clear that it would be impossible to produce a text that has the same effect on, or that pleases, everyone. For example, in 1992 I attended an ethnographic film festival in Granada (Spain). One of the films screened was *The Condor and the Bull* (Getzels and Gordon 1990), a film about an Andean village festival. During the festival the locals become drunk and a live condor, captured for the event by local men, is tied to the back of a bull. Discussions began during the session after the screening and continued later that night after dinner when the festival participants (mainly anthropologists and filmmakers from Europe and Latin America) sat around a large table in the open air. Some viewers found this film, made by a British woman and a North American man, problematic. They felt it represented Latin American villagers as drunken and their festivals as primitive and chaotic. Filming people when they are drunk always raises ethical issues, but whether these create ethical problems also depends on how the film is interpreted. Other viewers had a different impression of the film. Some felt the villagers' drunkenness was only to be expected as people in many places get drunk at festivals. They did not feel it was a negative representation of the villagers or their festival.

I noted above that reflexivity has already been incorporated in ethnographic filmmaking practice in films that recognize filmmakers' roles and intentions and the constructedness of the reality they represent. Some have also begun to consider how a self-conscious approach to viewing ethnographic documentary may be developed or guided through novel narrative forms (see Mermin 1997) and this is important reading for aspiring ethnographic filmmakers. Here, however, I am not concerned with ethnographic film narrative, but to suggest uses of video in reflexive ethnographic representations that may themselves be read reflexively.

Video representations of ethnography

There are various options for using video in ethnographic representation: for example, ethnographic documentary, showing clips in conference presentations, video installations in exhibitions or electronic representations (see Chapter 8), combining moving and still images, voiceover and text in edited documentaries, or printing video stills and transcripts alongside descriptive passages in books or journals. Some of these are discussed below.

Producing an ethnographic documentary about a piece of research

While good ethnographic documentaries can sometimes be edited from footage not intended for documentary making, successful documentaries are usually carefully planned and shot with a documentary narrative in mind. In such projects video making becomes part of the research narrative itself. However, while there are some parallels between ethnographic research and ethnographic video making, some ethnographic filmmakers would argue that ethnographic documentary making requires specialist study and training in practice and theory. Moreover, whereas ethnographic documentary making is often likened to participant observation in that it involves a long-term association with the film's subjects, ethnographic films are not always shot during long-term fieldwork. Television documentaries like Granada Television's *Disappearing World* and the BBC's *Under the Sun* series were based on an ethnographer's existing work and shot as a collaboration between ethnographers, filmmakers and the film subjects. Thus documentary designs may be informed by existing knowledge of people and cultures. Sometimes existing research can support funding applications or encourage the collaboration of trained filmmakers (if this is needed). Video footage shot during original fieldwork can help potential collaborators or sponsors assess a project's potential and provide examples of visual work for the film's potential participants to view. Ethnographers who work with commercial filmmakers may find that academic, practical and ethical conflicts arise when different agendas of filmmakers and social scientists clash (see Barbash and Taylor 1997; Loizos 1993; Lydall 1990; Woodhead 1987; Marvin 2005). Another option is for ethnographers to collaborate with specialist ethnographic filmmakers (for example the ethnographic documentary *Faces in the Crowd* (Henley 1994) represents the sociologist Ann Rowbottom's research but was shot by ethnographic filmmaker Paul Henley).

(Edited) clips

Footage of activities, actions, events, interviews, landscapes, artefacts or other visual aspects of culture can be carefully edited or simply selected as unedited footage. While a set of clips may not fit together coherently as a full-length documentary narrative, they may be combined with written or spoken words, sound or stills to tell another story. Each clip may itself represent a short story, demonstrate an activity, or represent an informant's spoken narrative or visual self-representation. Some clips may be realist references to actions and events that respect the order these occurred in. Others might be edited to represent 'real' sequences of events that divert from the original chronology of the footage. There are multiple options, depending on what researchers intend video clips to represent and how clips are situated in relation to other texts that represent aspects of the same ethnographic project.

Each such set of video clips that tells its own ethnographic story may also be part of a larger representation. This wider narrative might include still images, sound and different styles of written text. Rather than photographs and videos serving as illustrations to the written or spoken text, it may be led by any of these media. The same set of video clips may also be used to represent the work in different ways. For example, from my collaborative video tours in one of my research projects about the home I produced about 40 hours of video tape. I used clips selected from these videos to present the work in three different ways. First in my applied presentations to Unilever, who had funded the project, I presented clips to the research team in both spoken presentations and in a series of CD ROMs I produced. Secondly, I used clips from the videos of informants who had agreed that I might do so to present my work in more public academic contexts as part of seminar papers that I gave in academic departments. These showings gave me an opportunity to hear other academics' comments and feedback on both my written and visual materials. Thirdly, I developed two experimental CD ROM projects in which I included selected clips. These were disseminated in a limited way and with the approval of those who had appeared in them and viewed the projects themselves.

Within these presentations I used video in both realist and expressive ways. For example, on one level they were intended to be realist representations of individuals and their material homes. They also portrayed people performing domestic tasks in their homes, which could be interpreted as (my) representations of (their) domestic performances. Because the video tours also recorded the interaction between researcher and informant, the clips also function as reflexive texts that reveal the relationships and processes through which the research produced ethnographic knowledge. Some clips I have shown have been selected specifically for this purpose. As evocative texts the video clips are also intended to communicate something of materiality of specific homes and of people's sensory and embodied experiences of them. Finally, I have used the clips to give my informants a voice – to enable them to express themselves directly to an audience through words and actions (although of course mediated by my camera work, selection and editing of clips). As I have analysed in detail elsewhere (Pink 2004b, 2005), these clips have some ethnographic documentary video qualities and would not conform to Barbash and Taylor's definition of research footage (above). Yet neither are they ethnographic documentary; they tell only very short stories that need to be situated in a wider more informative ethnographic context to be meaningful. These video clips sit between realist and expressive representations since they are short visual documents that form part of constructed ethnographic narratives where they are situated by spoken or written words and other clips. By using video clips in this way, I have been able to avoid having to use spoken and written words to describe visual knowledge. Digital video clips can now easily be inserted into PowerPoint presentations (see also El Guindi

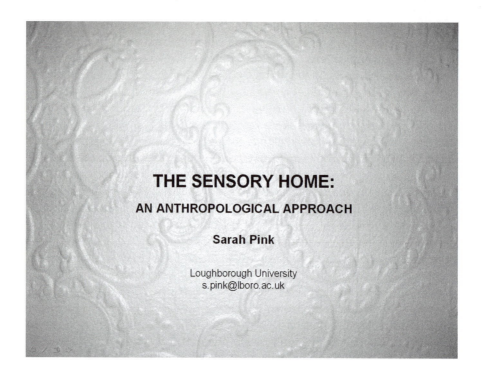

THE SENSORY HOME:

AN ANTHROPOLOGICAL APPROACH

Sarah Pink

Loughborough University
s.pink@lboro.ac.uk

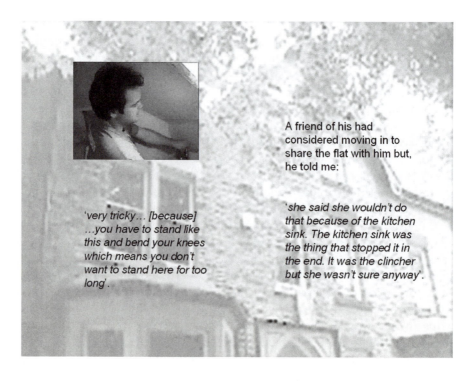

A friend of his had considered moving in to share the flat with him but, he told me:

'very tricky... [because] ...you have to stand like this and bend your knees which means you don't want to stand here for too long'..

'she said she wouldn't do that because of the kitchen sink. The kitchen sink was the thing that stopped it in the end. It was the clincher but she wasn't sure anyway'.

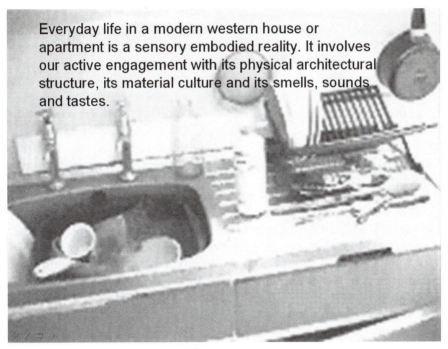

Everyday life in a modern western house or apartment is a sensory embodied reality. It involves our active engagement with its physical architectural structure, its material culture and its smells, sounds and tastes.

© *Sarah Pink 2005*

Figure 7.1
When I presented a paper at the Interior Insights symposium at the Royal College of Art (2005) I used a PowerPoint presentation to combine video, photographs and written text. I was not alone in this, as several of the other speakers also used the same range of different media in their own PowerPoint presentations. In the slides reproduced here I show how I used close-up photographs of the textures of home (slide 1) and a video still background foregrounded with a video clip, contextualizng words and quotations from the video transcript (slide 2) and a video still of an everyday domestic reality overlaid with academic writing (slide 3).

During the presentations an interesting ethical issue arose: some of the members of the audience were practising a form of visual note-taking during the presentations. They were photographing the slides from the speakers' presentations as they were screened. This raises another layer of issues relating to consent. A research participant may have agreed that a specific researcher may show a video clip of her or him in public, but not that another individual may subsequently copy it by photographing or video recording the presentation. I asked these members of the audience not to photograph during my presentation.

2004), which are now becoming a quite standard presentation format amongst social scientists. These, like web page design (see Chapter 8), offer us exciting opportunities to present visual texts, written and spoken words *in relation to each other* in public contexts (see Figure 7.1).

Ethnographic representation is not just books and films. Whereas these are more permanent ways of making statements about ethnographic experiences and theoretical concerns, conference and seminar presentations are also an important part of academic work and offer opportunities to present ideas to wider audiences. Conferences and seminars are also ideal situations for presenting short video clips in combination with other images and texts. Moving images (and sound) can distinguish a dry paper, read to an audience that has already listened to other speakers for hours, from a lively, evocative presentation that engages its audience visually, as well as in words, inviting them to participate in interpreting visual knowledge and view images that were part of the research experience described in the paper. Video clips can also be used in ethnographic exhibitions, where they may be set alongside written texts, photographs or other artistic installations. When planning video and/or PowerPoint presentations it is important to ensure in advance that appropriate video screening, compatible computing facilities and projection facilities are available.

Video narratives that combine ethnographic footage with other media

Video clips that are combined with other visual, spoken and written text for conference presentations and ethnographic exhibitions may also be edited with these other materials into a more complete video for dissemination. Video offers an option that follows a linear narrative constructed by the video editor. Such ethnographic videos differ from conventional ethnographic documentaries as they consist of not only observational documentary footage but also other visual sources and spoken narratives that might include voice over, written text inserts, photographic stills, the researcher's 'talking head', or acted-out reconstructed scenes. They may include novel uses of video footage that challenge conventional ethnographic documentary formats, but explore the potential of the medium further. For example in his documentary *Passing Girl, Riverside*, Braun (1998) used the same video clip of a girl passing his camera repeatedly to the voiceover of the video maker reflecting on the power relations involved in producing that image. The composition of such documentary videos emphasizes their constructedness and their authors' selectivity. A more recent example is Jay Ruby's use of video as part of his CD ROM series *Oak Park Stories*. Here his video texts include scenes in which he is alternatively in front of and behind the camera; photographic slides from his informants' digital and printed collections; and scrolling text (see Pink 2005: ch. 6 for a fuller analysis of Ruby's work). Here in a way quite different from Braun, Ruby creates a video narrative that also reflects on the context of its own production and contains contextualizing written knowledge.

Description, transcripts and video stills

Some would predict that in the near future print publishing will be superseded by the ever-increasing on-line publishing. Nevertheless, at the beginning of the twenty-first century, book and journal publishing is still the dominant medium for disseminating ethnography as well as for advancing academic careers, thus obliging researchers to represent their work in written words. For some researchers who work extensively with video, publishing their work in printed form can be understandably frustrating. For projects that really require that moving images form part of their representations on-line CD-ROM and DVD publications provide one option. I discuss these in Chapter 8. Another possibility is to include still photographs or video stills and written text in the printed form and the video clips on a related website, as Cristina Grasseni has done (see Grasseni 2004 and www.lboro.ac.uk/departments/ss/workingimagesbook/ch2.htm). Here, in this section, I discuss how video may form part of printed ethnography as written description, transcripts of video conversations and captured video stills. In contrast to the idea that visual knowledge should be interpreted and translated into written words, this approach emphasizes the presence of video in research and representation. While written description, transcription and stills do not act on the reader of written text in the same way that screening ethnographic video can, they allow the visual and spoken knowledge of video to become part of ethnographic representation. Existing printed texts that use video stills or transcripts tend to reflect on the role of video in the research and make the process of analysis and the relationship between research and representation explicit.

In Chapter 4 I described Lomax and Casey's use of video in research about midwives' home visits. This work is published in an on-line article that embeds video transcripts, digitized sound tracks and video stills in the written text. Lomax and Casey take a realist approach, arguing that '[v]ideo generated data is an ideal resource ... as it can provide a faithful record of the process as an aspect of the naturally occurring interaction that comprises the research topic' (1998: 1). Their sociological approach incorporates a response to anticipated criticisms from 'traditional' sociology (as do Prosser and other visual sociologists discussed in Chapter 1), that suggests that greater reflexivity can be achieved by including video in the text. Justifying their use of video against 'scientific' sociological opposition they argue that: 'Far from being a distraction or unimportant a reflexive analysis of the research process can contribute to an understanding of the phenomenon under investigation' (1998: 6). In addition to video materials, Lomax and Casey also provide lengthy quotations from field notes where the use of video was discussed, thus situating video within the wider research process. Each line of their transcribed conversations is numbered and submitted to a conversation analysis method by which the transcripts and digitized sound presented in the text are analysed. By presenting field notes, video transcripts and stills in the same text, the processes of research and analysis are evoked in the text. Lomax and Casey also make good use of video stills to discuss how midwives and their clients managed the camera during examinations of genitalia and other personal body parts by either switching it off or using their bodies to obstruct its view. The authors also participate in this strategy of concealment by blurring their informants' faces to guard their privacy. Lomax and Casey succeed in representing the visual and verbal qualities of video without including moving video images themselves in the text. Tim Dant (2004) has also used video stills to represent aspects of work practices. In his study video-recording was used extensively to research the everyday practices of car mechanics working in garages. To represent this work he combines video stills, written descriptions of the activity visually and aurally represented on the video-recording (which reference the stills included in the text) and sections of transcriptions of the spoken interactions that are recorded on the video (between mechanics and between mechanics and researcher). Dant complains that 'when still images are used to illustrate text, the crucial flow of action is lost (hands gesturing, holding the wiper as it moves)', but suggests that one quotation technique would be to 'use series of still "frames" in sequence that show how non-verbal forms of communication are integrated within talk' (2004: 58).

In Chapter 4 I discussed Ferrándiz's use of video in his research with a Venezuelan spirit cult. In his (1998) essay about using video in this research, Ferrándiz includes descriptive passages about the video footage, sometimes quoting words spoken by the video's subjects and including still images captured from the video. Ferrándiz attempts to evoke the *experience* of video research in his text in a different way to the more realist approaches employed in the examples discussed in the previous paragraph. The article begins with the following text alongside a video still of a fingerprint and the handwritten name 'ELOY':

> 'What is this fellow doing?'
> 'He is filming, *compadre*'.
> 'Filming what, a paper or something?'
> 'Yes'
> 'Find me a feather, and ink, and all that stuff, so I can also film. Let me show you how I film, *carajito*'.
> (Ferrándiz 1998: 19)

Having attended a presentation of this project, accompanied by a screening of some 20 minutes of the footage that Ferrándiz describes (at a conference organized by the *Taller de Antropologia Visual* in Madrid, in 1996), my own reading of the article was inevitably influenced by my experience of seeing the footage. However, even without an accompanying screening, the text succeeds in interlinking a narrative that represents the experiential elements of video production and viewing with theoretical and ethnographic narratives about the visual and spirit possession. Ferrándiz includes 12 still images from the video tapes. In one section of the article, where he describes how his informants used and interacted with the technology when being filmed by him and when filming one another, he includes a series of video stills from footage shot by himself and different informants. These are either captioned with quotes from tapes in which video subjects addressed the camera verbally, or with Ferrándiz's descriptions. For example, an image of a woman videoed by 'Ruben' is captioned: 'Ruben as cinematographer, interacting with Carmencita la Canelita (possessing Teresa) through the camera' (1998: 28). In this project video images and technology became a medium of communication and representation between and among researcher and informants. As video was so important to Ferrándiz's research narrative his written text would be incomplete without it: the video images could not be translated into words. The video stills are not merely 'I was there' images or realist recordings, but fragments of the video images through which meanings were created and communicated in the research. These video stills play at the edge of realism and fiction. They challenge the idea of visual truth as, in the case of the caption I have quoted above, some of the stills are of people who are not there, but whose bodies are possessed by spirits and are therefore someone else. In other contexts video might be represented through written description and printed extracts from transcripts. In the book based on my own video ethnography *Home Truths* (Pink 2004b) I used this strategy in order to preserve the privacy of those informants who had given me access to the intimate spaces of their homes, but did not want to be identified in public.

Further uses of video stills may include constructing visual narratives, as in a photo-essay (see Chapter 6), montage images, or poster presentations. Photographic narratives or montage might be composed, for example, of video stills that represent a series of points or themes from the research. Arranged together in the same montage image or as a series of captioned images, stills can create expressive representations that interlink different moments and themes in the research. Presented in this way, stills can also allow people to view a visual research narrative differently, without demanding that it is viewed in a linear video narrative. Expressive montage images and poster presentations offer possibilities for further creativity – montage or posters may combine video stills, photographs and other depictions, interview quotations and academic commentaries.

Video stills and transcripts may be used in printed text as both realist and expressive representations. As the examples I have discussed demonstrate, ethnographers have used stills as evidential data, claims of the ethnographer's authority, as well as symbolic or evocative images of the context in which they were produced, the social relationships this involved and the knowledge associated with it.

Collaboration

As Barbash and Taylor point out, 'Documentary filmmaking is by nature collaborative. Quite simply, it's impossible to make a film about other people completely on your own' (1997: 74). Video research is equally collaborative. However, the final stages of making finished ethnographic representations tend to involve less collaboration and, as Barbash and Taylor note for film, there is a danger 'the film maker will remain the real author, with the participants simply being brought in to legitimate a collaborative rubber stamp' (1997: 89). Indeed, in the case of documentary films made for television, and using broadcast practices, control of the editing process is usually the domain of the film company, even if film subjects are invited to comment on or have some input into the editing. As Garry Marvin puts it: 'Here what is generally required is that those who participate in a documentary must sign a "release form" that allows the producers of the film to use the person's voice and image in any way, within the limits of the law, they chose' (2005: 199). Ethnographic documentaries made by academic researchers, however, tend to work according to more collaborative methods. In some ethnographic documentary projects the film's subjects have participated in editing or commented on how they and their cultures are represented. For example, the film *Zulay Frente al Siglo XXI* (Prelorain et al. 1992) represents the experiences of Zulay, who travels from Ecuador to Los Angeles in the USA to participate in editing an ethnographic film from footage shot of her. When documentaries cover sensitive topics this may help ensure that a film's political or other implications are not problematic for its subjects. For instance, the Spanish *A Buen Común* ethnographic documentary making team (Camas et al. 2004) describe how their collaborative approach revealed that one of their film's protagonists was not comfortable with the edited version of a documentary he appeared in. Their videos are developed through a process of constant feedback from both informants and team members. They describe, how when making their documentary *La Piel del Monte*

> (w)e were surprised to discover that one of the main protagonists was not satisfied with the final video. After watching and discussing the film with him we concluded that he did not like how he came across and, worse still, he was worried about the repercussions his words could have on his public image in a community of less than 1,000 inhabitants. (Camas et al. 2004: 138)

In this work the video subjects had the right to 'paralyse the editing process and eliminate the fragments that were most compromising for them' (2004: 138), thus giving them significant control over how they would be represented in the final film product. In Figure 4.1 I discussed Zemirah Moffat's work, another example of an ethnographic documentary project in which the film's protagonists (of which she herself is also one) comment on the process of representation. Here, in the film making process, and in the film itself, the question of trust and the relationship the filmmaker develops with the other people in the film is brought to the surface at the outset.

Often though ethnographers might find that they have to edit their video clips or documentary and write up their texts alone or with the support of technical specialists. Particularly for students and unfunded researchers, it could be costly to return to a distant research site, or to host informants at home after returning, thus making it difficult to show people how they are represented and receive their impressions of rough-cuts.

Researchers who work in areas close to their own homes might have more opportunities to collaborate with informants, whose participation may not solely let them influence how they are represented in the public domain, but may also increase the researcher's understanding of them. In some cases, however, I have found that people I have video-recorded have told me that they do not mind me editing and showing images of them and they do not wish to see these before they are screened in public. While this allows me freedom to work as I like with the materials, my own experience is that because the burden of judging whether a representation is appropriate then falls completely on me as the video maker, then my position is one in which I must take total responsibility for getting it right. Thus the burden is greater.

A final form of collaboration in the representation of ethnographic video is when the video subjects, or protagonists, are also involved in the public presentation of the video. In some cases ethnographic filmmakers have been able to source funding to bring the people who are in their documentaries to the film festivals they are screened at. The benefit of this is that they can also participate in introducing the film and in the sessions where questions are asked about the film and its production (see for example Camas et al. 2004: 136).

The examples discussed in this section have referred mainly to work that has been produced as part of edited ethnographic documentary films. However, the issues raised apply equally to using short edited or unedited clips or video stills.

Ethics

General ethical concerns were discussed in Chapter 2. In this chapter the examples I have discussed above have highlighted some ethical issues specific to using video in ethnographic representation and demonstrate how these were dealt with in existing projects. For example, Lomax and Casey (1998) have blurred their informants' faces to conceal their identities and Braun's (1998) video raised the question of whether, when people consent to be filmed, they are really 'informed' about how they will be represented and how others will interpret this. As I noted for photography in Chapter 6, using consent or release forms can help clarify intentions in some contexts but they do not necessarily resolve the ethical issues that ethnographers are confronted with at the point of representing others on video. Some ethnographers have tried to resolve this by showing their video footage to the people represented in it, inviting them to participate in the process of editing and representation. Finally, as I noted in Chapter 2, an ethical approach also involves attempting to anticipate how one's representations will be interpreted by a range of other individual, institutional, political and moral subjectivities.

Summary

In this chapter I explored some of the issues and potentials of video for ethnographic representation. As I have demonstrated, there are many more possibilities for video representation than simply ethnographic documentary production. Nevertheless, while I have departed from the emphasis on finished ethnographic documentary videos or films, the debates surrounding ethnographic documentary provide a background for understanding video in ethnographic representation. These existing debates will inevitably inform how other academics receive video representations of ethnography. Moreover, the theory that informs discussions of contemporary ethnographic documentary is well developed and can inform other video representations. Producers of video representations can also learn from the attention ethnographic filmmakers and critics have recently begun to pay to the audiences of their representations.

FURTHER READING

Barbash, I. and Taylor, L. (1997) *Cross Cultural Filmmaking: A Handbook for Making Documentary and Ethnographic Films and Video*, London: University of California Press. (a practical guide to ethnographic filmmaking)

Camas, V., Martínez, A., Muñoz, R. and Ortiz, M. (2004) 'Revealing the hidden: making anthropological documentaries', in S. Pink, L. Kürti and A. Afonso (eds), *Working Images*, London: Routledge. (An example of collaborative filmmaking practice)

Henley, P. (2004) 'Beyond observational cinema', in S. Pink, L. Kürti and A.I. Afonso (eds) *Working Images*, London: Routledge.

MacDougall, D. (2005) *The Corporeal Image*, Princeton: Princeton University Press. (Includes a useful discussion of MacDougall's 'Doon School' project)

Marvin, G. (2005) 'Research, representations and responsibilities: an anthropologist in the contested world of fox hunting', in S. Pink (ed.), *Applications of Anthropology*, Oxford: Berghahn. (A useful discussion of ethical issues in the context of the making of a television documentary based on the author's work)

8

Ethnographic Hypermedia Representation

Digital media and ethnographic representation

The internet and digital technologies are part of the everyday personal and professional lives of most researchers and students of ethnography. During the past 10 or so years, visual ethnographers in social sciences and humanities have published an increasing number of hypermedia texts in on-line journals, individual and project-based websites, CD ROM and DVD. Hypermedia offers exciting possibilities for ethnographic representation. Some of these are demonstrated in existing ethnographic hypermedia texts. Nevertheless, this remains an emergent field of practice and new work is constantly developing alongside changing theoretical and technical innovations. Here I outline existing possibilities and practices as a basis that researchers might wish to build on and depart from to develop their own contributions. New technologies generate new research areas and debates in social science, including the study of digital media as representation, ethnographic studies of media practices and experiences, and theories of electronic communication. Attention has now turned away from the postmodern theories of decentred identities that dominated internet studies during the 1990s (e.g. Poster 1995), towards ethnographic studies rooted in the everyday internet practices of individuals and communities (e.g. Miller and Slater 2000; Postill 2005). Methodologically, as on-line, hypermedia and digital ethnography have developed through a series of project-based case studies (e.g. Hine 2000; Biella 2004; Ruby 2004: CD; Dicks et al. 2005), a more mature literature on the use of electronic media in ethnographic research and representation has also emerged (see also Banks 2001: ch. 6).

In this chapter I suggest a reflexive approach to knowledge may be applied to hypermedia. First, by embedding reflexivity in the text itself as an element of hypermedia *representation* and, secondly, by encouraging hypermedia users to take a reflexive approach to how they create knowledge through their own interactions with hypermedia, thus developing reflexivity as *practice*. In the second part of the chapter I discuss three different areas of hypermedia practice, each of which produces a different category of text: on-line journal articles; on-line resources; and CD-ROM and DVD publications. Although most readers will be familiar with internet and multimedia texts, I recommend examining some actual ethnographic hypermedia texts alongside reading this chapter.

What is ethnographic hypermedia text?

While lengthy debates raged over ethnographic film (see Chapter 7), ethnographic hypermedia representation has been quietly accepted by social scientists (if not yet broadly engaged with). Although hypermedia representations can differ radically from printed text, they can also imitate and reproduce the conventions and objectives of printed words and images. They do not necessarily dramatically challenge existing styles of representation, but can embody continuities with established forms. Most existing hypermedia representations simultaneously imitate and transgress written text, photography and film. In fact such continuities are essential to the ability of ethnographic hypermedia representations to contribute to existing bodies of empirical and theoretical work (see Pink 2005).

Interactive hypermedia publications usually consist of sets of interlinked files that contain written words, still or moving images, sound, or a combination of these. The interlinkages between files, or points (e.g. words and images, theoretical sections and ethnographic description) within files, support the interactivity of hypermedia. But in addition to this, 'the links themselves have meaning' (Biella 1996: 595). As Dicks et al. put it, 'Hyperlinking means that multimedia ... is no longer simply the juxtaposition of image, text and sound, but the creation of multiple interconnections and pathways (or traversals) among them' (2005: 85). Users move between files through hyperlinks embedded in their text as well as using other navigation tools. Hyperlinks are represented with words or visual symbols and by clicking on one users move from one point in a text to another point in that or another text. The ways users can interact with texts depends on how their authors have used the software to construct links between different text files. As such, hypermedia *design* is fundamental to the ethnographic and academic meanings that the text can evoke.

Here I discuss internet, CD ROM and DVD representations. Although each medium can represent similar types of text, there are crucial differences. CD ROM, and more so DVD, has higher storage capacity and faster retrieval of higher-quality photographic and video images than internet. Internet publications are more widely accessible and, published on-line, can be less bounded than CD ROMs and DVDs. Despite this, many e-journal versions of subscription journals have restricted access. I do not discuss these here since, like e-books, they are usually published electronically in pdf files that replicate the printed versions. While they benefit from on-line access (albeit only to paying subscribers), they do not usually exploit the possibilities on-line publishing might offer for innovative uses of hyperlinks or visual media. To capitalize on the potential of both on-line and circumscribed CD or DVD publishing, a CD or DVD containing higher quality images might be embedded with hyperlinks that take users outside the boundaries of the CD ROM to access other internet materials. However, my emphasis here is not on the technical qualities of on-line versus CD ROM or DVD for electronic publishing. These are rapidly developing or being superseded by higher capacity technologies.

The ethnographicness of hypermedia texts should be judged in ways similar to ethnographic photography or film. No hypermedia text is essentially ethnographic. Different approaches might label the same text (or parts of it) ethnographic, or not. Hypermedia texts may contain different texts and narratives, some of which may conform to conventional styles of ethnographic writing or visual representation, whereas other parts of the text represent 'experimental' forms created by the author, informants' texts, or other research documents of various origins. Some texts may be composed completely of ethnographic research materials and reports; in others only certain strands will represent the ethnographic element of a project. In this sense the ethnographicness of hypermedia texts is determined partially by the intentions of its authors and users and the routes that they choose to imply and take through it. The relationship of an ethnographic hypermedia text to an academic discipline is also contingent on the design and intentions of its author. While one might imagine a simply ethnographic text that solely reports on ethnographic realities encountered during fieldwork, it is unlikely it could ever be *purely* ethnographic and uninformed by the methodological and theoretical approaches of any academic discipline(s). The more appropriate distinction to make is between, on the one hand, those ethnographic hypermedia texts that are simply informed by academic ideas and, on the other, those that actually explicitly engage in and contribute to existing discourses already ongoing within academia. This might involve referencing an existing ethnographic documentary filmically through imitation or another strategy, or it might mean including a theoretical written text that contributes to a theoretical debate within one or across several disciplines. Combining different types of knowledge and media offers a promising way forward for visual ethnographic representation. As part of this the continuities between existing forms of academic communication and those represented in a hypermedia text form essential links between existing academic practice and debate and the enhanced possibilities offered by hypermedia.

Multilinearity, montage and multivocality: hypermedia as experimental and collaborative text

In the Introduction to Part 3, I noted how calls for reflexive and multivocal approaches to ethnographic representation questioned the authenticity and authority of conventional ethnographic representations. In Chapters 6 and 7 I described how ethnographic writers and video makers have responded to these criticisms. Hypermedia, with its capacity to represent multiple media, in multiple narratives, offers exciting possibilities.

Hypermedia can represent ethnographic knowledge multilinearly. By creating a series of different strands, hypermedia authors can represent simultaneous but different narratives and knowledge and use hyperlinks to connect these strands. While printed text can also be accessed non-linearly, it has been argued that conventional linear ethnographic texts do not appropriately represent the complexity or diversity of contemporary culture, society and experience. Howard, an early advocate of ethnographic hypermedia, pointed out that 'where connections between phenomena are as interrelated as they are in human communities, the job of orchestrating even a limited degree of interconnectivity in the written medium is a struggle at best' (1988: 305). More recently, Marcus argued that anthropologists should 'come to terms with multiple agencies in varying locales' and study the relationship between elements of an increasingly deterritorialized 'culture' that is 'the product of parallel diverse and simultaneous worlds operating consciously and blindly with regard to each other' (Marcus 1995: 51). He suggested that the conventional linear narrative of anthropological writing should be re-thought and that the cinematic technique of montage offered a better template for representing the multiple locations in which culture and individuals simultaneously exist (1995: 53). While Marcus proposes this effect should be developed in printed ethnographies, hypermedia can also develop multilinear texts that can simultaneously represent narratives told from different standpoints, by different 'voices' in different media, as well as the connections between these narratives.

Multilinearity is a common feature in ethnographic hypermedia design, although, as the examples discussed below reveal, less so in on-line journal publishing and more so in CD ROM and DVD representations. Forms of montage are likewise developing in ethnographic hypermedia; a good example is Coover's (2003: CD) *Cultures in Webs*, also discussed below. However, perhaps surprisingly, multivocal and co-authored hypermedia ethnographies have been slower to develop. There are, nevertheless, two existing examples of how this might develop, in the work of Stephen Lyon and Jay Ruby, discussed in the section on on-line resource sites.

Between design and experience:
hypermedia texts and their users

Like readers and viewers of written and filmic ethnography, ethno-graphic hypermedia users participate in interpreting ethnographic representations. This raises issues that should inform how ethnographers design the structure and navigation of hypermedia representations. Ethnographic hypermedia design is a new practice and an analysis of the texts produced during the past 10 years shows that as yet there is no standard design format as exists, for example, for academic books (Pink 2005).

Initial concerns about ethnographic hypermedia representation referred to their potential incoherence and threadlessness. In the late 1990s Henley criticized a 'tendency for CD ROMs to be presented as authorless aggregates of objective information which the user can wander over at will, creating his or her own narrative threads' (Henley 1998: 55). Likewise, Biella agreed with Banks (1994) and acknowledged that 'disorientation can affect [hypermedia] users who do not follow a plan, a coherent itinerary' (Biella 1994: 6). Henley's and Banks's criticisms do represent genuine concerns. Nevertheless, these criticisms do not refer to a characteristic of hypermedia itself. Rather, they imply issues of authorship, design and navigation, and raise the question of the reader/viewer/user. Indeed, these issues could apply equally to montage styles in printed text, which were also characterized as chaotic and lacking a structuring narrative; Marcus warned that 'extreme montage' may lose both its coherence and its audience (1995: 46). In fact, the examples discussed below suggest ethnographic hypermedia projects developed since tend to be highly structured and conspicuously authored. In different ways they manage to, as Dicks et al. recommend, enable 'the reader to access *both* the data *and* the researcher's interpretations of them' (2005: 164).

Henley and Banks both identified the relationship between hyper-media texts and their users as key to the coherence of ethnographic hypermedia. The question of coherence cannot be resolved by simply interrogating hypermedia representations themselves, but needs to account for the dynamic between user and text. Readers/users/viewers of ethnographic text have frequently been neglected in existing discussions of representation that focus largely on ethnographers, informants, texts and their construction. Although slightly more concern has been directed to ethnographic film audiences (see especially Crawford and Hafsteinsson 1996; Martinez 1990, 1992, 1996; Stoller 1997; and Chapter 7 of this book), the creativity of readers, lone students, academics, ex-informants, whoever, who experience ethnographic text, scribble in margins, underline, draw on photographs and participate in producing ethnographic knowledge has received little attention. While some work has considered interactive hypermedia users (e.g. Orr Vered 1998), ethnographic hypermedia users' experiences are largely unknown (apart from Biella 1994 and Pink 1999c). Nevertheless, for at least two reasons it is important to understand how ethnographic hypermedia is received: first, because as Howard suggested, 'hypermedia has the potential for establishing an entirely new kind of relationship between authors and readers' (1988: 311); secondly, since Martinez (2004) demonstrated students might not interpret ethnographic films as intended by the filmmakers, it is important to attend to the strategies and intentionalities of ethnographic hypermedia users.

A focus on ethnographic hypermedia users can also inform questions about how and why hypermedia becomes chaotic or coherent and how users might appropriate different types of structure and design. The coherence of ethnographic hypermedia is created in the relationship between the design of the text and its interpretation. It depends on authors' creativity for the former and users' for the latter. Howard suggested hypermedia would challenge ethnographers to provide readers with theoretically informed multiple pathways constructed with 'a sense of interconnectivity that is based on a theory of multi-stranded relationships' (1988: 311). Nevertheless, as Biella emphasized, users also play a crucial role in making hypermedia coherent as '[l]inks incline: they do not impel. Disciplined users must resist tantalizing distractions if only to pursue with greater fervour those links that reward their research passions all the more' (Biella 1994: 6). While hypermedia texts, properly designed and constructed, offer coherent narratives (see Biella 1994: 6), it is also up to users to construct coherence. However much ethnographers tailor hypermedia representations, without the creative collaboration of their users, texts are only ever implied and partial because while hypermedia representation might be constructed as multilinear texts, individuals use them to create linear narratives. As Orr Vered pointed out, non-linearity refers to a situation where 'access to information is not dependent on serial sequencing or reflection on the order of a mirror'. Nevertheless, 'linearity is the end result of this process, despite the order in which information is acquired' (Orr Vered 1998: 42; see also Biella 1994: 6). Therefore, if the user's task is to create his or her own linear narrative through a multilinear text, the author's role is to facilitate this. By obliging users to participate in this way, hypermedia differs from books and films. New texts demand or inspire new types of user engagement.

Our understanding of how individual users interpret hypermedia representations can be informed by considering how digital media are consumed and appropriated in the practices and discourses of contemporary culture and society (see Banks 1994: 2; Silverstone and Hirsch 1993). In Chapter 7 I discussed intersubjectivity between filmmakers, film texts and audiences, and how viewing contexts may impact on how individuals interpret ethnographic films. To understand how users interpret ethnographic hypermedia representations implies questions of how they experience and appropriate technologies, software and multi-linearity as well as a text's actual content. In the 1990s grand proposi-tions that digital photography would rupture existing practices and beliefs about photographic truth bringing about the 'death of photogra-phy' (Robbins 1995: 29) could not be substantiated when one looked at the continuities between 'new' digital photographic practices and con-ventions and those that had already existed (T. Wright 1998: 207). Likewise Poster's 1990s argument that placed us in a 'second media age' (1995: 4), where electronically mediated communication 'enacts a radi-cal reconfiguration of language, one which constitutes subjects outside the pattern of the rational, autonomous individual' and where '[t]his familiar modern subject is displaced by the mode of information in favour of one that is multiple, disseminated and decentered, continu-ously interpellated as an unstable identity' (Poster 1995: 57) is quite untenable when one studies ethnographically what people actually *do* with new media (see for instance the work of Postill 2005; Miller and Slater 2000). The relationship between electronic technologies and indi-viduals can be more usefully understood by focusing on practice, expe-rience and the continuities between how individuals experience their identities when using hypermedia and traditional texts. Since individu-als interact with and experience hypermedia differently, hypermedia authors might wish to account for the various strategies in which users engage. Research about users' actual practices and experiences can inform this, and projects designed to test existing ethnographic hyper-media projects have shown how some users describe their experiences. For instance, my research into users' experiences of *The Bullfighter's Braid* CD ROM indicated that some felt 'empowered' by the freedom it offered them to choose their own routes through the materials. Others, who found this choice disorientating, did not engage with the possibil-ity of selecting a route self-consciously, but followed the path they thought the author had made most obvious (see Pink 1999c).

In Chapter 1 I argued that ultimately ethnographic knowledge is produced through the concrete personal experience of researchers. Here I apply the same ethnographic approach to the question of how individuals experience, interpret and produce knowledge with electronic hypermedia. Following Cohen (1994), individuals' experiences of everyday life can be seen as a matter of assimilating and making sense out of diverse experi-ences, constantly adapting themselves to these while maintaining intact a sense of their own selves. Therefore, individuals and their sense of self and identity also hold together the multiple narratives of their experi-ences of hypermedia. Thus hypermedia users produce knowledge by making sense of different types of information presented in multiple narratives, and making the text coherent by producing their own linear narratives from it. Each individual user may follow a different route through the multiple narratives of a hypermedia representation, creating their own narratives and unique, experience-based knowledge, which will be inevitably informed by their wider biographical experiences.

Publishing on-line: hypermedia journal articles

For visual ethnographers who need to publish in peer-refereed journals, but also want to include photographic and video materials in their articles, on-line journal publishing presents one possibility. In this section I discuss the potential and limitations of existing formats.

Despite the enormous potential of hypermedia for visual representation, many electronic journals imitate word-processed printed styles. Electronic journals that emerged in the 1990s, such as *Sociological Research On-line* and *The Journal of Music and Anthropology*, are largely dominated by conventions governing printed text, whereby written words lead and structure the text and frame uses of visual and audio files. In on-line journals hyperlinks facilitate some strategies that readers may already practise, such as hyperlinks that take readers directly from a reference in the text to a full citation in the bibliography (e.g. *Sociological Research On-line*). Hypermedia also responds well to serving readers' established expectations. Biella has pointed out that one of the conventional requirements of scholarly work is that it 'must be inscribed in a medium that allows rapid, non-linear access to all its components' (Biella 1993: 144), suggesting authors should assume that their texts will be read non-linearly (1993: 145). Comparing electronic text to printed and film representations, Biella noted how '[r]andom-access navigation is often attributed exclusively to electronic media, but it is clearly a property which facilitated scholarship in books [but not in film] long before the computer revolution' (1993: 144). Nevertheless there are differences between printed and hypermedia text since, as Howard pointed out, the linearity of printed text imposes constraints because 'writers are forced into linear sequential mode and are compelled to choose which aspects of a total experience are to be placed first, second, third, etc. The only way to vitalize interconnections that are nonsequential, or multisequential, is to refer back to previous pages' (Howard 1988: 305). Clearly, hypermedia supports and can even encourage non-linear approaches to creating and reading seemingly conventional ethnographic representations. In doing so, Howard argued '[h]ypertext thus articulates with actual modes of thinking far better than linearly written materials' (1988: 306). This suggests the linear narrative of printed text is not conversant with how we produce or use ethnographic knowledge. Some would take this further to argue that the very construction and content of ethnographic texts should challenge the notion of linearity (e.g. Marcus 1995). As yet, articles published in on-line journals have not engaged fully with the multilinear potential of hypermedia.

Articles published in on-line, refereed journals also imitate printed versions in that they are presented as 'complete'. This limits how their authors can respond to the possibilities of on-line publishing. Once published, journal articles are not updated or altered. Moreover, subscription-based on-line journals are usually discrete entities, isolated from other internet resources or websites, and can only be accessed through routes created by their publisher. Although this is necessary for the economic viability of journal publishing, it limits the potential of internet publications to be interconnected with, and accessed from, other websites. There have been some exceptions. In the late 1990s the journal *iNtergraph* (formerly at www.intergraphjournal.com but unavailable at the time of writing) was set up by social anthropologists at the University of Hull, UK. The journal was freely accessible and provided open spaces for dialogue with users. *iNtergraph* was also interesting because it included photographic exhibitions as part of its publications brief. Current free access on-line journals, such as *Anthropology Matters* (www.anthropologymatters.com) appear more conventional in their use of photographs within texts, published as pdf files. However, it should be noted that in most existing cases this may not be due to the agenda-setting of the journal's editors but related to the type of contributions that are submitted. One on-line journal project that has attempted to take this further is a special issue of *Sociological Research On-line* edited by Susan Halford and Caroline Knowles, focusing on visual research.

This special issue aims to go beyond written text, and seeing photography and video as ways to represent the performative nature of everyday life, the editors characterize it as a text 'in which the authors use visual imagery in a variety of ways' and that 'captures a live sociology of performances that is not possible without photography and video' (Halford and Knowles 2005: 1.3). They are also conscious of the role of the reader/viewer of sociological text and make it clear that underlying its production was the assumption that its users would also experience it and participate in the creation of meanings from it in new ways. The essays, they write, 'also seek to transform sociological participation, drawing the audience "inside": engaging us, as embodied, sensual beings in the living details of the thing we seek to understand' (Halford and Knowles 2005: 1.9). The different articles included in the issue develop this to different degrees, some simply using the capacity of electronic publication to include an extended number of colour photographs and other scanned images framed by a written argument (e.g. Chaplin 2005; Farrar 2005). Even these articles go beyond the possibilities of a journal like *Visual Studies* (discussed in Chapter 6) in their use of colour.

The article that expands the possibilities of hypermedia most creatively, however, is Monika Büscher's 'Social life under the microscope?', which discusses both the embodied work practices of designers and the use of video to research these. Büscher points out that 'Design sessions ... draw to our attention that formulating is not restricted to talk, as drawing, gesturing, enactments, and embodied reference to images, plans or features in the surroundings can all reflexively formulate the imagined object and the scenic intelligibility of the activity' (2005: 3.3). Here the ability of video to represent the embodied and sensory nature of human practice and experience is key. Büscher's article is also worth reading as an example of video methodology, although here I reflect on it as an example of a hypermedia article. Büscher makes interesting and extensive use of the potential of hypermedia to include video, still images and composite images within a written narrative.

Her text in many ways follows the conventional structure of a written essay. It is produced in a linear form and divided into sections, following the established style of *Sociological Research Online*. However, linked to this written narrative, in a way that is acutely aware that 'Neither video nor microscopes can provide a way of seeing through to an independent natural or social reality' (2005: 11.1), she uses video, animations, photographs and other images (e.g. maps, examples of design drawings) both as realist images of what is done and what actually happened and to bring examples of her data into the text and make aspects of her analysis explicit. The introduction of so much of the visual data into the text also invites the viewer to several possibilities, including: to engage with the experiences of the people represented on a personal and empathetic level; to re-analyse the data her- or himself; to reflect on not only the design process as it is represented in the text, but also on the research process as it is embedded in the video data. In addition to video clips, Büscher also makes creative and interesting uses of video transcripts and still images to represent aspects of the design process. In these representations that combine writing and image she is able to emphasize aspects of the design process in ways that would not be achievable by simply playing a video clip on-line.

Because Büscher's article follows existing conventions established for written on-line articles it is easily accessible to mainstream academics. It does not demand that the reader/viewer's initial form of engagement with the text involves vastly unfamiliar practices. Nevertheless, within this familiar frame it invites the new forms of engagement I suggested above, and as such allows the reader/viewer access to forms of knowledge that could not be evoked in a conventional printed text. This work provides an excellent example of how hypermedia can extend and enhance the capabilities of existing publishing conventions without challenging existing practices of academic communication. It is nevertheless limited in that by adopting the linear narrative of conventional academic writing (which it only transgresses to 'branch out' into hyperlinked visual examples) it does not take full advantage of the creative possibilities offered by hypermedia.

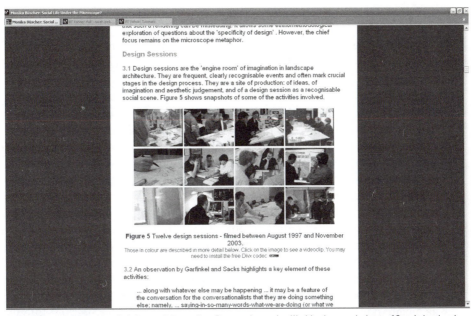

Each image here is a link to a video clip. Reproduced with kind permission of Sociological Research Online

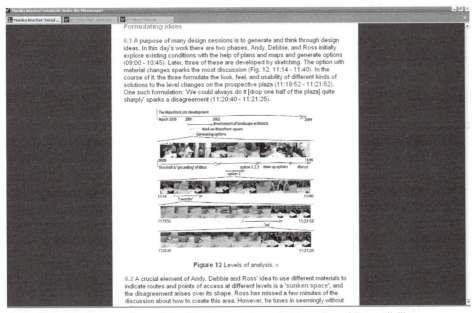

The sequences here are hyperlinked to transcripts and video clips of the activities represented. Reproduced with kind permission of Sociological Research Online

Figure 8.1

Uses of video in Monika Büscher's article published in *Sociological Research Online* (2005).

On-line visual ethnography resources

The art of creating a structured, bounded and finished written or visual narrative is one of the skills of conventional ethnographic writing and filmmaking. Many ethnographers recognize that the capacity of these bounded, linear texts to represent a reality that is in fact continuous and subjectively experienced is limited; at best ethnographers can only reconstruct fragments of a subjective experience of reality. While hyper-media cannot resolve this, it can be used to develop texts that emphasize and recognize the selectivity and specificity of processes of representa-tion and allow their authors to connect 'complete' ethnographic repre-sentations to contextualizing materials and wider resources. For example, finished documentaries might be linked to unedited footage or finished photographs may be contextualized by video clips that repre-sent the research or other photographs that informed the composition of the exhibited or published photograph (such as photographs not selected for exhibition, or informants' own photographs). The notion of open-endedness can also be taken further to regard hypermedia texts as permanently 'unfinished'. Theoretically, this means neither knowl-edge itself nor representations of knowledge are ever complete; inter-pretations are open to re-interpretation and representations may be re-represented. Practically, this means that, unlike printed books and finished films, on-line hypermedia texts may be up-dated, added to, or altered. Video sequences may be re-edited, photographs manipulated in new ways, written words changed and the hyperlinks between them modified. Hypermedia representations are also open-ended because their users can slip over their boundaries and explore their relationship to other texts. Whereas book and journal readers can also do this by cross-referencing other texts, the experience and ease of doing so on-line is different. If authors create hyperlinks between their ethnographic web pages and other existing sites, users can follow links to sites of related interest. These may be sites that are not 'ethnographic' but are of ethno-graphic interest.

There are a number of existing visual ethnography resource sites on-line. Banks (2001) discusses his Haddon project (www.bodley.ox.ac.uk/external/isca/haddon/HADD_home.html), which contains photographic, film and written materials about Alfred Cort Haddon's 1898 British expedition to the Torres Straits Islands. Another significant site is Paul Stirling's *Turkish Village* (discussed below), which contains pho-tographs, field diaries, book and PhD manuscripts produced throughout Stirling's life-time of involvement with the village (at www.lucy.ukc.ac.uk). More recently created is the *Visualising Ethnography* website (www.lboro.ac.uk/departments/ss/visualising_ethnography/) that I pro-duced in 2001. This site was developed as a gateway resource that both publishes its own introductory texts, interviews and articles and provides links to other on-line visual ethnography resources (see Figure 8.5).

While such resource sites may include texts that are 'complete' or 'finished', they are not necessarily presented as complete, discrete or finished texts in themselves. Rather, they are open-ended representations whose form and content may be up-dated, added to and altered. Their authors may create or delete hyperlinks to other websites, in doing so re-situating the resource in relation to other web resources and sites and therefore creating new meanings. In contrast to the 'finished' electronic essay, open-ended hypermedia representations challenge existing forms of ethnographic representation. Their boundaries and form are arbitrary and changing and they lend users greater freedom to organize and structure knowledge and narratives.

Other on-line resource sites are developed to support, or in relationship with, printed books. Often they contain additional resources and images that could not be included in the printed text. For example, Banks's (2001) *Visual Images in Social Research* book was published with a website that provided links and other materials specifically to support the book. Dicks et al.'s (2005) *Qualitative Research and Hypermedia* is also related to a website, although in a less structured way. The book relates to and elaborates on questions represented in the *Digital Ethnography* website, developed by Dicks and her colleagues at Cardiff University, UK (www.cf.ac.uk/socsi/hyper/). The website promises to include examples of their practical work which will allow readers of the book to engage with their hypermedia practice in ways that cannot be achieved through reading a printed text. Finally, Pink et al.'s *Working Images* (2004) is accompanied by a dedicated website that provides additional visual resources and exhibitions to the book on a chapter-by-chapter basis (www.lboro.ac.uk/departments/ss/workingimagesbook/cover.htm). The colour photographs and drawings, video clips and hypermedia samples provided on-line could not be included in the printed text and they allow readers deeper insights into the contributors' visual practice. Other examples include the website of the journal *Visual Anthropology Review*, where similarly visual resources linked to journal articles are posted (http://etext.virginia.edu/VAR/).

The content of the sites discussed above is produced exclusively by academic researchers. However, one of the most exciting possibilities of on-line hypermedia ethnography publishing is its capacity to bring ethnographic research into dialogue with a broader public. Such sites may have restricted access for only research participants or known commentators. However two existing websites that achieve this have unlimited access. One is a website developed by Stephen Lyon while doing his PhD fieldwork in Pakistan in 1998–9 (http://anthropology.ac.uk/Bhalot). Lyon regularly published materials on his fieldwork, including his own notes and photographs, local people's contributions, music and local cultural texts and a selection of comments and questions from visitors to the website. Another is Jay Ruby's *Maintaining Diversity* (http://astro.temple.edu/~ruby/opp/), where he reports on the progress of his ethnographic study of Oak Park, a neighbourhood in the United States (for a discussion of Ruby's CD ROM projects that are also based on this work see above and for an in-depth analysis of this work, see Pink 2005: ch. 6). In the introduction to the site Ruby states that 'This web page is primarily designed for Oak Parkers in the hope that I can get a continuing dialogue from people in the community about this work. In addition it is designed for my graduate students at Temple and for my academic colleagues'. The site contains written and photographic reports of the research from June 2000 to the present (at the time of writing) and Ruby invites his readers to contact him with comments by e-mail. While both Lyon's and Ruby's websites are researcher-driven and authored, by making their work available for the scrutiny of others they demonstrate important moves towards a transparent and public approach to producing ethnographic knowledge. By inviting informants, and a wider (mainly academic) public, to comment on the work, they create possibilities for visual ethnographers to work in dialogue with others.

Ethnographic hypermedia publishing with CD ROM and DVD

Since the late 1990s, interest in ethnographic CD ROM and DVD publishing has gradually developed amongst social scientists and artists using ethnographic approaches. Nevertheless, during the past 10 years still only a handful of projects have emerged. Amongst these, those that stand out are Biella, Chagnon and Seaman's (1997) *Yanomamö Interactive: The Ax Fight*, Coover's (2003) *Cultures in Webs*, Ruby's (2004, 2005) *Oak Park Stories* series, Joanna Kirkpatrick's (2003) *Transports of Delight*, and Hubbard et al.'s (2003) *Sexual Expression in Institutional Care Settings*. In the late 1990s I also developed two CD ROMs *The Bullfighter's Braid* (1998a), and *Interweaving Lives* (1998b) and from 2000 to 2002 developed two further experimental CD ROMs, *Gender at Home* and *Women's Worlds* (discussed in Pink 2005), which I eventually decided to treat as learning processes rather than for publication. In chapter 6 of my book *The Future of Visual Anthropology* I discuss several of these projects in detail in an analysis of the implications of anthropological hypermedia 'for the relationship between visual and written anthropology in academic and applied visual anthropology in the twenty-first century' (Pink 2005: 105; see also S. Harper 2004 for a review of recent projects).

Rather differently, in this section I discuss ethnographic hypermedia CDs and DVD designs that have been developed to date. Then, below I discuss how video and photography have been used in ethnographic hypermedia representations. The examples discussed here are not exhaustive, but rather cases of existing practice that readers might learn from. Since no standard conventions for ethnographic hypermedia publishing have yet developed (Pink 2005), they are diverse in their subject matters, design and aims. Most work in this area has been developed by visual anthropologists, although most recently ethnographic hypermedia texts have also been based on work in visual sociology, social policy and video documentary. My intention is that readers use my comments as an introduction to their own explorations of these texts.

Biella et al.'s *Yanomamö Interactive: The Ax Fight* (1997) is the most established and discussed of these existing texts (Banks 2001: 164–7; Biella 2004; Pink 2005: 109–10; Dicks et al. 2005: 61). Its screen is divided into four sections from which users may access a series of interlinked resources: photographs, historical, descriptive and analytical written texts, film footage, biographical details of 51 people, kinship diagrams, maps, figures and charts. It is an excellent example of a text that takes advantage of the multimedia, multilinear, interactive and reflexive potential of hypermedia. It allows students to view materials in different media simultaneously, interrogate the data themselves, read the reflexive discussions of how knowledge was produced, and view and listen to examples of this from the film footage. While the text is highly structured and authored it allows users to create their own routes through the materials. While this relatively early hypermedia text has been influential in discussions of hypermedia ethnography, later texts do not appear to have been modelled on it. This may be because although *Yanomamö Interactive* contains resources useful to researchers, its primary use is as a teaching text. With the exception of my own *The Bullfighters' Braid* and *Interweaving Lives,* which also had didactic aims, the primary focus of later ethnographic hypermedia projects has been to represent research.

Different authors have approached this in different ways, with some features in common with *Yanomamö Interactive*. For example, hypermedia provides great possibilities for creating structured archives that provide users access to visual and written materials. Kirkpatrick's *Transports of Delight*, a CD ROM about ricksha decorative arts in Bangladesh, contains over 1,000 colour photographs along with videos, music and written texts of different kinds. Making excellent uses of local music, it is divided into three narratives composed of written texts, an annotated photographic gallery and video clips of street scenes. Jay Ruby's *Oak Park Stories* series CD ROMs, *The Taylor Family* (2004) (discussed in Pink 2005: 110–15) and *Rebekah and Sophie* (2005), are also multilinear texts. They are divided into three narratives of Introductory, Text and Video modules. In the first two written words dominate, accompanied by photographs, and some slide shows. In the third moving images dominate in video clips that also reference the value of multimedia in ethnographic representation since some scrolling written text and still images are edited into the video. These narratives and the subsections within them are themselves interlinked and cross-referenced. This also makes the navigation of the text easy as its structure is made explicit from the outset and remains as a constant guide to the user: it is hard to get lost. The CD ROMs are not presented as data archives, although they do

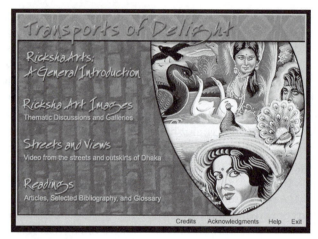

Joanna Kirkpatrick's Transports of Delight (*2003*). © *Joanna Kirkpatrick 2003*

Rod Coover's Cultures in Webs (*2003*). © *Rod Coover 2003*

Jay Ruby's Rebekah and Sophie (*2004*). © *Jay Ruby 2004*

Figure 8.2
Although each of these three CD ROMs is divided into three narratives, in fact the content of these narratives, their treatments of photography, video and writing, and the ways in which the narratives are interlinked with each other, varies considerably between them.

contain video material that, because it takes us directly into the context in which it was produced, inevitably invites re-analysis.

Yet another approach to structure and presentation is provided by Rod Coover's *Cultures in Webs* (2003) – a beautifully designed text that shows appreciation for the relationship between ethnographic representation and aesthetics. This text is also divided into three narratives: a written essay embedded with digitalized clips from ethnographic films discusses montage in ethnographic documentary; a photographic essay represents grape picking in Burgundy (France) (discussed in Coover 2004a); and a more fully multimedia montage essay based on Coovers' travel and video documentary work in Ghana combines photographic stills, video clips and different styles of writing (discussed in Coover 2004b; Pink 2005: 120–5). However, the navigation of Coover's project is quite different from that presented by Ruby's text, as each of these narratives forms a quite linear strand set by the author. While the user can scroll or navigate back and forwards, with the exception of Coovers' Photographic essay, there is limited multilinear access to different sections of the narratives.

Another innovative CD ROM project has been developed by Hubbard et al. (2003) as part of a project about the sexual identities of older people in care homes. This work is structured around a narrative of academic writing in a report style, accessible in sections, from which the user is invited to browse video and transcripts (see Pink 2005: 125–7 for a fuller discussion). Other CD ROMs have taken a less ambitious approach to ethnographic representation. For example, Steiger's *En Route*, published on CD ROM as an addition to the journal *Visual Sociology*, contains only a slide show of a series of photographs already published in the journal and an electronic version of the written text that accompanies them.

Photography in ethnographic hypermedia

A review of existing ethnographic hypermedia publishing indicates that uses of digital photographs often follow the conventional realist approaches I described in Chapter 6 (e.g. Banks n.d.; Lomax and Casey 1998). Other digitized photographs are treated as products of 'photographic moments' rooted in fieldwork experience (e.g. Biella's *Masaai Interactive* and my own *The Bullfighter's Braid*). In earlier hypermedia projects these were scanned prints, now they are usually taken with a digital camera. Existing examples often follow the conventions of using captioning, and written references to give meanings to photographs I discussed in Chapter 6 (see, for example, Chaplin 2005). Some more recent innovations are discussed below.

First, however, I address one of the concerns underlying the use of digital photography: manipulation. While digital manipulation certainly offers ethnographers opportunities to use photography in new ways rather than simply rupturing existing approaches, it also allows researchers to enhance how their photographs represent ethnographic information in conventional ways. Digital manipulation gives ethnographers more autonomy over how their photographs are presented. These techniques of manipulation (such as cropping, or changing the colour mix, hue or brightness) do not necessarily go beyond the results an experienced colour printer could achieve. While theoretically it can be argued that the very manipulability of digital images implies doubt that they are realist representations, many ethnographic digital photographs do not break with realist conventions and are treated (and often interpreted) as realist representations. As Wright points out, '[r]ather than limiting photography's ability to record a "truthful" image, computer manipulation has the potential to broaden the repertoire of the photographic system and to enrich photography's scope and ability to describe the visual world' (T. Wright 1998: 217).

In Chapter 6, I emphasized that the way photographs are situated in relation to other texts or images determines the ethnographic meanings they represent. Hypermedia presents opportunities to depart from the layouts, captions and referencing systems of printed text described in Chapter 6 and offers new ways of interconnecting visual and written knowledge. Embedded in hypermedia text, digitized images can be presented and situated in new ways. For example, they may be enlarged, linked to other images and theoretical texts, connected to visual and written information about the research context, or shown in sequence to correspond with oral narratives. In my CD ROM *The Bullfighter's Braid,* for instance, I linked video clips of myself taking group photographs with the actual photographs and a written discussion. These sequences show how groups united and dispersed for their 'photographic moments', and represent the social and material context of those 'moments'. The fixity of visual meanings may be questioned by presenting the same images in different narratives, in each of which they may take on a new significance. While in printed text photographs occupy one single position and the same photograph is rarely printed more than once, hypermedia allows the same photograph to appear in any number of different narratives so that the multiple contexts in which the photograph becomes meaningful and the arbitrary nature of these meanings can be made explicit. By using the same photographs in different narratives the photographs themselves can also be used as symbols of and meeting points between the different narratives and experiences they refer to. Montage uses of still images in hypermedia can also exploit their potential to create meanings. Coover's *Cultures in Webs* provides excellent examples of this. In his 'Performance' narrative he combines video, writing and still photographs on the same page to build up layers of visual and written meanings of different kinds (see Coover 2004a; Pink 2005). In his 'Practice' text about wine making in Burgundy (France), Coover has created an unusual horizontal text with four narratives. Each horizontal narrative contains a different type of

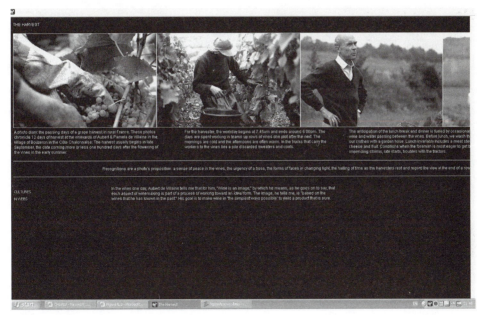

Figure 8.3

A screen capture from the 'Practice' narrative of Rod Coover's *Cultures in Webs*. Note the unusual horizontal narrative.

visual or written knowledge that is interrelated with that represented in the others (see Figure 8.3).

Ways of presenting photographs digitally often reference archive, gallery and exhibition settings. Kirkpatrick's gallery of over 1,000 photographs of rickshas and related objects and practices, is organized on the basis of both local (emic) themes and some additionally discerned by the author (or etic themes). The photographs are annotated as they are combined with a written narrative that situates them. Presented as thumbnails alongside the text, the user is invited to click on the photographs to enlarge and view them (see Figure 8.4).

Slide shows, also produced with similar effects in gallery installations, are also easily produced in digital texts. One example is Steiger's CD ROM *En Route*. Comparing the CD version of the photographic sequence to that printed in the journal the obvious difference is that presented as a slide show this sequence of images of travel and movement are experienced differently: the increased authorial control imposed through the timing and ordering of the slide show prevents the reader from engaging in a more eclectic viewing process that might transgress the linear sequence presented in the printed text. In short, the CD slide show invites us to engage in a way that produces a particular sense of the experience of movement.

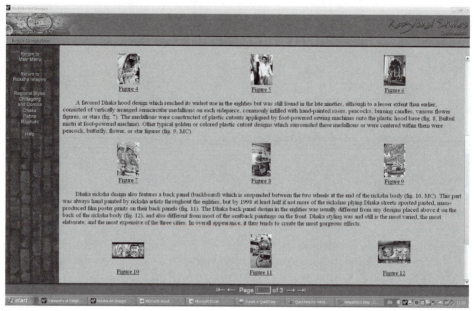

© Joanna Kirkpatrick 2003

Figure 8.4

Part of the photographic gallery from Joanna Kirkpatrick's *Transports of Delight* (2003).
See also Kirkpatrick's website 'The Ricksha arts of Bangladesh' at www.ricksha.org/.

An example of an on-line slide show can be reviewed on the *Visualising Ethnography* website. Here in the 'experiences' section slide shows, which form just one part of a screen that also contains written text, are used to visually represent parts of the ethnographic projects discussed. Here, by the visual and written narratives beings both separated and published on the same page, the constant visual loop of the photographs makes them ever-present through the article, rather than being simple illustrations that are linked to one specific statement or section of the text (see Figure 8.5).

Hypermedia representations and ethnographic video/film

As I described in Chapter 4, digital video implies new relationships between video makers and subjects as well as new viewing possibilities during fieldwork, and in Chapter 7 I suggested how video clips and stills produced during fieldwork might be used in conventional presentation and printed texts. Hypermedia presents a further opportunity for linking moving and still images, sound and written words, in the

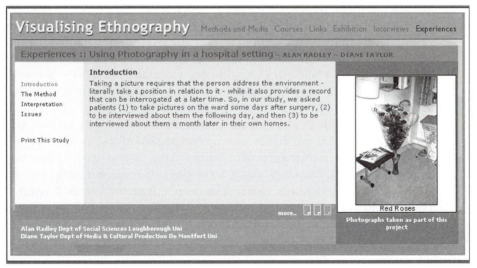

Written text and photograph © Alan Radley and Diane Taylor 2001

Figure 8.5

A screen capture from the *Visualising Ethnography* website, showing a slide show of photographs alongside sections of written text from Radley and Taylor's work, also discussed in Chapter 3.

same text. As for digital photography, many ethnographic video and filmmakers have appropriated digital video for their existing practice. In contrast, visual hypermedia ethnographers are introducing new digital video practices in their representations. These change the viewing options. Whereas a linear ethnographic documentary would be viewed from start to finish continuously, in hypermedia video can be viewed in closer relationship to written texts, still images and other video clips, thus making changes in the meanings it can be used to produce. This offers various options.

One of the earlier uses of digitalized ethnographic film was to enable new forms of ethnographic film scrutiny and critique. In 1996 Biella wrote that, '[i]n the past no simple techniques existed to question and explore ethnographic film *inch by inch*.' Now, however, '[i]nteractive media has begun to make critiques, reviews and follow-up studies precise and feasible' (1996: 599; original italics). He describes how his close analysis of Fruzzetti and Östör's (1994) laser disc version of their ethnographic film *Seed and Earth* revealed problematic subtitling and explanatory information given in an alternative soundtrack that gave misplaced significance to conversations, scenes and activities represented in the film. Another example of close film scrutiny enabled through digitalization is the use of the film *The Ax Fight* in *Yanomamö Interactive* (Biella et al. 1997), discussed above. More recently, Robert Gardener's film *Dead Birds* has been published on DVD, presenting new options for dissemination, viewing (on computer screen) and analysis. Digitalized films can also be more easily visually quoted by other authors when permissions are given for the citation of clips in a hyper-media essay. However, my interest here is less with the publication or re-publication of whole ethnographic documentaries on DVD than with the use of digital video to represent ethnographic realities in multimedia contexts.

There are some important differences between ethnographic film and hypermedia narratives. Biella has proposed that hypermedia has two key quantitative advantages over linear film: it has greater storage capacity and it allows more rapid access to information (1994: 241–2). Film, and by implication video, has been characterized as having a linear narrative: 'there is the capacity of film, noted by Pinney, to lead the viewer, merely by the (not necessarily chronological) succession of images, along one particular narrative and explanatory path' (Crawford and Turton 1992: 5). The ability of film and video to represent particular narratives and specific aspects of human experience is one of its advantages. However, as Biella points out, this linearity also has the disadvantage that the elements that are selected for inclusion in them must be divorced from their own contextual surroundings (Biella 1994: 241). Biella notes an advantage of hypermedia is that whole edited ethnographic films may be stored and viewed in their linear form, but in hypermedia text there is also space to 'include materials that video-makers would reject as outtakes' (Biella 1994: 241), thus providing more visual context. Hypermedia ethnographies may combine clips, unedited footage and full-length documentaries, offering users quicker access to different sections of these texts (see Biella 1994: 242). *Yanomamö Interactive* is a good example of this. It might enable users to play multiple clips from a video archive on the same monitor and could be designed to allow users to blow up video stills and re-edit original digitized footage. Video may be connected by hyperlinks to written texts, photographs, transcripts and footnotes about the video-recording process (see Biella 1993, 1994). Therefore the possibilities for working with and using full ethnographic documentaries are enhanced by hypermedia. However, since Biella's 1990s discussions of these possibilities, these practices have not been further developed. Rather, more recent innovations in hypermedia have used short video clips in multimedia hypermedia contexts, rather than full films, and have done so in ways that create explicit links between the processes of research and representation. Existing examples are varied and present interesting models which new researchers might want to respond to when developing their own work.

Above I have discussed some examples of on-line uses of videos in linear essays. Coover's essay 'Metaphors, montage and worldmaking' in *Cultures in Webs* (2003) is a similar example of how video clips might be embedded in a written scholarly essay. However, in this case Coover has embedded not his own footage in the essay, but digitalized clips of the existing well-known ethnographic films that he discusses. This use of video as audio-visual 'quotation' is very effective as it allows one to communicate about an audio-visual form without having to resort entirely to written description. In another of Coover's *Cultures in Webs* essays, 'Concealed Narratives', he uses his own video footage shot in Ghana in a very different way. Here his clips are embedded in a sequence of web pages and used in both realist ways (e.g. interviews, performance videos) and as evocative expressive texts (video and audio edited in innovative ways to evoke sensory experience) to represent themes related to performance and politics in contemporary Ghana (see Pink 2005 for a full analysis of this). Ruby's (2005) CD *Rebekah and Sophie* demonstrates a very different use of video clips. Here Ruby includes video footage of his research interviews with his informants, in which his own questions and presence are made explicit. This reflexive use of video allows the viewer access to elements of the research context and to view the data that Ruby himself would have worked with (see Murdock and Pink 2005b for a fuller analysis of this).

Reflexive text: hypermedia and the relationship between research and representation

Reflexivity about how ethnographic knowledge is created can be achieved in printed text or film (Chapters 6 and 7). Hypermedia's capacity for multilinearity and layering information allows reflexivity to be developed differently and can represent the historical development of ethnographic research and interpretation in ways written text and film cannot. Dicks et al. (2005) have explored the possibility of using CAQ-DAS to develop hypermedia texts that bridge the gap between analysis and representation. However, as yet existing software does not facilitate this. Instead, existing ethnographic hypermedia texts tend to 'go back' into the research process by creating hyperlinks between academic or report-style texts and files that represent the research documents and experiences these 'final' reports are based on – thus aiming to make the relationship between research and representation explicit. As Fischer and Zeitlyn pointed out in the 1990s, the 'fieldwork experience' is important for the development of an 'anthropological understanding' but was rarely reproduced in printed articles. Their *Experience Rich Anthropology* Project at the University of Kent addresses this through hypermedia texts that represent the results of research and the fieldwork experiences on which published articles and books were based (see www.era.anthropology.ac.uk/index.htm/). These include photographs, field diaries, video clips and other written texts. One of the most significant projects is *45 years in the Turkish village 1949–1994*, an internet resource of Professor Paul Stirling's *Ethnographic Data Archives* (see www.lucy.ukc.ac.uk/TVillage), which includes Stirling's book *Turkish Village* (1998 [1965]), articles and PhD thesis, as well as his field notes, letters, photographs and data base. This transparent presentation of Stirling's work allows other researchers to interpret the historical development of his ideas as well as his ethnographic research materials. It also recognizes the importance of photography in Stirling's research, which was largely undertaken in a period when ethnographic photography remained 'hidden behind' written text and was rarely discussed in published work.

There are various ways that hypermedia can represent historical development and reflexivity. Stirling did not impose his own reflexive authorial narrative on *45 years in the Turkish village*, yet the relationship between research and representation is implicit in the text. In contrast, other hypermedia authors have developed texts that specifically reflected on how individual ethnographers produced, interpreted and represented their knowledge. Sometimes analysis is explicitly represented in the text, rather than treated as a hidden practice of 'translation'. Biella's CD ROM project *Masaai Interactive* was developed from a six-week period of fieldwork among the Masaai people in 1980, during which a series of interviews were filmed and recorded and photographs were taken. Biella shows how interactive hypermedia can represent and annotate the historical development of ethnographic work, thoughts, ideas and interpretations, using visual, verbal and written texts. He aimed 'to explore how digital technology can enhance the understanding of anthropological research in which camera and tape recorder play an important role' (Biella 1997: 60). His comments on this, made in 1997, are of continuing relevance:

> The new technology permitted audio recordings, photographs and texts to be integrated on one study-screen. Through electronic footnotes, texts could instantly 'call up' for review any moment of the audio, any photograph, and any text. Translations, studio and photographs could themselves nonlinearly access additional texts, such as my annotations of the Ilpoarakuyo materials ... (1997: 61)

The interview scenes in the CD ROM are contextualized with annotations written over several years and dated to show how Biella's analysis progressed and how some of his earlier interpretations were misguided. He saw this as a challenge to the conventional strategies of ethnographic representation:

> I leave traces of the different drafts because I think it is important to affirm that 'meaning has history'. ... This counterposes a dominant conceit in the discipline

that advocates non-contradiction in ethnography by the erasure of history, uncertainty, and change from texts. (Biella 1997: 61)

However, the annotations do not force users to disrupt their enjoyment of the ethnographic scenes (scripted like a play) in the text. Rather, they can be clicked on and referred to at will. Thus users of Biella's text would be allowed freedom to take their own personal narratives through it, to access different resources of information when they need to and take responsibility for developing their own routes to understanding. Biella et al.'s (1997) *Yanomamö Interactive* also works as a reflexive text (see Banks 2001; Biella 2004; Pink 2005). Biella's work involves complex and detailed annotated representations; most other ethnographic hypermedia texts do not go down this route, tending to provide representations that bridge the gap between research and representation by revealing the contexts of their production, rather than such extensive archives of data. For example, in *The Bullfighter's Braid* CD ROM (Pink 1997) I developed a less ambitious strategy, publishing an article about photographic research methods with a set of related visual and written texts (similar to Büscher's 2005 work discussed above). An earlier version of the article, published in Spanish (Pink 1996), included only one photograph, however the hypermedia publication has links to over 30 photographs and several video clips produced during my research. My intention was that by following these different routes and hyperlinks users of the CD would not only read an article about research methodology as well as less academic pieces, but also go 'behind' it to view the photographic materials produced and interpreted in the project. The CD ROMs produced by Ruby (2004) and Hubbard et al. (2003), through the written text and particularly in their uses of video, as noted above also provide reflexive routes to understanding the contexts in which the knowledge represented in their texts was produced.

Ethics

Different hypermedia texts allow their users different degrees of control over the materials they include. The idea of empowering hypermedia users to create their own narratives and stories with other people's images and words also raises ethical issues. While Biella has suggested hypermedia authors may be able to guide the way people use and experience electronic representations (see above), as I noted in the Introduction to Part 3 ultimately authors cannot control how their work is interpreted once it is subjected to other gazes. As for photography and video, this demands that ethnographers be informed about the ethical implications that their hypermedia publications raise.

In Chapter 2 I argued that ethnographers should be committed to representing their informants' images and words appropriately and responsibly. While the internet offers unsurpassed opportunities for global dissemination of ethnography, it also raises some concerns. Authors of electronic representations of ethnography cannot necessarily control how other people appropriate their images. Digital photographs and video can be copied from CD ROMs. On the internet, where copyright is difficult to regulate, ethnographic still and moving images can be copied and reproduced in new and possibly inappropriate contexts. Ethnographic film or video footage published on-line might be downloaded, re-edited and represented in contexts that might produce negative or harmful meanings or consequences for the people represented in it, which could also be disseminated globally on-line. However, to keep this in perspective, illegal copying and re-editing of ethnographic video, like manipulation of photographs, has always been possible and the main difference of on-line publishing is easy accessibility.

Copyright regulations, and the technologies that can be used to protect or locate misused images, constantly change and there would be little point in setting out guidelines here. Up-to-date information may be best found on the internet itself or should be accessed in consultation with experts. It is also likely to be country-specific.

Practical concerns

This book is not a practical skills manual; step-by-step guides to digitizing and manipulating video and photographs and using hypermedia software would not only merit a whole book in itself, but would soon be out of date. Hypermedia design and production skills are best gained from appropriate manuals, on-line resources, training groups or university courses. My own experience of making hypermedia representations has shown me that each project is a learning experience. It is important to take a critical approach to one's own and other existing works. To shift from writing ethnography to creating image-led hypermedia texts that exploit the multilinear, multimedia and interactive potential of hypermedia means thinking about ethnographic representation in new ways.

Summary

Hypermedia ethnography is an exciting practice that invites visual ethnographers to explore a number of creative options for representation. There is now a growing list of examples of good practice in ethnographic hypermedia production. Nevertheless, there are still no set conventions for ethnographic hypermedia, leaving a fertile field for innovation and experimentation open for visual ethnographers.

FURTHER READING

Biella, P. (2004) 'The Ax Fight on CD-ROM', in E.D. Lewis (ed.), Timothy Asch and Ethnographic Film, London: Routledge. (An analysis of CD ROM The Ax Fight that also provides insights that inform wider understandings of hypermedia)

Dicks, B., Mason, B., Coffey, A. and Atkinson, P. (2005) Qualitative Research and Hypermedia: Ethnography for the Digital Age, London: Sage. (A general review and project-based report on multimedia and hypermedia ethnography)

Pink, S. (2005) The Future of Visual Anthropology: Engaging the Senses, London: Routledge, Chapter 6. (An analysis of recent academic and applied anthropological hypermedia texts)

REFERENCES

Alasuutari, P. (1995) *Researching Culture*. London: Sage.

Amit, V. (2000) (ed.) *Constructing the Field*. London: Routledge.

Appadurai, A. (1986) 'Introduction: commodities and the politics of value', in A. Appadurai (ed.), *The Social Life of Things: Commodities in Cultural Perspective*. Cambridge: Cambridge University Press.

Ardevol, E. (2003) 'Teaching anthropology virtually: learning communities at work', *Anthropology in Action*, 9 (2): 32–42.

Ardevol, E. (2005) 'Dream gallery: online dating as a commodity', http://www.philbu. net/media-anthropology/ardevol_catalogodesuenos.pdf. Paper presented to the EASA Media Anthropology Network e-seminar.

Askew, K. and Wilk, R. (eds) (2002) *The Anthropology of Media: A Reader*. Oxford: Blackwell.

Back, L. (1998) 'Reading and writing research', in C. Seale (ed.), *Researching Culture and Society*. London: Sage.

Banks, M. (1992) 'Which films are the ethnographic films?', in P.I. Crawford and D. Turton (eds), *Film as Ethnography*. Manchester: University of Manchester Press.

Banks, M. (1994) 'Interactive multimedia and anthropology – a sceptical view', http://www.rsl.ox.ac.uk/isca/marcus.banks.01.html.

Banks, M. (2001) *Visual Methods in Social Research*. London: Sage.

Banks, M. (n.d) 'Visual research methods', in *Social Research Update*, http://www. soc.surrey.ac.uk/sru/SRU11/SRU11.html.

Banks, M. and Morphy, H. (1997) *Rethinking Visual Anthropology*. London: Yale University Press.

Barbash, I. and Taylor, L. (1997) *Cross Cultural Filmmaking: A Handbook for Making Documentary and Ethnographic Films and Video*. London: University of California Press.

Barndt, D. (1997) 'Zooming out/zooming in: visualizing globalisation', *Visual Sociology*, 12 (2): 5–32.

Barnes, D.B., Taylor-Brown, S. and Weiner, L. (1997) '"I didn't leave y'all on purpose": HIV-infected mothers' videotaped legacies for their children', in S.J. Gold (ed.), *Visual Methods in Sociological Analysis*, special issue of *Qualitative Sociology*, 20 (1).

Barry, C.A. (1998) 'Choosing qualitative data analysis software: Atlas/ti and Nudist compared', *Sociological Research Online*, 3 (3), <http://www.socresonline.org.uk/ socresonline/3/3/4.html>.

Bateson, G. and Mead, M. (1942) *Balinese Character: A Photographic Analysis*. New York: New York Academy of the Sciences.

Baudry, P. (1996) 'Happy tapes', in P.I. Crawford and S.B. Hafsteinsson (eds), *The Construction of the Viewer*. Aarhaus: Intervention Press.

Becker, H. (1986) 'Photography and sociology', in *Doing Things Together*. Evanston, IL: North Western Press.

Becker, H. (1995) 'Visual sociology, documentary photography or photojournalism (almost) all a matter of context', *Visual Sociology*, 10 (1–2): 5–14.

Bell, D., Caplan, P. and Jahan Karim, W. (1993) *Gendered Fields: Women, Men and Ethnography*. London: Routledge.

Bergamaschi, M. and Francesconi, C. (1996) 'Urban homelessness: the negotiation of public spaces', *Visual Sociology*, 11 (2): 35–44.

Berger, J. and Mohr, J. (1967) *A Fortunate Man*. Cambridge: Granta Books.

Berger, J. and Mohr, J. (1982) *Another Way of Telling*. Cambridge: Granta Books.

Biella, P. (1993) 'Beyond ethnographic film', in J.R. Rollwagen (ed.), *Anthropological Film and Video in the 1990s*. Brockport, NY: The Institute Inc.

Biella, P. (1994) 'Codifications of ethnography: linear and nonlinear', http://www.usc.edu/dept/elab/welcome/codifications.html.

Biella, P. (1996) 'Interactive media in anthropology: *Seed and Earth* – promise of rain', *American Anthropologist*, 98 (3): 595–616.

Biella, P. (1997) 'Mama Kone's possession: scene from an interactive ethnography', *Visual Anthropology Review*, 12 (2): 59–95.

Biella, P. (2004) '*The Ax Fight* on CD-ROM', in E.D. Lewis (ed.), *Timothy Asch and Ethnographic Film*. London: Routledge.

Bloustien, G. (ed.) (2003) En-visioning ethnography: exploring the complexity of the visual methods in ethnographic research, *Social Analysis*, 47 (3).

Bourdieu, P. (1990 (1965)) *Photography: A Middle-Brow Art*. Cambridge: Polity Press.

Bowman, G., Grasseni, C., Hughes-Freeland, F. and Pink, S. (eds) (forthcoming) *The Frontiers of Visual Anthropology*, a guest edited double issue of *Visual Anthropology*.

Brandes, S. (1997) 'Photographic imagery in Spanish ethnography', *Visual Anthropology Review*, 13 (1): 1–13.

Burgess, R.G. (1984) *In the Field*. London: Routledge.

Büscher, M. (2005) 'Social life under the microscope?', *Sociological Research Online*, 10 (1), <http://www.socresonline.org.uk/10/1/buscher.html>.

Camas, V., Martínez, A., Muñoz, R. and Ortiz, M. (2004) 'Revealing the hidden: making anthropological documentaries', in S. Pink, L. Kürti and A. Afonso (eds), *Working Images*. London: Routledge.

Cerezo, M., Martinez, A. and Ranera, P. (1996) 'Tres antropólogos inocentes y an ojo si parpado', in M. Garcia Alonso, A. Martinez, P. Pitarch, P. Ranera and J. Fores (eds), *Antropologia de los Sentidos: La Vista*. Madrid: Celeste Ediciones.

Chalfen, R. (1987) *Snapshot Versions of Life*. Bowling Green, OH: Popular Press.

Chalfen, R. (2005) 'Looking at Japanese society: Hashiguchi George as visual sociologist', *Visual Studies*, 20 (2): 140–58.

Chalfen, R. and Rich, M. (2004) 'Applying visual research: patients teaching physicians about asthma through video diaries', in S. Pink (ed.), *Applied Visual Anthropology*, a guest edited issue of *Visual Anthropology Review*, 20 (1): 17–30.

Chaney, D. (1993) *Fictions of Collective Life*. London: Routledge.

Chaplin, E. (1994) *Sociology and Visual Representations*. London: Routledge.

Chaplin, E. (2005) 'The photograph in theory', *Sociological Research Online*, 10 (1) at <http://www.socresonline.org.uk/10/1/chaplin.html>.

Clifford, J. (1986) 'Introduction: partial truths', in J. Clifford and G. Marcus (eds), *Writing Culture: The Poetics and Politics of Ethnography*. Berkeley, CA: University of California Press.

Clifford, J. and Marcus, G. (1986) *Writing Culture: the Poetics and Politics of Ethnography*. Berkeley, CA: University of California Press.

Coffey, A., Holbrook, B. and Atkinson, P. (1996) 'Qualitative data analysis: technologies and representations', *Sociological Research Online*, 1 (1), <http://www.socresonline.org.uk/socresonline/1/1/4.html>.

Cohen, A. (1992) 'Self-conscious anthropology', in J. Okely and H. Callaway (eds), *Anthropology and Autobiography*. London: Routledge.

Cohen, A. (1994) *Self Consciousness: An Alternative Anthropology of Identity*. London: Routledge.

Cohen, A. and Rapport, N. (1995) *Questions of Consciousness*. Routledge: London.

Cohen, C.B., Wilk, R. and Stoeltje, B. (1996) *Beauty Queens on the Global Stage.* London: Routledge.

Collier, J. (1967) *Visual Anthropology: Photography as Research Method.* Albuquerque, NM: University of New Mexico Press.

Collier, J. (1973) *Alaskan Eskimo Education.* New York: Holt, Rinehart, Winston.

Collier, J. (1995 (1975)) 'Photography and visual anthropology', in P. Hockings (ed.), *Principles of Visual Anthropology.* Berlin and New York: Mouton de Gruyter.

Collier, J. and Collier, M. (1986) *Visual Anthropology: Photography as a Research Method.* Albuquerque, NM: University of New Mexico Press.

Concise Oxford Dictionary (1982) J.B. Sykes (ed.). Oxford: Clarendon Press.

Connell, R.W. (1987) *Gender and Power.* Cambridge: Polity Press.

Connell, R.W. (1995) *Masculinities.* Cambridge: Polity Press.

Cooke, L. and Wollen, P. (eds) (1995) *Visual Display: Culture Beyond Appearances.* Seattle, WA: Bay Press.

Coover, R. (2004a) 'The representation of cultures in digital media', in S. Pink, L. Kurti and A. Afonso (eds), *Working Images.* London: Routledge.

Coover, R. (2004b) 'Using digital media tools in cross-cultural research, analysis and representation', *Visual Studies,* 19 (1): 6–25.

Cornwall, A. and Lindisfarne, N. (1994) 'Introduction', in A. Cornwall and N. Lindisfarne (eds), *Dislocating Masculinity: Comparative Ethnographies.* London: Routledge.

Crawford, P.I. (1992) 'Film as discourse: the invention of anthropological realities', in P.I. Crawford and D. Turton (eds), *Film as Ethnography.* Manchester: Manchester University Press.

Crawford, P.I. and Hafsteinsson, S. (eds) (1996) *The Construction of the Viewer.* Aarhaus: Intervention Press.

Crawford, P.I. and Turton, D. (1992) 'Introduction', in P.I. Crawford and D. Turton (eds), *Film as Ethnography.* Manchester: Manchester University Press.

Crawshaw, C. and Urry, J. (1997) 'Tourism and the photographic eye', in C. Rojek and J. Urry (eds), *Touring Cultures.* London: Routledge.

Crotty, M. (1998) *The Foundations of Social Research: Meaning and Perspective in the Research Process.* London: Sage.

Dant, T. (2004) 'Recording the "habitus"', in C. Pole (ed.), *Seeing is Believing?* Oxford: Elsevier.

Dant, T. and Bowles, D. (2003) 'Dealing with dirt: servicing and repairing cars', *Sociological Research Online,* 8 (2), <http://www.socresonline.org.uk/8/2/dant.html>.

Da Silva, O. (2000) *In the Net,* exhibition catalogue. Porto, Portugal: Rainho and Neves Lda.

Da Silva, O. and Pink, S. (2004) 'In the Net: ethnographic photography', in S. Pink, L. Kurti and A. Afonso (eds), *Working Images.* London: Routledge.

Davis, J. (1992) 'Tense in ethnography: some practical considerations', in J. Okely and H. Callaway (eds), *Anthropology and Autobiography.* London: Routledge.

Desjarlais, R. (2003) *Sensory Biographies: Lives and Death Among Nepal's Yolmo Buddhists,* London: University of California Press.

Devereaux, L. (1995) 'Experience, representation and film', in L. Devereaux and R. Hillman (eds), *Fields of Vision: Essays in Film Studies, Visual Anthropology and Photography.* Berkeley, CA: University of California Press.

Devereaux, L. and Hillman, R. (eds) (1995) *Fields of Vision: Essays in Film Studies, Visual Anthropology and Photography.* Berkeley, CA: University of California Press.

Dicks, B., Mason, B. Coffey, A. and Atkinson, P. (2005) *Qualitative Research and Hypermedia: Ethnography for the Digital Age.* London: Sage.

Edensor, T. (1998) *Tourists at the Taj: Performance and Meaning at a Symbolic Site.* London: Routledge.

Edgar, I. (2004) *Guide to Imagework: Imagination-Based Research Methods.* London: Routledge.

Edwards, E. (ed.) (1992) *Anthropology and Photography.* New Haven, CT: Yale University Press.

Edwards, E. (1997a) 'Beyond the boundary: a consideration of the expressive in photography and anthropology', in M. Banks and H. Morphy (eds), *Rethinking Visual Anthropology.* London: Routledge.

Edwards, E. (ed.) (1997b) Special issue of *History of Photography,* 21 (1).

Edwards, E. (2001) *Raw Histories.* Oxford: Berg.

El Guindi, F. (2004) *Visual Anthropology: Essential Theory and Method.* Walnut Creek, CA: Altamira Press.

Ellen, R. (1984) *Ethnographic Research: A Guide to General Conduct.* London: Academic Press.

Emmison, M. and Smith, P. (2000) *Researching the Visual.* London: Sage.

Engelbrecht, B. (1996) 'For whom do we produce?', in P.I. Crawford and S.B. Hafsteinsson (eds), *The Construction of the Viewer.* Aarhaus: Intervention Press.

Evans, J. and Hall, S. (eds) (1999) *Visual Culture: The Reader.* London: Sage.

Fabian, J. (1983) *Time and the Other: How Anthropology Makes Its Object.* New York: Columbia University Press.

Farrar, M. (2005) 'Photography: making and breaking racialised boundaries: an essay in reflexive, radical, visual sociology', *Sociological Research Online,* 10 (1), <http://www.socresonline.org.uk/10/1/farrar.html>.

Fernandez, J. (1995) 'Amazing grace: meaning deficit, displacement and new consciousness in expressive interaction', in A. Cohen and N. Rapport (eds), *Questions of Consciousness.* London: Routledge.

Ferrándiz, F. (1996) 'Intersubjectividad y vídeo etnográfico. Holguras y textxuras en la grabación de ceremonias espiritistas en Venezuela', in M. Garcia, A. Martinez, P. Pitarch, P. Ranera and J. Fores (eds), *Antropologia de los sentidos: La Vista.* Madrid: Celeste Ediciones.

Ferrándiz, F. (1998) 'A trace of fingerprints: displacements and textures in the use of ethnographic video in Venezuelan spiritism', *Visual Anthropology Review,* 13 (2): 19–38.

Fetterman, D. (1998) *Ethnography,* 2nd edn. London: Sage.

Fischer, M. and Zeitlyn, D. (n.d.) 'Mambila Nggwun – the construction and deployment of multiple meanings in ritual', http://lucy.ukc.ac.uk/dz/ Nggwun /nggwun_1.html.

Flick, U. (1998) *An Introduction to Qualitative Research.* London: Sage.

Flores, C. (2004) 'Indigenous video, development and shared anthropology: a collaborative experience with Maya-Q'eqchi' filmmakers in post-war Guatemala', in S. Pink (ed.), *Applied Visual Anthropology,* a guest edited issue of *Visual Anthropology Review,* 20 (1): 31–44.

Fortier, A. (1998) 'Gender, ethnicity and fieldwork: a case study', in C. Seale (ed.), *Researching Culture and Society.* London: Sage.

Fruzzetti, L., Guzzetti, A., Johnston, N. and Östör, Á. (1994) *Seed and Earth.* Video and Laser Disc. Middletown, CT: Wesleyan University.

Gilroy, R. and Kellett, P. (2005) 'Picture me: place, memory and identity in the lives and names of older people'. Paper presented at the AHRC symposium: *Interior Insights, Design, Ethnography and the Home.* Royal College of Art.

Ginsburg, F., Abu-Lughod, L. and Larkin, B. (eds) (2002) *Media Worlds: Anthropology on New Terrain.* Berkeley, CA: University of California Press.

Goffman, I. (1979) *Gender Advertisements.* London and Basingstoke: Macmillan.

Gold, S.J. (1995) 'New York/LA: a visual comparison of public life in two cities', *Visual Sociology,* 10 (1–2): 85–105.

Gold, S.J. (ed.) (1997) 'Visual methods in sociological analysis', special issue, *Qualitative Sociology,* 20 (1).

Goldfine, R. and Goldfine, O. (2003) 'Hunters and healers: social change and cultural conflict in rural Maine', *Visual Studies,* 18 (2): 96–111.

Goopy, S. and Lloyd, D. (2005) 'Picturing cosmopolitanism – identity and quality of life among older Italo-Australians', in D. Ellison and I. Woodward (eds), *Sites of Cosmopolitanism: Citizenship, Aesthetics, Culture,* Centre for Public Culture and Ideas, Griffith University, pp. 133–9.

Grady, J. (1991) 'The visual essay and sociology', *Visual Sociology,* 6 (2): 23–38.

Grady, J. (1996) 'The scope of visual sociology', *Visual Sociology,* 11 (2): 10–24.

Grasseni, C. (2004) 'Video and ethnographic knowledge: skilled vision and the practice of breeding' in S. Pink, L. Kürti and A.I. Afonso (eds), *Working Images.* London: Routledge.

Grimshaw, A. (2001) *The Ethnographer's Eye.* Cambridge: Cambridge University Press.

Grimshaw, A. (2004) 'Eyeing the field: new horizons for visual anthropology', in A. Grimshaw and A. Ravetz, *Visualizing Anthropology.* Bristol: Intellect.

Grimshaw, A. and Ravetz, A. (2004) *Visualizing Anthropology.* Bristol: Intellect.

Gullestad, M. (1993) 'Home decoration as popular culture: constructing homes, genders and classes in Norway', in T. del Valle (ed.), *Gendered Anthropology.* London: Routledge.

Halford, S. and Knowles, C. (eds) (2005) 'More than words: some reflections on working visually', themed issue of *Sociological Research Online,* 10 (1) <http://www.socreson-line.org.uk/10/1/knowleshalford.html>.

Hall, S. (ed.) (1997) *Representation: Cultural Representations and Signifying Practices.* London: Sage.

Hammersley, M. and Atkinson, P. (1995) *Ethnography: Principles in Practice,* 2nd edn. London: Routledge.

Harper, D. (ed.) (1994) 'Cape Bretton 1952: the photographic vision of Tim Asch', special issue, *Visual Sociology,* 9 (2).

Harper, D. (1998a) 'An argument for visual sociology', in J. Prosser (ed.), *Image-based Research: A Sourcebook for Qualitative Researchers.* London: Falmer Press.

Harper, D. (1998b) 'On the authority of the image: visual methods at the crossroads', in N. Denzin and Y. Lincoln (eds), *Collecting and Interpreting Qualitative Materials.* London: Sage.

Harper, D. (2002). 'Talking about pictures: a case for photo-elicitation', *Visual Studies,* 17 (1): 13–26.

Harper, D., Knowles, C. and Leonard P. (2005) 'Visually narrating post-colonial lives: ghosts of war and empire', *Visual Studies,* 20 (1): 4–15.

Harper, S. (2004) 'Multimedia and visual research: a review essay', *Visual Sociology* (19) 1: 112–15.

Harvey, P. (1996) *Hybrids of Modernity: Anthropology, the Nation State and the Universal Exhibition.* London: Routledge.

Hastrup, K. (1992) 'Anthropological vision: some notes on visual and textual authority', in P.I. Crawford and D. Turton (eds), *Film as Ethnography.* Manchester: Manchester University Press.

Heider, K. (1976) *Ethnographic Film.* Austin, TX: University of Texas Press.

Henley, P. (1998) 'Filmmaking and ethnographic research', in J. Prosser (ed.), *Image-based Research.* London: Falmer Press.

Henley, P. (2000) 'Ethnographic film: technology, practice and anthropological theory', *Visual Anthropology,* 13: 207–26.

Henley, P. (2004) 'Beyond observational cinema ...', in S. Pink, L. Kürti, and A. Afonso (eds), *Working Images.* London: Routledge.

Hine, C. (2000) *Virtual Ethnography.* London: Sage.

Hockings, P. (ed.) (1975) *Principles of Visual Anthropology.* The Hague: Mouton.

Hockings, P. (1992) 'The yellow bough: Rivers' use of photography in *The Todas*', in E. Edwards (ed.), *Anthropology and Photography.* New Haven, CT: Yale University Press, pp. 179–86.

Hockings, P. (ed.) (1995) *Principles of Visual Anthropology,* 2nd edn. The Hague: Mouton.

Holliday, R. (2001) 'We'e been framed – visualizing methodologies', *Sociological Review,* 48 (4): 503–21.

Holliday, R. (2004) 'Reflecting the self', in C. Knowles and P. Sweetman (eds), *Picturing the Social Landscape.* London: Routledge.

Homberger, E. (1992) 'J.P. Morgan's nose: photographer and subject in American portrait photography', in G. Clarke (ed.), *The Portrait in Photography.* London: Reaktion Books.

Hoskins, J. (1993) '"Why we cried to see him again": Indonesian villagers' responses to the filmic disruption of time', in J. Rollwagen (ed.), *Anthropological Film and Video in the 1990s.* Brockport, NY: The Institute Inc.

Howard, A. (1988) 'Hypermedia and the future of ethnography', *Cultural Anthropology,* 3 (3): 387–410.

Howes, D. (2005) *Empire of the Senses: The Sensory Culture Reader.* Oxford: Berg.

Hughes-Freeland, F. (ed.) (1997) *Ritual, Performance, Media.* London: Routledge.

Hughes-Freeland, F. and Crain, M. (eds) (1998) *Recasting Ritual.* London: Routledge.

Hutnyk. J. (1990) 'Comparative anthropology and Evans – Pritchard's Nuer photography: photographic essay', *Critique of Anthropology,* 10 (1): 81–102.

Hutnyk, J. (1996) *The Rumour of Calcutta.* London: Zed Books.

Hyde, K. (2005) 'Portraits and collaborations: a reflection on the work of Wendy Ewald', *Visual Studies,* 20 (2): 172–90.

Ihde, D. (1995) 'Image technologies and traditional culture', in A. Feenberg and A. Hannay (eds), *Technology and the Politics of Knowledge.* Bloomington and Indianapolis: Indiana University Press.

Jacknis, I. (1984) 'Franz Boas and photography', *Studies in Visual Communication,* 10 (1): 2–60.

James, A., Hockey, J. and Dawson, A. (1997) *After Writing Culture: Epistemology and Praxis in Contemporary Anthropology.* London: Routledge.

Jenks, C. (1995) *Visual Cultures.* London: Routledge.

Jhala, J. (2004) 'In a time of fear and terror: seeing, assessing, assisting, understanding and living the reality and consequences of disaster', *Visual Anthropology Review,* 20 (1): 59–69.

Josephides, L. (1997) 'Representing the anthropologist's predicament', in W. James, J. Hockey and A. Dawson (eds), *After Writing Culture: Epistemology and Praxis in Contemporary Anthropology.* London: Routledge.

Knowles, C. and Sweetman, P. (eds) (2004) *Picturing the Social Landscape: Visual Methods and the Sociological Imagination.* London: Routledge.

Kulick, D. (1995) 'The sexual life of anthropologists: erotic subjectivity and ethnographic work', in D. Kulick and M. Willson (eds), *Taboo: Sex, Identity and Erotic Subjectivity in Anthropological Fieldwork.* London: Routledge.

Kulick, D. and Willson, M. (eds) (1995) *Taboo: Sex, Identity and Erotic Subjectivity in Anthropological Fieldwork.* London: Routledge.

Kürti, L. (2004) 'Picture perfect: community and commemoration in postcards', in S. Pink, L. Kürti and A.I. Afonso (eds), *Working Images.* London: Routledge.

Lakoff, G. and Johnson, M. (1980) *The Metaphors We Live By.* Chicago, IL: University of Chicago Press.

Larson, H.J. (1988) 'Photography that listens', *Visual Anthropology,* 1: 415–32.

Lister, M. (1995) *The Photographic Image in Digital Culture.* London: Routledge.

Lister, M. and Wells, L. (2000) 'Seeing beyond belief: cultural studies as an approach to analysing the visual', in T. van Leeuwen and C. Jewitt (eds), *The Handbook of Visual Analysis.* London: Sage.

Loescher, M. (2004) 'Cameras at the Addy: speaking in pictures with city kids', in A. Grimshaw and A. Ravetz (eds), *Visualizing Anthropology.* Bristol: Intellect.

Loizos, P. (1993) *Innovation in Ethnographic Film*. Manchester: Manchester University Press.

Lomax, H. and Casey, N. (1998) 'Recording social life: reflexivity and video methodology', *Sociological Research Online*, 3 (2), http://www.socresonline.org.uk/socresonline/3/2/1.html.

Lury, C. (1998) *Prosthetic Culture: Photography, Memory and Identity*. London: Routledge.

Lydall, J. (1990) 'Filming *The Women Who Smile*', in P.I. Crawford and J.K. Simonsen (eds), *Ethnographic Film Aesthetics and Narrative Traditions*. Aarhaus: Intervention Press.

MacDougall, D. (1995) 'The subjective voice in ethnographic film', in L. Devereaux and R. Hillman (eds), *Fields of Vision: Essays in Film Studies, Visual Anthropology and Photography*. Berkeley, CA: University of California Press.

MacDougall, D. (1997) 'The visual in anthropology', in M. Banks and H. Morphy (eds), *Rethinking Visual Anthropology*. London: Yale University Press.

MacDougall, D. (1998) *Transcultural Cinema*. Princeton, NJ: Princeton University Press.

MacDougall, D. (2001) 'Renewing ethnographic film: Is digital video changing the genre?', *Anthropology Today*, 17 (3): 15–21.

MacDougall, D. (2005) *The Corporeal Image*, Princeton, NJ: Princeton University Press.

Macintyre, M. and Mackenzie, M. (1992) 'Focal length as an analogue of cultural distance', in E. Edwards (ed.), *Anthropology and Photography*. London: Yale University Press.

Marcus, G. (1995) 'The modernist sensibility in recent ethnographic writing and the cinematic metaphor of montage', in L. Devereaux and R. Hillman (eds), *Fields of Vision: Essays in Film Studies, Visual Anthropology and Photography*. Berkeley, CA: University of California Press.

Martinez, W. (1990) 'Critical studies and visual anthropology: aberrant vs. anticipated readings of ethnographic film', *CVA Review*, Spring: 34–47.

Martinez, W. (1992) 'Who constructs anthropological knowledge? Toward a theory of ethnographic film spectatorship', in P.I. Crawford and D. Turton (eds), *Film as Ethnography*. Manchester: Manchester University Press.

Martinez, W. (1996) 'Deconstructing the "viewer": from ethnography of the visual to critique of the occult', in P.I. Crawford and S.B. Hafsteinnson (eds), *The Construction of the Viewer*. Aarhaus: Intervention Press.

Marvin, G. (2005) 'Research, representations and responsibilities: an anthropologist in the contested world of fox hunting', in S. Pink (ed.), *Applications of Anthropology: Professional Anthropology in the Twenty First Century*. Oxford: Berghahn.

McGuigan, J. (ed.) (1997) *Cultural Methodologies*. London: Sage.

McQuire, S. (1998) *Visions of Modernity: Representation, Memory, Time and Space in the Age of the Camera*. London: Sage.

Mead, M. (1995 (1975)) 'Visual anthropology in a discipline of words', in P. Hockings (ed.), *Principles of Visual Anthropology*. The Hague: Mouton.

Mermin, S. (1997) 'Being where? Experiencing narratives of ethnographic film', *Visual Anthropology Review*, 13 (1): 40–51.

Miller, D. (1995) *Acknowledging Consumption*. London: Routledge.

Miller, D. (1998) *Material Cultures*. London: Routledge.

Miller, D. (ed.) (2001) *Home Possessions*. Oxford: Berg.

Miller, D. and Slater, D. (2000) *The Internet: An Ethnographic Approach*. Oxford: Berg.

Mitchell, W. (1995) *City of Bits*. London: Routledge.

Mizen, P. (2005) 'A little "light work"? Children's images of their labour', *Visual Studies*, 20 (2): 124–39.

Moore, H. (1994) *A Passion for Difference: Essays in Anthropology and Gender*. Cambridge: Polity Press.

Morley, D. (1996) 'The audience, the ethnographer, the postmodernist and their problems', in P.I. Crawford and S.B. Hafsteinsson (eds), *The Construction of the Viewer*. Aarhaus: Intervention Press.

Morphy, H. (1996) 'More than mere facts: repositioning Spencer and Gillen in the history of anthropology,' in S.R. Morton and D.J Mulvaney (eds), *Exploring Central Australia: Society, Environment and the Horn Expedition*. Chipping Norton: Surrey Beatty and Sons.

Morphy, H. and Banks, M. (1997) 'Introduction: rethinking visual anthropology', in M. Banks and H. Morphy (eds), *Rethinking Visual Anthropology*. London: Routledge.

Mulvey, L. (1989) 'Visual pleasure and narrative cinema', in *Visual and Other Pleasures*. Basingstoke: Macmillan.

Murdock, G. and Pink, S. (2005a) 'Picturing practices: visual anthropology and media ethnography', in Eric Rothenbuhler and Mihai Coman (eds), *Mass Media Anthropology*. London: Sage.

Murdock, G. and Pink, S. (2005b) 'Ethnography bytes back: digitalising visual anthropology', *Media International Australia,* 116: 10–23.

Nencel, L. and Pels, P. (1991) *Constructing Knowledge: Authority and Critique in Social Science*. London: Sage.

Nichols, B. (1994) 'The ethnographer's tale', in L. Taylor (ed.), *Visualizing Theory*. London: Routledge.

Nuemann, M. (1992) 'The travelling eye: photography, tourism and ethnography', *Visual Sociology,* 7 (2): 22–38.

Okely, J. (1994) 'Vicarious and sensory knowledge of chronology and change: ageing in rural France', in K. Hastrup and P. Hervik (eds), *Social Experience and Anthropological Knowledge*. London: Routledge.

Okely, J. (1996) *Own or Other Culture*. London: Routledge.

Okely, J. and Callaway, H. (1992) *Anthropology and Autobiography*. London: Routledge.

O'Neill, M. (2002) in association with Giddens, Breatnach, Bagley, Bourne and Judge, 'Renewed methodologies for social research: ethno-mimesis as performative praxis', *Sociological Review,* 50 (1): 69–88.

Orobitg, G. (2004) 'Photography in the field: word and image in ethnographic research', in S. Pink, L. Kürti and A. Afonso (eds), *Working Images*. London: Routledge.

Orr Vered, K. (1998) 'Plotting new media frontiers: myst and narrative pleasure', *Visual Anthropology Review,* 13 (2): 39–47.

Patton, J. (2004) 'Multiple worlds on Oakland's streets: social practice and the built environment', *Visual Anthropology Review,* 20 (2): 36–56.

Pauwels, L. (1996) 'Managing impressions on visually decoding the workplace as a symbolic environment', *Visual Sociology,* 11 (2): 62–74.

Pauwels, L. (2002) 'The video- and multimedia-article as a mode of scholarly communication: toward scientifically informed expression and aesthetics', *Visual Studies,* 17 (2): 150–59.

Pels, P. (1996) *EASA Newsletter,* 18: 18, http://www.ub.es.easa.netethic.htm.

Pink, S. (1993) 'La mujer en el toreo: reflexiones sobre el éxito de una mujer novillero en la temporada de 1993', *La Tribuna,* Spain, December.

Pink, S. (1996) 'Excursiones socio-visuales en el mundo del toro', in M. Garcia, A. Martinez, P. Pitarch, P. Ranera and J. Fores (eds), *Antropologia de los sentidos: La Vista*. Madrid: Celeste Ediciones.

Pink, S. (1997a) *Women and Bullfighting: Gender, Sex and the Consumption of Tradition*. Oxford: Berg.

Pink, S. (1997b) 'Visual histories of success', in E. Edwards (ed.), *History of Photography*. London and Washington, DC: Taylor & Francis.

Pink, S. (1998) 'Report on the Göttingen International Ethnographic Film Festival 1998', *Anthropology Today,* 14 (4): 23–4.

Pink, S. (1999a) '"Informants" who come "home"', in V. Amit-Talai (ed.), *Constructing the Field*. London: Routledge.

Pink, S. (1999b) 'A woman, a camera and the world of bullfighting: visual culture, experience and the production of anthropological knowledge', *Visual Anthropology*, 13: 71–86.

Pink, S. (1999c) 'Students at the centre: non-lineal narratives and self conscious learning', *Journal of Computer Assisted Learning*, 15: 244–54.

Pink, S. (ed.) (2004a) *Applied Visual Anthropology*, a guest edited issue of *Visual Anthropology Review*, 20 (1).

Pink, S. (2004b) *Home Truths: Gender, Domestic Objects and Everyday Life*. Oxford: Berg.

Pink, S. (2004c) 'Performance, self-representation and narrative: interviewing with video', in C. Pole (ed.), *Seeing Is Believing? Approaches to Visual Research*. Studies in Qualitative Methodology – Volume 7. Oxford: Elsevier Science.

Pink, S. (2005) *The Future of Visual Anthropology: Engaging the Senses*. London: Routledge.

Pink, S. (ed.) (forthcoming) *Visual Interventions: Applied Visual Anthropology*. Oxford: Berghahn.

Pink, S., Kürti, L. and Afonso, A.I. (eds) (2004) *Working Images*. London: Routledge.

Pink, S. and Martinez Perez, A. (2006) 'A fitting "social model": culturally locating telenadre.com', *Home Cultures*, 3 (1): 63–86.

Pinney, C. (1992) 'Montage, doubling and the mouth of God', in P.I. Crawford and J.K. Simonsen (eds), *Ethnographic Film Aesthetics and Narrative Traditions*. Aarhaus: Intervention Press.

Pinney, C. (1997) *Camera Indica: The Social Life of Indian Photographs*. London: Reaktion Books.

Pinney, C. and Peterson, N. (eds) (2003) *Photography's Other Histories*. Durham and London: Duke University Press.

Pitt-Rivers, J. (1954) *The People of the Sierra*. New York: Criterion.

Pole, C. (ed.) (2004) *Seeing Is Believing? Approaches to Visual Research*. Studies in Qualitative Methodology – Volume 7. Oxford: Elsevier Science.

Pollock, G. (1988) *Vision and Difference: Femininity, Feminism and the Histories of Art*. London: Routledge.

Poster, M. (1995) *The Second Media Age*. Cambridge: Polity Press.

Postill, J. (2005) 'A few comments on media and sociation'. Paper presented to the EASA Media Anthropology Network 'Media, Anthropology, Theory' workshop, at Loughborough University, http://www.philbu.net/media-anthropology/lboro_postill.pdf.

Pratt, M.L. (1986) 'Fieldwork in common places', in J. Clifford and G. Marcus (eds), *Writing Culture*. Berkeley, CA: University of California Press.

Press, I. (1979) *The City as Context*. Urbana, IL: University of Illinois Press.

Price, D. and Wells, L. (1997) 'Thinking about photography: debates, historically and now', in L. Wells (ed.), *Photography: A Critical Introduction*. London: Routledge.

Prosser, J. (1996) 'What constitutes an image-based qualitative methodology?', *Visual Sociology*, 11 (2): 26–34.

Prosser, J. (ed.) (1998) *Image-based Research: A Sourcebook for Qualitative Researchers*. London: Falmer Press.

Prosser, J. and Schwartz, D. (1998) 'Photographs within the sociological research process', in J. Prosser (ed.), *Image-based Research: A Sourcebook for Qualitative Researchers*. London: Falmer Press.

Radley, A, Hodgetts, D. and Cullen, A. (2005) 'Visualizing homelessness: a study in photography and estrangement', *Journal of Community and Applied Social Psychology*, 15: 273–95.

Radley, A. and Taylor, D. (2003a) 'Images of recovery: a photo-elicitation study on the hospital ward', *Qualitative Health Research*, 13 (1): 77–99.

Radley, A. and Taylor, D. (2003b) 'Remembering one's stay in hospital: a study in recovery, photography and forgetting', *Health: an Interdisciplinary Journal for the Social Study of Health, Illness and Medicine*, 7 (2): 129–59.

Ragazzi, R. (2006) 'Memory, resistance and speaking the "self": migrant children's accounts of a shifted place–time', in Metje Postma and Peter I. Crawford (eds), *Reflecting Visual Ethnography: Using the Camera in Anthropological Research.* Leiden & Hoejbjerg: CNWS-Press and Intervention Press.

Raggl, A. and Schratz, M. (2004) 'Using visuals to release pupils' voices: emotional pathways into enhancing thinking and reflecting on learning', in C. Pole (ed.), *Seeing Is Believing?: Approaches to Visual Research.* Oxford: Elsevier.

Ramos, M.J. (2004) 'Drawing the lines: the limitations of cultural *ekphrasis*', in S. Pink, L. Kürti and A.I. Afonso (eds), *Working Images.* London: Routledge.

Rapport, N. (1997) *Transcendent Individual: Towards a Literary and Liberal Anthropology.* London: Routledge.

Reiger, J. (1996) 'Photographing social change', *Visual Sociology,* 11 (1): 5–49.

Rich, M., Lamola, S., Gordon, J. and Chalfen, R. (2000) 'Video intervention/prevention assessment: a patient-centered methodology for understanding the adolescent illness experience', *Journal of Adolescent Health,* 27 (3): 155–65.

Robins, K. (1995) 'Will the image hold still', in M. Lister (ed.), *The Photographic Image in Digital Culture.* London: Routledge.

Rollwagen, J. (1988) *Anthropological Film Making.* New York: Harwood Academic Press.

Rose, G. (2001) *Visual Methodologies.* London: Sage.

Rothenbuhler, E.W. and M. Coman (eds) (2005) *Media Anthropology.* Thousands Oaks, CA: Sage.

Ruby, J. (1982) 'Ethnography as *trompe l'œil*: film and anthropology', in J. Ruby (ed.), *A Crack in the Mirror: Reflexive Perspectives in Anthropology.* Philadelphia, PA: University of Pennsylvania Press <http://www.temple.edu./anthro/ruby/trompe.htm>.

Ruby, J. (2000) *Picturing Culture: Explorations of Film and Anthropology.* Chicago: University of Chicago Press.

Schneider, A and Wright, C. (2005) *Contemporary Art and Anthropology.* Oxford: Berg.

Schwartz, D. (1992) *Waucoma Twilight: Generalizations of the Farm.* 'Series on Ethnographic Inquiry'. Washington, DC: Smithsonian Institution Press.

Schwartz, D. (1993) 'Superbowl XXVI: reflections on the manufacture of appearance', *Visual Sociology,* 8 (1): 23–33.

Seaman, G. and Williams, H. (1992) 'Hypermedia in Ethnography' in P.I. Crawford and D. Turton (eds), *Film as Ethnography.* Manchester: Manchester University Press.

Secondulfo, D. (1997) 'The social meaning of things: a working field for visual sociology', *Visual Sociology,* 12 (2): 33–46.

Sekula, A. (1982) 'On the invention of photographic meaning', in V. Burgin (ed.), *Thinking Photography.* London: Macmillan.

Sekula, A. (1989) 'The archive and the body', in R. Bolton (ed.), *The Contest of Meaning.* Cambridge, MA: MIT Press.

Shanklin, E. (1979) 'When a good social role is worth a thousand pictures', in J. Wagner (ed.), *Images of Information.* London: Sage.

Silva, E. (2000) 'The politics of consumption @ home'. PAVIS Papers in Social and Cultural Research, No. 1. Milton Keynes: Faculty of Social Sciences, The Open University.

Silverstone, R. and Hirsch, E. (1993) *Consuming Technologies.* London: Routledge.

Simoni, S. (1996) 'The visual essay: redefining data, presentation and scientific truth', *Visual Sociology,* 11 (2): 75–82.

Slater, D. (1995) 'Domestic photography and digital culture', in M. Lister (ed.), *The Photographic Image in Digital Culture.* London: Routledge.

Stirling, P. (1998 (1965)) *Turkish Village.* http://lucy.ukc.ac.uk/TVillage/Stirling Contents.html

Stirling, P. (n.d) 'Paul Stirling's ethnographic data archive', http://www.lucy.ukc.ac.uk/TVillage/notes.html.

Stoller, P. (1997) *Sensuous Scholarship.* Philadelphia, PA: University of Pennsylvania Press.

Strecker, I. (1997) 'The turbulence of images: on imagery, media and ethnographic discourse', *Visual Anthropology,* 9: 207–27.

Suchar, C. (1993) 'The Jordaan: community change and gentrification in Amsterdam', *Visual Sociology,* 8 (1): 41–51.

Sutton, D. (2001) *Remembrance of Repasts.* Oxford: Berg.

Taussig, M. (1993) *Mimesis and Alterity: A Particular History of the Senses.* New York and London: Routledge.

Tayler, D. (1992) '"Very lovable human beings": the photography of Everared and Thurn', in E. Edwards (ed.), *Anthropology and Photography.* London: Yale University Press.

Taylor, L. (1996) 'Iconophobia: how anthropology lost it at the movies', *Transition,* 69: 64–88.

Thomas, H. (1997) 'Dancing: representation and difference', in J. McGuigan (ed.), *Cultural Methodologies.* London: Sage.

Trias i Valls, M.A. (2003) 'Online teaching: the role of visual media in the delivery of anthropology online', *Anthropology in Action,* 9 (2): 43–51.

Tyler, S. (1987) *The Unspeakable: Discourse, Dialogue, and Rhetoric in the Postmodern World.* London: Academic Press.

Tyler, S. (1991) 'A post-modern in-stance', in L. Nencel and P. Pels (eds), *Constructing Knowledge: Authority and Critique in Social Science.* London: Sage.

Urry, J. (1990) *The Tourist Gaze.* London: Sage.

Van Leeuwen, T. and Jewitt, C. (eds) (2000) *Handbook of Visual Analysis.* London: Sage.

Van Mierlo, M. (1994) 'Touching the invisible', *Visual Sociology,* 9 (1): 43–51.

Wagner, J. (1979) 'Avoiding error', in J. Wagner (ed.), *Images of Information.* London: Sage.

Walsh, D. (1998) 'Doing ethnography', in C. Seale (ed.), *Researching Culture and Society.* London: Sage.

Weaver, A. and Atkinson, P. (1994) *Microcomputing and Qualitative Data Analysis.* Aldershot: Avebury.

Weaver, A. and Atkinson, P. (1995) 'From coding to hypertext', in R.G. Burgess (ed.), *Computing and Qualitative Research: Studies in Qualitative Methodology 5.* Greenwich, CT: JAI Press, pp. 141–68.

Wendl, T. (2001) 'Entangled traditions – photography and the history of media in Southern Ghana', *Res Journal of Anthropology and Aesthetics,* 39 (Spring): 78–101.

White, S. (2003) *Participatory Video: Images that Transform and Empower.* London: Sage.

Woodhead, L. (1987) *A Box Full of Spirits: Adventures of a Film-maker in Africa.* London: Heinemann.

Wright, C. (1998) 'The third subject: perspectives on visual anthropology', *Anthropology Today,* 14 (4): 16–22.

Wright, T. (1998) 'Systems of representation: toward the integration of digital photography into the practice of creating visual images', *Visual Anthropology,* 12 (1): 207–30.

Wright, T. (1999) *The Photography Handbook.* London: Routledge.

Young, M.W. (1998) *Malinowski's Kiriwina: Fieldwork Photography 1915–1918.* Chicago and London: University of Chicago Press.

CD ROMs and DVDs

Biella, P., Changon, N. and Seaman, G. (1997) *Yanomamö Interactive: The Ax Fight* (book and CD ROM). Wadsworth: Thompson Learning.

Coover, R. (2003) *Cultures in Webs* (CD ROM). Watertown: Eastgate Systems.

Hubbard, G., Cook, A., Tester, S. and Downs, M. (2003) *Sexual Expression in Institutional Care Settings: an Interactive Multi-media CD ROM.* Stirling: University of Stirling, Department of Applied Social Science, UK.

Kirkpatrick, J. (2003) *Transports of Delight: The Ricksha Arts of Bangladesh* (CD ROM). Bloomington and Indianapolis: Indiana University Press.

Pink, S. (1998a) *The Bullfighter's Braid: Unravelling Photographic Research* (CD ROM). University of Derby.

Pink, S. (1998b) *Interweaving Lives, Producing Images, Creating Knowledge: Video in Ethnographic Research* (CD ROM). University of Derby.

Ruby, J. (2004) *The Taylor Family* (CD ROM). Oak Park Stories series. Distributor Documentary Educational Resources, Watertown, MA, USA.

Ruby, J. (2005) *Rebekah and Sophie* (CD ROM) *Oak Park Stories series*. Distributor Documentary Educational Resources, Watertown, MA, USA.

Steiger, R. (2000) *En Route* (CD ROM). Distributed with *Visual Sociology*, 15.

Filmography

Braun, K. (1998) *Passing Girl, Riverside: An Essay on Camera Work*. Documentary Educational Resources, Watertown, MA, USA.

Engelbrecht, B. (1993) *Copper Working in Santa Clara del Cobre*. IWF, Goettingen, Germany.

Getzels, P. and Gordon, H. (1990) *The Condor and the Bull*. National Film and Television School, UK.

Henley, P. (1994) *Faces in the Crowd*. Granada Centre Productions (filmmaker Paul Henley, anthropological consultant Ann Rowbottom).

Lydall, J. and Head, J. (1990) *The Women Who Smile*. BBC *Under The Sun* Series.

MacDougall, D. and MacDougall, J. (1979) *Lorang's Way*. Documentary Educational Resources, Watertown MA, USA.

MacDougall, D. and MacDougall, J. (1991) *Photo Wallahs: An Encounter with Photography in Mussorie: a North Indian Hill Station*. Berkeley, CA: Oxhard Film Productions.

Martinez Perez, A. (1997) *Cronotopo*. Taller de Antropologia Visual, Spain.

Moffat, Z. (2006) *Mirror Mirror*. Made in association with University of Westminster, UK.

Pink, S. (1991) *Home from Home*. Granada Centre for Visual Anthropology.

Prelorain, J., Prelorain, M. and Saravino, Z. (1992) *Zulay Frente el Siglo XXI*, Department of Film and Television, University of California, Los Angeles.

Strecker, I. and Lydall, J. (1995) *Sweet Sorghum*. IWF, Goettingen, Germany.

Wendl, T. and Du Plessis, N. (1998) *Future Remembrance*. IWF, Goettingen, Germany.

Websites

http://www.socresonline.org.uk/socresonline/Sociological Research OnLine, an online journal.

http://www.lucy.ukc.ac.uk   The website of the Anthropology Department of the University of Kent at Canterbury. This has links to the *Experience Rich Anthropology* website, *The Virtual Institute of Mambila Studies*, *The Ascoli Project* (Colclough, Bagg, Hosking Coluccelli), *Making Tradition in the Cook Islands* (Fischer) and many other interesting examples of ethnographic hypermedia.

http://www.soc.surrey.ac.uk/sru/SRU11/SRU11.html   *Social Research Update*, a set of online research methods guides.

http://www.rsl.ox.ac.uk/isca/   The website of the Anthropology Department at the University of Oxford where links can be found to the Haddon Project as well as to papers on ethnographic hypermedia by Marcus Banks.

http://www.lucy.ukc.ac.uk/TVillage/notes.html   Stirling, P. (n.d.) 'Paul Stirling's ethnographic data archive'.

http://www.copyrightservice.co.uk.

http://anthropology.ac.uk/Bhalot   Lyon, S.M. (n.d) Social organisation, economy and development.

http://www.lucy.ukc.ac.uk/dz   The Virtual Institute of Mambila Studies.

http://www.cf.ac.uk/socsi/hyper/   Hypermedia and qualitative research at Cardiff University.

http://astro.temple.edu/~ruby/opp/   Jay Ruby's Maintaining Diversity website.

http://www.lboro.ac.uk/departments/ss/newwisite/newworkingimages.htm   The Working Images web pages – the website of the Visual Anthropology Network of the European Association of Social Anthropologists.

http://www.lboro.ac.uk/departments/ss/visualising_ethnography/ The Visualizing Ethnography website.

http://etext.virginia.edu/VAR/   The web site of the journal *Visual Anthropology Review*.

http://www.anthromethods.net   A very useful website that includes advice and information about software for computer-assisted ehtnographic research, including software for visual research and representation.

INDEX

Index by Caroline Eley